RECKLESS DISREGARD

RECKLESS DISREGARD

How Liberal Democrats Undercut Our Military,
Endanger Our Soldiers, and Jeopardize Our Security

Lt. Col. Robert "Buzz" Patterson
USAF (Ret.)

Since 1947
**REGNERY
PUBLISHING, INC.**
An Eagle Publishing Company • Washington, DC

Library of Congress Cataloging-in-Publication Data on file with the Library of Congress

ISBN 0-89526-086-7

Published in the United States by
Regnery Publishing, Inc.
An Eagle Publishing Company
One Massachusetts Avenue, NW
Washington, DC 20001
Visit us at www.regnery.com

Distributed to the trade by
National Book Network
4720-A Boston Way
Lanham, MD 20706
Printed on acid-free paper
Manufactured in the United States of America

10 9 8 7 6 5 4 3 2 1

Books are available in quantity for promotional or premium use. Write to Director of Special Sales, Regnery Publishing, Inc., One Massachusetts Avenue, NW, Washington, DC 20001, for information on discounts and terms, or call (202) 216-0600.

*For the men and women of the armed forces of the United States of America,
past, present, and future. For the soldiers, sailors, airmen, and Marines,
for it is you "whom we shall send." God bless you, your families,
and your service to our country.*

CONTENTS

RECKLESS DISREGARD

Wherein lies our security? It is the American man at arms. From personal experience I know how well he guards us. I have seen him die at Verdun, at St. Mihiel, at Guadalcanal; in the foxholes of Bataan, in the batteries of Corregidor, in the battle areas of Korea; on land, on sea, and in the air; amidst jungle and swamp, hot sands and frozen reaches, in the smoldering mud of shell-pocked roads and dripping trenches.

He was gaunt and he was ghostly; he was grieved and he was loused; he was filthy and he stank; and I loved him.

He died hard, that American fighting man. Not like a dove which when hit, folds its wings gently and comes down quietly. But like a wounded wolf at bay, with lips curled back in a snarl.

He left me with an abiding faith in the future of this nation; a faith that our beloved land will once more know the serenity of hope without fear; a faith in the course of our destiny as a free, prosperous, and happy people.

—*General Douglas MacArthur, as quoted by General Alexander M. Haig at the Nixon Library, Yorba Linda, California, on July 29, 2003*

by Thomas S. Winter, president and editor in chief of HUMAN EVENTS

White House political advisor Karl Rove created a stir on Capitol Hill in January 2002 when he told a group of Republicans that the GOP should use national security as an issue in the upcoming midterm elections.

"We can go to the country on this issue," Rove said, "because they trust the Republican Party to do a better job of protecting and strengthening America's military might and hereby protecting America."

Democratic House Minority Leader Dick Gephardt of Missouri immediately condemned these remarks as "shameful," adding, "I hope the president will set the record straight. This is not a partisan issue."

Rove had violated a new principle that liberals now want everyone in politics to embrace uncritically: that in the post–September 11 world, it is going too far to question the other party's commitment to national security.

Yet when it comes to such an important issue as national security, sensitivity and comity between the political parties are obviously less important than actual results. The question is not whether Rove was insensitive, but whether Rove was right: Are Republicans really that much better on the issue of national security? And conversely, are Democrats so bad on the issue that they can never be trusted to defend America?

In this strongly argued book, Lieutenant Colonel Buzz Patterson (U.S. Air Force, Retired), answers with a resounding "Yes." I must agree with his assessment. In my forty-three years of covering policy and politics in Washington, D.C., for *Human Events*, I have seen this thesis borne out again and again on nearly every defense issue, vote after roll call vote. It is not a question of how many historical examples one can give of liberal weakness on national security issues, but rather of how many one can fit into a single book.

It is no exaggeration to say that the United States won the Cold War despite the best efforts of the American Left. Beginning especially with the Vietnam era, liberals have consistently done everything in their power to ensure America's military defeat. And despite their frequent active alliances with America's Communist enemies throughout the Cold War, many liberal Democrats have successfully duped much of the American public into supporting them politically. Each election, Democrats ask for still more of the same power they have repeatedly demonstrated they are not worthy of exercising.

THE DODGER PRESIDENT

If there was ever any doubt about the truth of this conclusion, the Clinton presidency sufficiently answered it for all time. It is difficult enough to forgive Bill Clinton for dodging the draft and making some other young man from Hope, Arkansas, serve and perhaps die in his place in Vietnam. It is outright impossible, however, to forgive him for gravely abusing his power as commander in chief—using the military for political ends, dramatically cutting back the size of our forces to pay for wasteful social programs, and turning what should be an elite fighting force into a laboratory for social experimentation.

Despite lacking any clear mandate after his plurality victory in the election of 1992, (a fact that would only come crashing down on him later in the GOP electoral sweep of 1994), Clinton, once in office, immediately moved to undermine military morale and effectiveness by trying to force acceptance of homosexuality on the military. In doing this, Clinton again showed that all too often liberals' top priority is not to strengthen the military, but rather to force political correctness on America's soldiers.

Along these lines, Clinton made it a priority to put women in situations closer and closer to actual combat. In 1994, Secretary of Defense Les Aspin revoked the so-called "risk rule," which barred female soldiers from roles in which there was substantial risk of capture. This culminated in the Nasiriyah incident in Iraq last year, in which two women service members were captured and one killed. These women—two of them single mothers and the other a mere girl of nineteen years—were in maintenance roles close behind the front lines, in a place they never would have been had the Clinton administration not altered the rules for women in combat. The fact that women were serving in that specific location did not make America's military any stronger—quite the contrary, in fact—but it did serve to further a social goal of the Left: to obliterate sex roles, even at the expense of American security and strength.

Clinton also introduced sex-integrated training into the Army—a policy frowned upon as "not efficient" in a January 2003 study by the Army itself. Although co-ed training does not improve the military's strength, the study stated, it "improved female performance ... increases acceptance of women in the Army" and "provides shared training experience." All very nice, but hardly the way to build military might in an age of global terrorism.

Of course, given that human nature is real—not the societal construct that leftist theorists claim—a more highly sex-integrated military produces increasing rates of pregnancy in the services (especially aboard ships at sea) as well as aberrations such as the sadistic, pornographic photographs and videos that have come out of the Abu Ghraib prison in Iraq. It is noteworthy that as the first explanations of the prison abuse incident trickle out of Iraq, we learn that the co-ed guard staff was practically running a sex club right under the nose of their incompetent female commander, Brigadier General Janis Karpinski.

The liberals accompanied their social experimentation on the armed forces with an outright dismantling of America's military might. In the 1990s, as American servicemen were undergoing sensitivity training thanks to Clinton's leadership, the commander in chief was cutting the armed forces nearly in half. As Republican House Armed Services chairman Duncan Hunter of California told *Human Events'* Terry Jeffrey last October, "We had eighteen Army divisions in 1991. Today we have ten. So, when Bill Clinton left the White House we had cut the Army at that point almost in half. We had twenty-four active fighter air wings in the Air Force. Today we have thirteen. So we cut our tactical airpower almost in half. We had 546 ships in 1991. Today we are down to three hundred. So we cut the ship force massively."

By the time terrorists hit the United States on September 11, 2001, America was in a desperate situation and needed an enormous boost in military funding just to rebuild. "I think it's clear that we've cut our force structure too deeply, and that's being reflected in the op tempo and personnel tempo that are required now to support our commitments around the world," said Hunter.

Later in his presidency, Clinton showed a sick and cynical knack for using the military to suit his own political ends. Take, for example, his famous diversionary missile strikes of August 20, 1998, to distract Americans on the same day Monica Lewinsky testified in the Paula Jones sexual harassment trial, and three days after his own mendacious testimony. It was a sickening case of life's imitating art— namely the 1997 movie *Wag the Dog*. Fourteen months later, the administration was still defending its missile strikes on an aspirin factory in Sudan that, as it turns out, had no readily discernable connection to the terrorists who were supposedly the real target.

Then came the Kosovo conflict, a truly shameful episode in the history of our foreign policy. This aerial bombardment of Yugoslavia was more about giving Clinton a legacy than it ever was about serving American interests. In the end it accomplished nothing positive, but it did simultaneously inflame anti-American sentiment worldwide and help Albanian Islamic extremists gain a base of support in south-eastern Europe.

When Clinton had a chance to do something good for America's security—capture Osama bin Laden, retaliate effectively for the attack on the USS *Cole* and the African embassy bombings, or pursue the international terrorist organizations behind the 1993 World Trade Center bombing—he inevitably passed it up. He continues to lie about his opportunity to apprehend bin Laden, even though he was caught on tape in 2002 explaining why he turned down the terrorist leader when Sudan's government offered him up in 1996.

Of all American presidents, Clinton was the least mindful of national security. His law enforcement apparatus was too often occupied in operations such as Waco, and his military was stretched thin, performing peacekeeping missions of questionable value for American interests in a variety of places, including Bosnia and Haiti.

A NEW MCGOVERN

As bad as Bill Clinton was, this year's election may be showcasing a candidate who rivals even George McGovern in his unworthiness to hold the position of commander in chief. That Democratic senator John Kerry of Massachusetts is all but certain to be the Democrats' official nominee for president this year speaks volumes about just how powerful the remnants of the 1960s radical anti-American Left remain within the Democratic Party.

As Patterson demonstrates, Kerry has a long history of proposing and voting for bills that would slash military and intelligence funding, sometimes gutting or eliminating key weapons systems. In 1997, Kerry said, "Now that [the Cold War] struggle is over, why is it that our vast intelligence apparatus continues to grow?" Naturally, this did not stop Kerry from complaining after September 11 of the failure of America's intelligence agencies to prevent terrorism.

On March 29, 2004, *Human Events* chronicled several of Kerry's votes on defense issues, comparing his record to that of a fellow

Vietnam veteran, John McCain, Republican senator from Arizona. The contrast is very striking, despite the fact that McCain is not considered a strong conservative by any stretch of the imagination. Kerry's anti-soldier, anti-military bias shines through again and again in his votes to take money away from the military for use in social programs. As icing on the cake, in the course of passing the 1993 motor-voter legislation, Kerry even voted against an amendment that would have helped new enlistees register to vote.

Perhaps more important, John Kerry has a long history of collaborating with America's enemies. He got to where he is today only by falsely besmirching the reputation of his country and undermining American morale during the Vietnam War. After returning from his very brief stint in Vietnam, Kerry became a stateside apologist for Communism. Kerry's former comrade-in-arms Robert Elder said it best about the anti-American activities Kerry engaged in after his return from Vietnam: "We didn't lose the war on the ground in Vietnam. We lost it at home, and at home John Kerry was the field general."

As Patterson notes, Kerry's April 22, 1971, testimony before the Senate Foreign Relations Committee bears the unmistakable scent of Communist propaganda, treating that vicious totalitarian system as if it were just another form of government, and dismissing as "bogus" the idea that it represented any threat to the United States and our freedoms.

On top of Kerry's radical rhetoric came the slanders that will surely dog him in this year's presidential election: his uncritical repetition, under oath, of undocumented, dubious allegations—many of them later discredited—of atrocious daily war crimes by American servicemen in Vietnam. Patterson shows how Kerry painted a picture of the American soldier as cruel and sadistic, asserting that there were somehow "200,000 a year who are murdered by the United States of America" in Vietnam. Kerry decried America's "hypocrisy in our taking umbrage in the Geneva Conventions and using that as justification for a continuation of this war, when we are more guilty than any other body of violations of those Geneva Conventions." He also made the claim—immediately retracted under questioning because of its sheer absurdity—that "a lot of guys, 60, 80 percent, stay stoned twenty-four hours a day" in Vietnam order to deal with the war.

Human Events has aggressively covered the story of Kerry's testimony, which came at the same time Republican congressman Sam Johnson of Texas was suffering as a POW in the so-called "Hanoi Hilton" prison camp. "When [Kerry] testified against the war, his testimony was un-American and untrue, and I think he lost all credibility as a real military man," Johnson recently told a *Human Events* reporter. As Kerry was decrying the U.S. as the world's worst violator of the Geneva Conventions, Johnson and other brave men such as Republican senator Jeremiah Denton of Alabama were experiencing true violations of the Conventions at the hands of their captors. (For all we know, aged, missing POWs might still be suffering, thanks to Kerry's offhand dismissal, when he served as chairman of the Senate Select Committee on POW/MIA Affairs, of thousands of examples of evidence that American servicemen remained captive in Vietnam.)

In the same Senate testimony, Kerry predicted that upon America's withdrawal from Vietnam, perhaps a few thousand anti-Communists might have to be evacuated from the country in order to escape retribution. He could not have been more wrong. America's early flight led to the brutal murder of millions in Vietnam, Cambodia, and Laos at the hands of the Communists.

There is even more to the story of Kerry's activist group, Vietnam Veterans Against the War (VVAW). Contrary to the story the mainstream media have peddled in this election year, VVAW was not in any sense just a group of concerned veterans who had returned from the war and had some reservations about its conduct. In addition to the fact that several of the group's "veterans" were later exposed as frauds who had lied about their service records, FBI files and eyewitnesses suggest a more nefarious organization. Patterson rightly draws attention to a November 1971 Kansas City meeting at which some of VVAW's leaders discussed a plot to murder pro-war U.S. senators.

While FBI informants' accounts contradict each other on some details, they agree that John Kerry was present at that meeting, a fact that has been bolstered by subsequent eyewitness accounts. Earlier this year, Kerry tried to deny he was there, but has since claimed memory loss in the face of overwhelming evidence that he was. And after attending this amazing meeting, he remained a member of VVAW and apparently did not even report this treasonous activity to the relevant authorities.

Kerry also acknowledged in his 1971 Senate testimony, under oath, that he had personally met in Paris with representatives of the North Vietnamese government and the Communist "provisional government" of South Vietnam to "negotiate" a private diplomatic solution for American withdrawal. As a Naval Reservist at the time, subject to the Uniform Military Code of Justice (Section 904 Article 104), Kerry could have faced the death penalty for this unauthorized contact with the enemy.

Instead, he could now become president of the United States.

QUESTION THEIR PATRIOTISM

The scariest thing about watching the Vietnam era end and roll into the 1980s is that many of those who did the most to hurt our soldiers and help our enemies suddenly became respected political figures in the Democratic Party. It is almost amusing to hear the now-fashionable protestation, "How dare you question my patriotism?" coming from politicians who actually collaborated with our enemies only a few decades ago.

Unfortunately, the public has such a short attention span that most Americans remain largely unaware that many of our elected officials come from this collaborationist brood.

If you find Kerry's constant self-serving references to his Vietnam service annoying today, you should look back to 1985, when the newly elected senator traveled to Nicaragua to help the Soviet-backed Communist regime there. A *Washington Post* reporter memorialized

Kerry's April 18 landing in Managua: "'Look at it,' Kerry said as their plane touched down here Thursday night. 'It reminds me so much of Vietnam. The same lushness, the tree lines.'"

And, as Kerry would try to portray it, the same quagmire and the same war atrocities. Kerry's trip to Managua was intended to score a propaganda coup against Ronald Reagan, who had just been reelected in a landslide. Reagan had been backing a counter-insurgency to keep the Soviets from exploiting the strategic foothold his predecessor, Jimmy Carter, had given them in the Americas.

Predictably, Kerry and Democratic senator Tom Harkin of Iowa took the other side of the debate from Reagan. They went to Managua to meet with Communist dictator Daniel Ortega and negotiate a "cease-fire" that was contrary at the time to American policy and interests. Kerry, who would denounce the anti-Communist fighters as "death squads" while visiting and cavorting with America's enemy, sought a "peace" agreement favorable to the Communists that he could take back to Washington and throw in Reagan's face. The White House denounced it as a "propaganda initiative."

The following week, after his return, Kerry would praise this phony plan he had brought back, which would have cut off all funding for the anti-Soviet resistance, handing total victory to the Communists and leaving America vulnerable in its own hemisphere.

"I share with this body the aide-mémoire which was presented to us by President Ortega," he said of the pro-Communist peace plan. "Here is a guarantee of the security interest of the United States.... My generation, a lot of us grew up with the phrase 'give peace a chance' as part of a song that captured a lot of people's imagination. I hope that the president of the United States will give peace a chance."

Fortunately, Reagan ignored this advice from the Democratic senators. His intransigence caused Harkin to complain of the administration, "They just have an ideological fanaticism with respect to Nicaragua that goes beyond any bonds of reasonableness."

Four years later, Reagan's fanatical unreasonableness would erase the Communist threat from the earth, despite the efforts of Harkin, Kerry, and others to prop it up and keep it alive.

The story of Democratic senator Ted Kennedy of Massachusetts goes even further to demonstrate liberal disloyalty. Unfortunately, many conservatives just laugh Kennedy off as a demagogue "whose car has killed more people than my gun ever will." Others remain angry at the thought of the Chappaquiddick incident thirty years ago, in which he left a young woman to drown after he drove his car off a bridge.

But how many of them know about Ted Kennedy's active collaboration with the KGB, the Soviet intelligence apparatus? No, this is not the stuff of conspiracy theory. It was revealed during the 1990s with the opening of the Soviet archives after the collapse of the Russian Communist dictatorship, and by files brought to U.S. intelligence services by courageous Soviet defectors.

As anti-Communist expert Herb Romerstein reported in *Human Events* last December, these files show that Kennedy used the KGB to advance his political ambitions and the business prospects of his friends, all at the expense of U.S. national interests.

The KGB files show that on March 5, 1980, using former Democratic senator John Tunney of California as an intermediary, Kennedy offered to speak out against President Jimmy Carter and his (albeit weak) condemnation of the Soviet invasion of Afghanistan.

In May 1983, the KGB again reported to their bosses that Kennedy was offering to "undertake some additional steps to counter the militaristic policy of Reagan and his campaign of psychological pressure on the American population." Kennedy requested a meeting with Yuri Andropov, the general secretary of the Soviet Communist Party, for the purpose of "arming himself with the Soviet leader's explanations of arms control policy so he can use them later for more convincing speeches in the U.S."

It is no surprise, then, that as Kennedy was secretly working with America's enemies, he and his friends on the Left were overtly undermining America's intelligence apparatus.

As Patterson notes, the intelligence sabotage by the likes of Kennedy and other liberals in Congress in the late 1970s unmistakably culminated in the terror attacks of September 11, 2001. Democratic senator Frank Church of Idaho, who famously described the CIA as a "rogue elephant," led the committee that created an absolute separation between the activities of domestic law enforcement and foreign intelligence investigations.

Kennedy and others helped pass the 1978 Foreign Intelligence Surveillance Act (FISA), which for the first time prevented the executive branch from monitoring foreign enemies operating in the United States without first demonstrating to a special court "sufficient specific and articulable facts to indicate that the individual's activities are in preparation for sabotage or international terrorism." This was an unprecedented restriction. President Franklin Roosevelt had freely wiretapped Nazis and Communists operating in the U.S., which only made sense, and his successors enjoyed the same inherent power.

But the liberals carried the day in 1978. Twenty-three years later, the FBI arrested Zacarias Moussaoui on immigration charges and wanted to search his computer. But thanks to the stringent statutory restrictions on our law enforcement personnel—a veritable wall—created by Kennedy, Church, and other liberals, their request for a warrant was rejected.

Attorney General John Ashcroft testified on this incident before the independent 9-11 Commission on April 13, 2004, and cited a note written by one frustrated FBI investigator at the time—and this was just weeks prior to September 11: "Someday someone will die—and wall or not—the public will not understand why we were not more effective and throwing every resource we had at certain 'problems.' "

Don't expect Ted Kennedy to apologize any time soon. He's already out there demanding to know why the FBI failed. A look in the mirror would explain a lot.

SHOOTING DOWN MISSILE DEFENSE

As President Ronald Reagan reached the end of his second term in 1988, he argued in favor of George H. W. Bush's candidacy by recalling the disastrous defense policies of his predecessor Jimmy Carter and the harm they caused to America's safety and world standing.

"Our national defense had been so weakened that the Soviet Union had begun to engage in reckless aggression," said Reagan. "The world began to question the constancy and resolve of the United States. Our leaders answered, not that there was something wrong with our government, but that our people were at fault because of some malaise."

Reagan's election in 1980 changed all of that. Unlike his predecessors—and certainly unlike his leftist adversaries—Reagan believed that the Cold War could be won, and he set out to do it. Today we take for granted Reagan's success, but nearly everyone has forgotten the lengths to which the Left went to prevent him from effectively countering the Soviet threat.

One of the clearest examples of this—well described by Patterson—is the fight by Kerry, Kennedy, and a whole host of other leftists to adopt a so-called "nuclear freeze" policy. This was a disastrous idea that would have put the United States at the mercy of an overwhelmingly superior Soviet nuclear power.

When Reagan entered office, there was great concern that the Soviets would permanently take the lead in the nuclear arms race and "bury" the free world, just as Nikita Khrushchev had promised in his famous diplomatic address of 1956. Between 1973 and 1983, the United States had increased its number of nuclear warheads only slightly, from 1,754 to 2,100. The Soviets, on the other hand, had

quadrupled their nuclear arsenal—from 1,527 to 6,000—and aggressively deployed missiles in Europe, training them on Western capitals.

Meanwhile, at the behest of their Soviet backers, the American Left
began to advocate a bilateral "nuclear freeze" that essentially
amounted to surrender. Their plan would have left Russia with a commanding numerical advantage in warheads. Naturally, Soviet premier
Yuri Andropov loved the idea, and spoke in its favor in a January
1983 interview with *Pravda*. The American "peace movement,"
bankrolled and controlled by the Soviets, staged rallies and marches
in several American cities in support of this plan.

House Democrats even passed a nuclear freeze bill in 1983, but
President Reagan ruled out such a move, instead beginning his own
nuclear buildup of intermediate-range Pershing II nuclear missiles. By
deploying these missiles throughout Western Europe to counter the
Soviet missiles, he immediately created a more favorable starting position for nuclear negotiations. In March 1983, Reagan went even further, unveiling the beginning of work on the Strategic Defense Initiative
(SDI)—a national missile defense system. Reagan argued that it was
morally superior to defend the nation against nuclear attack rather
than to base the nation's defense on mutually assured destruction.

"I know this is a formidable technical task, one that may not be
accomplished before the end of this century," Reagan said in a nation-
ally televised speech. "It will take years, probably decades, of effort
on many fronts.... But isn't it worth every investment necessary to
free the world from the threat of nuclear war?"

This did not sit well at all with the Soviets, who stood to lose the
nuclear threat they then held over the American people. And so their
left-wing allies in the U.S. Congress jumped at the chance to oppose
it. Kennedy derisively denounced "the misleading red scare tactics and
reckless Star Wars schemes of the president." (Recall that Kennedy
was in contact with the KGB at this time.)

Reagan pressed on anyway, and successfully pushed SDI through
Congress over strenuous Democrat objections. The program became

a key part of negotiations with Soviet premier Mikhail Gorbachev in 1986, giving Reagan a clear upper hand in these talks. As Gorbachev himself would later declare, Reagan's tough SDI stance signaled the beginning of the end for Soviet Communism. Still, throughout the 1980s, Reagan and his successor would have to battle liberals such as Kerry, Kennedy, and Harkin to preserve the missile defense program and resist what Reagan called a move "back toward the weakness and accommodation of the 1970s."

Since that time, national missile defense has come closer to reality, and its great need is accentuated by the threat of terrorists and rogue states such as North Korea, which has long-range missiles and a demonstrated willingness to use them. Yet liberals continue to oppose missile defense. They even argued that the September 11 attacks *prove* that a missile defense system is unnecessary, because the terrorists did not use ballistic missiles!

As *Human Events* reported exclusively in July 2002, Democratic Senate Armed Services chairman Carl Levin of Michigan led an effort to kill the missile defense program without leaving fingerprints by quietly removing key funding provisions without which the rest of the program would not function. As Republican senator Phil Gramm of Texas said at the time, "It's just like a guy who takes the ignition out of a car and says, 'Well, you've got 98 percent of your car.'"

To head off Levin, Republicans had to make secret plans to wheel ailing Republican senator Jesse Helms of North Carolina—still recovering from heart surgery—onto the Senate floor to cast the fiftieth vote in favor of full missile defense funding. Levin blinked, and the vote never took place, but his anti-defense crusade illustrates the problems Americans will always face as long as they entrust his ideological allies with the security of our nation.

BETRAYAL AGAIN

Many Americans believed in the weeks and months following the terror attacks of September 11, 2001, that the nation's politics would never be the same again. In the aftermath, it appeared that liberals would join conservatives in supporting military operations and domestic law enforcement aimed at decreasing the terror threat against America.

Unfortunately, the post–September 11 debate on Capitol Hill has only confirmed that liberals lack the will to fight America's enemies. Even the destruction of the World Trade Center and much of the Pentagon has not changed the permanently partisan nature of the Democrats on national defense issues or caused the liberals to back off their politically correct obsessions. Just as before, there is still only one increased military capability that Democratic legislators support in substantial numbers: to make taxpayers fund and military doctors perform abortions on our overseas bases.

In the war against the terrorists around the world, the bulk of America's leftists are not aligned with our enemy, as they were during the Cold War. Yet at best they are very uncomfortable with fighting a war against the Islamic fanatics who destroyed the World Trade Center and murdered three thousand Americans.

For one thing, the War on Terror makes them nervous because it threatens the very foundations of their "Blame America First" philosophy. The Left cannot stomach the possibility that other nations and cultures (besides our own) could somehow be deficient and inherently harmful to our peace and security.

This is why, just over one year after terror attacks ravaged our nation, Senator Kennedy, Democratic senator Russ Feingold of Wisconsin and Democratic congressman John Conyers of Michigan were already working to eliminate funding for what was at the time one of the most effective homeland security programs established after September 2001—the National Security Entry-Exit Registration System (NSEERS), which required the fingerprinting and registration of foreign visitors entering the United States from certain Muslim countries and state sponsors of terrorism.

In January 2003, Kennedy cleverly and quietly—with no one noticing—inserted an amendment to a spending bill that removed NSEERS funding from a supplemental spending bill. Kennedy, Feingold, and Conyers then wrote a joint letter calling the program "a second wave of roundups and detentions of Arab and Muslim males disguised as a perfunctory registration requirement."

Of course, they assumed this was a bad thing. In fact, NSEERS had by that time (after just four months of operation) led directly to the apprehension of seven terrorists and 341 other "law enforcement threats" trying to enter the United States, a Justice Department spokesman told *Human Events* at the time. Among those arrested were convicted drug traffickers, other felons (including a convicted Iranian child molester), and previous immigration violators.

Yet a survey of Democratic lawmakers by *Human Events* found almost universal opposition to this highly effective program. Political correctness, it turned out, was more important than national security.

"To the extent that it looks like racial profiling, I'm not in support of that," said Democratic congresswoman Denise Majette of Georgia.

"I think it's a very discriminatory policy," said Democratic senator Maria Cantwell of Washington.

"Just visualize this," said Democratic congressman Dennis Kucinich of Ohio. "Give me your tired, your free, your huddled masses—your fingerprints!"

Amazingly, even as liberals were seeking to end NSEERS, Democratic senator Hillary Clinton of New York was attacking the Bush administration for supposedly dropping the ball on homeland security. "Somewhere along the line, we lost our edge," she said. "We let our guard down."

Fortunately, Republicans later restored funding for NSEERS, which was later replaced by a more comprehensive immigration and visitor tracking system. But the lesson should be clear: When in power, liberals will leave our nation open to attack.

HOMELAND PORK AND ECO-WAR

It would seem almost tautological that money from the new Department of Homeland Security should be used to prevent future terrorist attacks. Unfortunately, Democrats don't see it that way. They have a strategy for Homeland Security money that has nothing to do with securing the homeland.

Their funding formula goes like this: political power, pork, and votes—not national defense. As Republican congressman Chris Cox of California wrote in the May 19, 2004, edition of *The Hill*: "Forty percent of the total state terrorism preparedness grants are being allocated with no regard for the threat of a terrorist attack, the vulnerability of key assets, the terrorists' known capabilities and intentions, or even state or regional population." The current funding levels, he continued, are "based not on threat assessment, nor on need, but on political formulas. . . . Homeland security is the essence of our national security. It cannot be burdened with pork and political formulas that fail to address our needs rationally."

Indeed, this is one of the most under-reported scandals of the post–September 11 era, mostly because Democrats have successfully concealed their disregard for public safety behind a façade of concern for "rescue workers" and "first responders." Unfortunately, these brave individuals can only help in the *aftermath* of a horrific terror attack. Yet rather than investing in a system of tough border enforcement, deportation of aliens who threaten our security, and expanded military strike capabilities to deter and combat terrorism, liberals prefer to pad the patronage payrolls of police and fire departments in rural Vermont, which will almost certainly never suffer a terrorist attack. Thanks to the hard work of pork-barreling Democratic senator Patrick Leahy of Vermont, the funding formula is set up such that Vermont will receive far more "homeland security" money on a per-capita basis than New York or California, which are far more likely to be targeted for such an attack.

In many cases, the programs to which liberals wish to dedicate anti-terrorism funding have nothing to do even with "first responders," and everything to do with certain lawmakers' desire to be reelected. In the spring of 2002, the Democrat-controlled Senate passed a so-called "emergency" supplemental spending bill for counter-terrorism that provided $2.5 million for mapping Hawaiian coral reefs, $11 million to bail out New England fishermen, $26.8 million for the U.S Geological Survey to map U.S. cities, $1 billion for Pell grants and $2 million for the Smithsonian to build a new warehouse for animal specimens preserved in formaldehyde.

Liberals also clearly show the low priority they put on national security as they repeatedly try to limit or abolish military training capabilities through imposition of draconian environmental laws. *Human Events* associate editor Joseph D'Agostino has extensively documented this abuse of environmental laws at the expense of national security. He noted in May 2003, for example, the Army's warning that "environmental laws now affect in some way 84 percent of the training land at Fort Hood, Texas, and that on 77 percent of the land, training practices are actually affected because of it."

At other bases, endangered species have become an issue, and liberals are always there to make a federal case of it. Environmentalists at the Natural Resources Defense Council are still suing to eliminate the training grounds of the 1st Marine Division at Camp Pendleton, near San Diego, California. As we reported in February 2003, they are trying to impose through litigation a 2000 proposal by the U.S. Fish and Wildlife Service "to designate 57 percent of the territory at that base as 'critical habitat' for creatures listed as threatened or endangered under ESA." The case is still pending, but a ruling against the Marines would be devastating for their training capabilities on the West Coast.

IRAQ: SAME OLD STORY

In 2002, the United States had every reason to take a tough diplomatic tack with Saddam Hussein and clear up, one way or another, the issue of his illicit weapons programs. Ever since 1998, there had been a strong bipartisan agreement that Hussein was a threat and that he had in his possession weapons of mass destruction.

President Bush was still seeking to settle the score with Hussein through diplomacy in 2002, but it did not help America's cause when three prominent Democratic lawmakers went to meet with Hussein and lend aid to his propaganda campaign against Bush. Democratic congressmen David Bonior of Michigan, Jim McDermott of Washington, and Mike Thompson of California went to Baghdad and then publicly called the president a liar, arguing from Iraqi soil against his aggressive policy toward Hussein.

Interviewed from Baghdad by satellite, Congressman McDermott told ABC's *This Week* in late September 2002, "I think you have to take the Iraqis on their value—at their face value." He also said, "I think the president would mislead the American people."

In other words, mass murderer Saddam Hussein could be trusted, but not George W. Bush. It was a singularly repulsive statement that smelled of treason, not even matched by Hillary Clinton's "Troop Demoralization Tour," recounted by Patterson in this book.

Human Events spoke with McDermott upon his return from Baghdad; he refused to back away from his pro-Hussein, anti-Bush remarks. McDermott remained completely unconcerned with whether his freelance foreign policy exploits—like those of John Kerry and Tom Harkin in 1985—were undermining and weakening U.S. government policy.

"Well, you know, the issue here is not those remarks," he said. "It's the issue of whether or not we're going to take the president's excuses for going to war rather than settling things diplomatically."

The same week, Republican congressman J. D. Hayworth of Arizona made it clear that it was not McDermott's antiwar position, but his ready embrace of an enemy's propaganda that made his remarks especially poisonous: "I'm very disappointed in Congressman McDermott," said Hayworth. "Not that people don't have the right to dissent, but that he would go to a foreign, hostile capital and express his disdain and distrust of the president of the United States, I find thoroughly despicable."

The phrase "thoroughly despicable" also describes the liberals' decades-long record on national defense and national security. As

Hayworth noted, dissent from government policy can indeed be patriotic. But anti-American sabotage—a term that often aptly describes liberals' consistent disdain for our nation's defense—is not.

Liberals have had enough chances to lead and to show their mettle, and they have failed. As Patterson argues convincingly, it is not time to put them back in control.

CHAPTER ONE

A SOLDIER KNOWS

"I do not know the dignity of their birth, but I do know the glory of their death. They died unquestioning, uncomplaining, with faith in their hearts, and on their lips the hope that we could go on to victory. Always for them: Duty, Honor, Country."

—General Douglas MacArthur

More than an act of terrorism, September 11, 2001, inaugurated a world war. Radical Islamists, as we know, killed Americans in New York, Washington, and Pennsylvania. They have killed Westerners in housing compounds in Saudi Arabia, in synagogues in Turkey and Tunisia, and on the railways of Spain. They have killed French sailors in Pakistan, Western tourists in Bali, Israelis in Kenya, and Russians in Moscow and Chechnya. They have killed American and allied troops on the battlefields of Afghanistan and Iraq. Their terrorist cells stretch from Pakistan to London to the Philippines to Detroit. A chemical weapons attack orchestrated by al-Qaeda, using weapons of mass destruction funneled through Syria (possibly originating in

Iraq), potentially killing tens of thousands, was thwarted in Jordan. Bomb plots have been foiled in England, France, Saudi Arabia, and the United States. And the war continues. As al-Qaeda operative Maulana Inyadullah put it, "The Americans love Pepsi-Cola, we love death."

The war was ongoing before September 11, but the Clinton administration didn't fight it, and many Americans barely noticed it. It took this second Pearl Harbor to shake every American out of the "roaring '90s" economic prosperity, the Nintendo-induced coma of affluence, the foolishness of believing in the "end of history." But soldiers knew; they always know. Our politicians—at least the ones who aspire to be statesmen—should know, but, as we'll see, an entire party in American politics, the Carter-Clinton-Kerry Democrats, never know, because they never focus on America's enemies. Instead, they always assume the enemy is us: America, her armed services, and her intelligence operations. This book is about these Democrats, about their reckless disregard for American security, and reveals that we cannot afford their mistakes again.

I write as a retired Air Force officer, a former White House military aide who carried the "nuclear football" for President Bill Clinton, and as an officer who has been ordered into harm's way by American presidents. I don't believe that we can any longer trust the Democratic Party of Carter-Clinton-Kerry with these life-and-death decisions; the Democratic Party has a demonstrated record of failure and irresponsibility when it comes to national security. September 11 helped bring that home to me. Everyone has his or her own September 11 story. But perhaps I should tell mine, because it was the fulfillment of a warning I personally witnessed given to President Clinton in the White House.

By then, I was a commercial pilot. I picked up my pilot kit and the black travel bag with red and blue embroidered Delta Air Lines logo, kissed my wife and daughter goodbye, and started toward the door. In my new position as a first officer on Delta's MD-88 aircraft, my flights would take me from Atlanta's Hartsfield Airport to LaGuardia in New York, back to Atlanta, and finally to West Palm Beach, Florida, for a layover.

I passed the living room television on the way to the car. A commercial airliner had slammed into one of the World Trade Center towers. The plane had erupted in flames and torched the top ten floors. The grayish black smoke characteristically produced by burning jet fuel billowed from the tower. Decades of training, thousands of hours of flying, and hundreds of safety classes do not prepare you for that instant when you see an aircraft crash.

Katie Couric, liberal America's sweetheart, was panicked, straining to comprehend and explain what had just occurred. She speculated that it might be pilot error or a failure on the part of the air traffic controllers. "No way," I thought. There was not a chance in hell that a commercial jet would inadvertently hit this tower on such a clear, cloudless, crystal blue sky day. Even in the very busy airspace of the New York metropolitan area, it was impossible.

I set my flight bags down and fell to the couch to watch. I still had an hour or so until my required sign-in at Delta's pilot lounge. I stared at the growing plume of smoke and wondered what airline this was. Were these pilots my friends, my peers? How many passengers were on board? How many people were working in the tower? What happened?

Unbelievably, in that instant, another jet appeared from the right of the screen and collided with the second tower. "What in the hell is going on?" I asked myself. I yelled for my wife to join me.

I immediately called Delta and was greeted by one of the flight operations managers. "Are you guys watching this?" I asked. "What do you want me to do? Should I come in?"

"Stay where you are until we call you," he said curtly.

As I watched the chaos in New York and Washington, D.C., I recalled being in the White House and retrieving a briefing paper given to President Clinton—it was the Presidential Daily Briefing—that described how the Filipino police had cracked Operation Bojinka ("loud bang" in Serbo-Croatian), an al-Qaeda plot to employ commercial airliners as weapons. That was in 1996. The Clinton administration had four years to act on this intelligence about al-Qaeda's methods. Operation Bojinka, I remembered, had implicated al-Qaeda bomb-builder Ramzi Ahmed Yousef, who had also been implicated in the first World Trade Center bombing in 1993. Yet nothing constructive had been done to prevent what I now saw on television—in fact, the idea of "profiling passengers" had been explicitly rejected by the Federal Aviation Administration during the Clinton years because of political correctness. The FAA, Vice President Al Gore, and the Janet Reno Justice Department did not want to single out people on the basis of "racial profiling." Such political correctness—and neglect about the intelligence information and its national security implications—cost three thousand lives.

I remembered the many terrorist attacks on American citizens during the 1990s. The first World Trade Center bombing, the attack on the U.S. military training center in Riyadh, Saudi Arabia, the bombing of the American military barracks in Dhahran, Saudi Arabia, the simultaneous bombings of the American embassies in Tanzania and Kenya, and the deadly attack on the USS *Cole*. The tragic scenes in New York City and at the Pentagon in Washington, D.C. were the horrible price we paid for President Clinton's reckless disregard for America's national security, and for the Democratic Party's decades of hostility towards the CIA and FBI that had left our intelligence operations toothless and legally restricted from sharing information.

Was the White House the next target? The President's Emergency Operations Center (PEOC) in the East Wing basement must be humming. I knew the protocol. They would be in crisis mode now. Because the president was out of town, Vice President Dick Cheney would be sequestered there, along with key senior staff members. The vaulted doors to what had been the White House World War II bomb shelter would be closed tight. The White House would be in "lock down."

I thought of the military aide with Bush right now and what was racing through his or her head: evacuation scenarios, the continuity of government (COG) plan, possibly breaking into the "nuclear football," and on and on.

I had been in that aide's shoes, and I thought of my brothers and sisters on active duty. I knew that President Bush would not treat this attack the way President Clinton had treated previous terrorist attacks. This was not a law enforcement matter alone; it was war. Our military would be launching into action.

The phone rang, jerking me from my numbed state. It was Delta Flight Operations. All flights were cancelled, most likely not just for today but for several days. "Stay home until we get back to you" were my orders.

The FAA was clearing the skies, ordering several thousand aircraft safely onto the ground in a matter of minutes—an event never contemplated before this day. It was a "national war emergency," the air traffic controllers claimed.

This is my generation's Pearl Harbor, I thought. *How will we respond?*

We have the answer now, from a president who has not flinched from the hard decisions, and from the courage and skill of the U.S. armed forces: the soldiers, sailors, airmen, and Marines who have volunteered for the fight. Today's soldier thinks of Khost, the Khyber Pass, Fallujah, and Ramadi, as his predecessors thought about the Ardennes, the Chosin Reservoir, Hue City, and Khe Sanh. On the battlefield, our soldiers are invincible; they know their enemy and can defeat him. But too many politicians will never understand the nature of the war we are in or what it means to lead.

The Constitution of the United States, Article II, Section II, declares "The President shall be Commander-in-Chief of the Army and Navy of the United States [the Air Force was established in 1947], and of the militia of the several States when called into the actual service of the United States." In time of war especially, the presidential job description requires a strong leader committed to our nation's defense. Liberal Democrats are not qualified.

The record of the last forty years shows that the Democratic Party cannot be trusted with the nation's defense. The party of George McGovern, Ted Kennedy, Jimmy Carter, Michael Dukakis, Bill and Hillary Clinton, Al Gore, and John Kerry treats America's national security—and the fortunes and fate of the American fighting man— with reckless disregard.

Strong words, I know, but I say this with no party animosity—it is a simple fact. I was born into a family of Southern Democrats. As a career Air Force officer, I was trained—in fact, legally bound—to refrain from engaging in partisan politics until retired and out of uniform. In my twenty years of active duty with the Air Force, I served under presidents of both parties, and I did so always with a sense of professionalism grounded in loyalty and patriotic faith in my country. That's what soldiers do.

The Democrats' record is clear and unmistakable: from the fiasco of John F. Kennedy's handling of the Bay of Pigs to Kennedy and Lyndon Johnson's disastrously managed intervention in Vietnam; from the humiliating Iranian hostage crisis during the administration of Jimmy Carter to the botched rescue attempt at Desert One; from President Clinton's spasmodic and pointless interventions in Somalia, Rwanda, Haiti, and Bosnia, to the litany of terrorist attacks against which he ordered no effective response.

All of these, and other ill-fated episodes under Democratic presidents, undermined America's national security in a variety of ways. All of them share this common theme: Democratic presidents placed American fighting men and women in harm's way without the resolve to support them, without the moral authority and courage to command them, and without clear mission objectives for them to achieve.

Democratic Congresses were just as bad. In the waning days of the Vietnam War and the Watergate scandal, liberal elements of the Democratic Party began the emasculation of our national defense. The Church Committee, led by Democratic senator Frank Church, the Pike Committee, led by Democratic congressman Otis Pike, and the antiwar liberals and partisans of the American Left "reformed" our intelligence services to the point of impotency. At the time, Church famously characterized the Central Intelligence Agency as a "rogue elephant rampaging out of control." The CIA was gutted and intelligence operations were neutered for the next thirty years. Today, congressional commissions scratch their heads and wonder why we didn't have "actionable" intelligence on al-Qaeda and the threat before September 11, 2001.

After the Democrats wrecked our intelligence services, President Jimmy Carter, the president who won't go away, assumed office and immediately slashed post-Vietnam military capabilities and, through his vacuous leadership, shattered military morale. Under his command, Americans were first introduced to the concept of the "hollow military." His "soft power" appeasement approach toward the Soviet Union and his repeated capitulations in Cold War negotiations led to instability in Central America (Nicaragua) and the Near and Middle East (Afghanistan and Iran). Most disastrous was when Carter turned his back on a longtime American ally, the shah of Iran, and watched the Ayatollah Khomeini create an "Islamic Republic." In doing that, Carter permitted the creation of state-sponsored Islamic fundamentalist terrorism that specifically targeted America as "the Great Satan."

In 1980, Henry Kissinger summarized Jimmy Carter's foreign policy: "The Carter administration has managed the extraordinary feat of having, at one and the same time, the worst relations with our allies, the worst relations with our adversaries, and the most serious upheavals in the developing world since the end of the Second World War."

President Bill Clinton was Jimmy Carter's natural successor and will be remembered as the most incompetent of all commanders in chief. He entered office an avowed draft dodger with a self-professed "loathing of the military." He left eight years later having as his legacy the most extreme and ill-advised defense reductions in our nation's history, the devastation of military morale across all branches of the armed forces, and, through his philandering and unscrupulous behavior, the complete abdication of his moral authority to lead men and women in uniform.

I served as an Air Force pilot under Clinton's command, flying in military operations in Somalia, the Persian Gulf, Bosnia, and Haiti, and served directly by his side from 1996 to 1998 as carrier of the "nuclear football," the black briefcase that must accompany the president at all times. As a pilot and a mid-level commander of men and aircraft, I experienced the dismay of my fellow officers and men that the president's top defense priority was not fighting terrorism or improving military performance and equipment but "gays in the military" and other liberal social-engineering programs. I witnessed the crushing effects of the Clinton budget cuts, poor unit morale resulting from them and from other Clinton policies, and repeated inane deployments at the direction of a president who never seemed to deploy us according to America's national interests. As his Air Force aide, I witnessed firsthand his irresponsible unraveling of our national security structure, his unconscionable leadership, which sent the military on operations solely to boost his personal popularity or divert attention from his personal scandals, and his failure to effectively deal with real national security threats such as the terrorist attacks of al-Qaeda.

Time after time, Clinton and his usual suspects, retreads from the Carter administration—Tony Lake, Sandy Berger, Warren Christopher, Madeleine Albright, and chief anti-terrorism advisor Richard Clarke—were confronted with terrorist attacks on Americans. Time after time, inaction, indecisiveness, and risk aversion followed politically expedient rhetoric.

I served with Richard Clarke in the White House. His specialty was pomposity, not effective counter-terrorism policy. Contrary to what Clarke was schlepping in his congressional 9-11 Commission testimony

of 2004; in his book, *Against All Enemies*; and in his many media interviews that followed, his policies were soft, impotent, and resulted in
nothing more than emboldening Osama bin Laden and al-Qaeda for
future attacks. As I will show in due course, Clarke is a fraud.

Today's liberal is yesterday's Vietnam War protester, the product
of the "New Left" or "The Movement." The genesis of the liberals'
ideology, the prism through which they view the military and national
security, was born on the streets of 1960s New York, Washington,
D.C., and San Francisco. Most marched against the war and skillfully
maneuvered for college or medical deferments to selfishly avoid having to serve their country.

They wore Communist red headbands and held up Mao's *Little
Red Book of Communism*. They marched in support of the Viet
Cong, the Sandinista Marxists in Nicaragua, the Communist guerril-
las in El Salvador, Fidel Castro, and, more recently, Saddam Hussein
and North Korea's repressive Communist dictator, Kim Jung Il.

They never march in support of their own country.

These antiwar protesters became the heart and soul of the new
Democratic Party and—in the case of the Clintons, Ted Kennedy,
John Kerry, Howard Dean, Dennis Kucinich, Ron Dellums, David
Bonior, and Pat Schroeder—eventually became the party's leaders.

John Kerry, senator from Massachusetts and 2004 Democratic
presidential nominee, is a prototypical example.

Kerry came home from the Vietnam War a decorated sailor, only
to immediately become a protester. Realizing that the radicalizing
politics of the Democratic Party would not support anything but an
antiwar stance, he seized that position for political bounty.

He allied with Jane Fonda, "Hanoi Jane," future wife of 1960s
radical activist Tom Hayden; with radical former attorney general
Ramsey Clark; and with a group of disgruntled veterans and
imposters denouncing not only the war but those still fighting it.

In 1971, he testified before Congress and charged his former brothers in arms, some three million Vietnam veterans all told, of being war criminals. He charged his compatriots with a series of ghastly crimes, none of which were true, none of which, he later admitted, he'd ever witnessed. He defamed, maligned, and mocked his fellow soldiers so he could bask in the plaudits of the likes of Jane Fonda.

But that's not all. His testimony was used by the North Vietnamese enemy as a propaganda tool and as a weapon with which to beat those American prisoners of war. Air Force Lieutenant Colonel Tom Collins, a POW for eight years in North Vietnam, told Jed Babbin of *The American Spectator* that speeches by the antiwar group Kerry led, Vietnam Veterans Against the War, were made an excuse for torture: "There was the old line [the interrogators] often used: 'There are two ways.' You can confess your crimes and denounce your government as . . . your fellow Americans [the protesters] did and things will be 'very good' for you or you can continue to 'have a bad attitude' and things will be 'very bad' for you. My common sense, logic, and the oath I took as an American fighting man left me, and most others, with only the second choice. So things continued to be 'very bad.'"

In what can only be characterized as treason, Kerry met in Paris with the Communist enemy our military was fighting—representatives of the North Vietnamese government and a Communist group from South Vietnam—just months after leaving the Navy and well before the eventual signing of the Paris Peace Accords in 1973. In May of 1970, Kerry traveled to Paris with his wife, Julia Thorne. There, according to his own testimony in 1971, "I have been to Paris. I have talked with both delegations at the peace talks, that is to say the Democratic Republic of Vietnam and the Provisional Revolutionary Government and all eight of Madam Binh's points."[1] Kerry was apparently dabbling at a low-level version of "independent diplomacy"—as Americans have grown accustomed to seeing from Jimmy Carter, Jesse Jackson, and other Democrats always eager to give a sympathetic ear to the enemies of the United States.

In Bill Clinton's case, he avoided serving his country in uniform during the Vietnam War, but in a way designed to "maintain his political viability within the system." He deftly worked an ROTC slot to buy some time, avoided the draft, and then ingloriously reneged on his agreement with University of Arkansas ROTC commander Colonel Eugene Holmes. Instead of serving his country, Clinton studied abroad, traveled to Communist countries, and helped organize the massive antiwar protests dubbed "The 1969 Student Moratorium" in Washington, D.C., and London, England.

College student and young lawyer Hillary Rodham Clinton marched against the war in Boston, pledged her support to the Black Panthers, and aligned herself with the Communist movement through her work with radical leftists like Robert Treuhaft, a former lawyer for the Communist Party; his wife, writer Jessica Mitford; and Robert Borosage of the Institute for Policy Studies, which supported Communist-backed groups in Africa, the Caribbean, and Latin America.

Vermont governor Howard Dean showed up for his draft physical with X-rays and doctor's note in hand. Once he'd secured his medical deferment for back pain, allowing him to avoid the draft, he was off to Aspen, Colorado, for a year of skiing. "I was in no hurry to get into the military," he said.

Ohio congressman Dennis Kucinich claimed a heart murmur, received a medical deferment, and went on to protest the war as well.

Protesting the Vietnam War was the shaping influence on these Democratic leaders and their fellow liberals. It is an influence that liberalism has never outgrown. Since the 1970s at least, the liberals of the Democratic Party have consistently chosen the wrong side of history, protesting Ronald Reagan's ultimately victorious Cold War policies toward the Soviet Union, George H. W. Bush's victorious war to oust Saddam Hussein from Kuwait, and now, George W. Bush's courageous efforts to defend America and take the War on Terror to the terrorists.

Today's liberal carries signs comparing Bush to Adolf Hitler—and believes it. One sign at an antiwar protest in San Francisco in March

2004 proclaimed, "I love New York... Even More Now That the
World Trade Center is Gone." Another sign called for "Violent Insurrection in Iraq," essentially championing the deaths of more American servicemen and women. A third declared, "We Support Our
Troops... When They Shoot Their Officers!"

For liberals, all of the Vietnam themes still play: America is evil,
her enemies are good. Democrats who don't buy that line have, over
time, woken up and left the party. In 1980, Ronald Reagan (a former
Democrat) attracted many conservative Democrats, the so-called
"Reagan Democrats," to the Republican Party. These were mainly
blue-collar working-class Catholics and Southerners for whom patriotism, religion, and traditional values (especially the opposition to
abortion) were important. They supported a strong anti-Communist
foreign policy, cracking down on crime, and social conservatism.
This was the voice of Middle America, the Middle America from
which the armed services draw their recruits—and the Middle America from which the Democratic Party has been divorcing itself.

Today, the Democratic Party is even weaker on terrorism than it
was on Communism. The party's socialist tendencies; the party's
appeal to the self-indulgent and irresponsible (the MTV/Hollywood
Left); and the party's claim, in defense of Bill Clinton, that character
doesn't matter, it was "only sex anyway," runs directly counter to the
fiber of the American military.

Today's Democratic Party, as I personally witnessed in my White
House experience, is socially liberal to the point of social decadence.
The principles and values that this country was founded on—morality,
integrity, honesty, and courage—have no home in the Democratic
Party that defended sex in the Oval Office, lying under oath, witness
tampering, suborning perjury, and sending soldiers into harm's way
with no concern for their safety, the effectiveness of their mission, or
its necessity to the nation's security. For liberals, character doesn't matter: The end justifies the means, and using the military in wag-the-dog

scenarios or to enforce socially liberal experiments is not only okay, but is the preferred tactic.

None of this is okay to the men and women in our armed services; to them, character most certainly does matter.

"Duty, honor, country" is the motto of the U.S. Military Academy at West Point, New York.

"Integrity first, Service before self, Excellence in all we do" are the core values of the Air Force.

"*Non sibi sed patriae*": "Not for self, but country" is engraved over the doors to the chapel at the U.S. Naval Academy in Annapolis, Maryland.

"*Semper Fidelis*": "Always faithful" is the battle cry of the Marine Corps.

"*Semper Paratus*": "Always ready" is the standard for the U.S. Coast Guard.

These are the hallowed words, the core beliefs, ingrained in all who wear the uniform of the United States of America. To our men and women in the armed forces, they are sacred. Much more than just concepts, these creeds are the words upon which our troops hang their heavy mantles of service.

These are the words that compel airmen to fly "downtown" over Baghdad or Hanoi or Dresden through a curtain of flak to shoot their missiles or drop their bombs.

These are the words that compel soldiers to shoulder a heavy ruck and march through the torturous cold and snow of the Ardennes or the Hindu Kush to engage the enemy.

These are the words that encourage the Cold War naval submariner who spent up to six months below the ocean's surface hunting and tracking the submarines of the Soviet Union.

These are the words that steel the heart of the Marine who withstood seventy-seven days of brutal, relentless Viet Cong siege atop the combat camp at Khe Sanh.

These are the words that send Coast Guard sailors into stormy swells at night to rescue American airmen who have ejected from disabled aircraft.

These are the words, as General Douglas MacArthur noted, that "build your basic character. They mold you for future roles as the custodians of the nation's defense. They make you strong enough to know when you are weak, and brave enough to face yourself when you are afraid."

This is the soul of a warrior, the life and existence of those who serve, whether in a stealth jet at 30,000 feet, in an armored personnel carrier moving quickly across the Iraqi desert, in a POW cell in Hanoi, as part of a special operations team searching the Afghanistan-Pakistan border, or on a Coast Guard cutter off the coast of Haiti.

Soldiers rely on each other with a trust that defies all odds. The rifleman relies on his buddy in a foxhole to keep a sharp eye on the enemy. The fighter pilot on the wing knows that his lead pilot will not fly him into a thunderstorm or, worse, a mountain. The tank crew depends completely on the wisdom and decision-making of their commander. And all 1.4 million members of the active duty armed forces and 900,000 members of the Reserves and National Guard trust that their commander in chief will not play politics with their lives.

Conservatives and military men and women know that self-sacrifice, personal responsibility, and unshakable moral character are necessities. For conservatives, they are the foundation of strong families and a just and decent society, and for the military they are absolutely essential to the bond of trust that the uniform requires.

That trust cannot exist with John Kerry. While former naval lieutenant Kerry was calling his military brothers "war criminals" and playing peacenik footsie with Jane Fonda, Air National Guard Lieutenant George W. Bush was flying supersonic F-102 fighter aircraft and answering 3:00 a.m. alerts.

The F-102 was an aging jet used during the Cold War to intercept aircraft, potentially Soviet bombers, and prevent them from entering

U.S. airspace. Bush spent a year of arduous, sometimes dangerous pilot training, to earn his silver wings and finished in the top 5 percent of his class. Pilot training, I can attest, is an intense year, and not without significant physical risk. Kerry was in the Navy for three and a half years; Bush served more than five years with the Air National Guard, but you would never know it, the way liberals talk.

Kerry, Democratic National Committee chairman Terry McAuliffe, and liberal Buddha Michael Moore (neither McAuliffe nor Moore served in the military), have likened Bush's service in the Air National Guard to "being AWOL," "desertion," or "avoiding" Vietnam. Kerry belittled National Guard service when he said, "I've never made any judgments about any choice somebody made about avoiding the draft, about going to Canada, going to jail, being a conscientious objector, going into the National Guard. Those are choices people make."[2] McAuliffe claimed, "George Bush never served in our military and our country."[3]

Comparing service in the Guard with desertion and committing crime shows both how ignorant liberals can be when it comes to the military and just how desperate they might be when it comes to winning an election. In today's armed forces, Guard and Reserve soldiers represent 97 percent of all the military's civil affairs units, 70 percent of all engineering units, 66 percent of all military police, and 50 percent of combat units. Tens of thousands of Guard and Reserve soldiers, about 25 percent of the total force, are fighting in Afghanistan and Iraq. During the Vietnam War, approximately 10 percent of those killed—6,100—were from the Guard and the Reserves.

The F-102, Bush's aircraft, was not used in Vietnam—it didn't have the capability to drop bombs—so his chances of being deployed there were slim to none. As a Cold War interceptor, F-102 pilots had a different role entirely; and though National Guard units could have been mobilized for Vietnam, Democratic president Lyndon Johnson never authorized mass mobilization for reasons of pure political expediency.

Political expediency is politics as usual for the Democratic Party. And in election year 2004, every terrorist cell, every terrorist hiding in a spider hole or cave complex, every phony business front used to launder terrorist money, and every rogue state willing to sponsor terrorism will be watching the results, hoping for the party of political expediency to win again.

Liberals would have us believe that September 11, 2001, was an anomaly, an aberration, and that we can return to preventing terrorism through law enforcement rather than military action—the official policy of the Clinton administration, and the policy laid out by candidate John Kerry. Liberals believe we will be safer if we transfer responsibility for fighting terrorism to the United Nations. Liberals believe that we can opt out of a war on terror. The terrorists are praying for that to happen.

Our choice is this: to treat terrorism as solely a matter for law enforcement and the United Nations—the Democratic Party's way— or to let the terrorist enemy know that no matter what spider hole or cave he might hide in, we will keep coming after him until he dies or surrenders—George W. Bush's way.

As an American fighting man, I choose the latter, because peace does not keep itself; conflict is prevented by vigilance and strength, not by appeasement and weakness. As I will show in the chapters that follow, the Democratic Party denies that truth and in doing so endangers American lives and security.

CHAPTER TWO

THE POLITICS OF TREASON I

"Whoever, owing allegiance to the United States, levies war against them or adheres to their enemies, giving them aid and comfort with the United States or elsewhere, is guilty of treason and shall suffer death, or shall be imprisoned not less than five years and fined under this title but not less than $10,000; and shall be incapable of holding any office under the United States."

—U.S. Code Title 18, Section 2381

"We know we can't beat you on the battlefield, but we can beat you on the streets of New York, Washington, D.C., and San Francisco."

—North Vietnamese camp commander, Son Tay POW camp, to Commander Paul Galanti, U.S. Navy, American prisoner of war

Operation Homecoming, the repatriation of American prisoners of war held during the Vietnam War, commenced on February 12, 1973. The night before, 112 American POWs received "going home clothes" from their North Vietnamese captors and cleaned the barbaric cells they'd called home one last time.

That morning, these American heroes joined together in the courtyard of the place they'd sarcastically named the "Hanoi Hilton." In fact the Hoa Lo prison, an archaic, dank, and dirty prison built by the French in 1901, it was still employed by the North Vietnamese seventy years later as their primary site for imprisonment, interrogation, and torture. Captured American warriors called it home from August 1964 to March 1973.

For the first time since their individual captures, the American servicemen walked out the front gate and into the sunlight without being blindfolded and handcuffed. One by one, in chronological order of their shootdowns, they climbed into camouflaged buses for the ride to Hanoi's Gia Lam military airfield.

For weeks, from their cells, they'd heard the sounds of B-52s high above the city and the rumbling thunder of explosions of American bombs finding their targets. It had been music to their ears. *Finally*, they thought. With this newfound U.S. resolve, the relentless bombing campaign directed by President Richard Nixon, the Communist regime was pressured to grant concessions. The POWs knew their release was imminent.

In stunned silence, they rode over Hanoi's bomb-damaged Paul Daumer Bridge. Most of the men had seen Hanoi from thousands of feet above, at the lightning speeds of high-performance jets as they flew their combat missions. Now, years later, they were seeing it from the ground.

The buses pulled onto the tarmac at Gia Lam, the military airport for this capital city. Three U.S. Air Force C-141A Starlifter aircraft awaited their arrival, each painted white with a large red cross on the tail signifying its peaceful intent. The Americans had been in captivity so long that most didn't recognize the C-141, although it had been in the Air Force inventory for years. They stepped off the buses with proud military bearing and discipline despite their physical scars, unhealed wounds, and malnutrition from years of Communist Third World incarceration. Two by two, they walked toward Colonel Al Lynn, the U.S. officer in charge of the repatriation. Each man stopped, crisply saluted Colonel Lynn, and, not yet believing, stepped onto the freedom birds. It was the moment each had hoped and prayed for, and it was finally happening.

The C-141s taxied for the runway, the tires of the heavy jet aircrafts straining as they rolled over the mismatched and dilapidated concrete slabs consistent with Soviet-built airfields. As the first C-141 pilot pushed forward on the throttles and the aircraft surged toward flying speed, the American warriors who had endured torture, starvation, and solitary confinement erupted in wild cheers and applause.

"We cheered when we felt the familiar acceleration and shouted with glee as we felt ourselves break ground for our destination," remembers Admiral James Stockdale, a naval aviator who was incarcerated for over seven years. The opportunity to rejoice in anything had become completely foreign to them.

Finally, they were going home.

In a similar moment decades later, I stood on the same decayed tarmac on a smoggy, steamy summer day. Only a handful of American aircraft had visited Vietnam since Operation Homecoming and the end of the war. Twenty-two years after our POWs had come home, my Air Force flight crew and a similar C-141 aircraft shared the same ground to retrieve the remains of five American servicemen who hadn't been as fortunate. They'd made the ultimate sacrifice for the war in Southeast Asia and, finally, they would receive the honors they had earned with the giving of their lives.

We formed a military cordon at the rear of our aircraft, paying our respects with smart salutes and silent prayers. Five pine boxes no larger than two feet by two feet, containing the remains of America's long-forgotten warriors, were boarded one by one.

With the humiliating conclusion of the war—the Democratic Congress's failure to meet its obligations to support our South Vietnamese allies during the final Communist offensive—the Communists took every opportunity to claim victory's spoils. As the mission commander, I paid the Vietnamese official the ten thousand dollars he required for the privilege of bringing these men home. He wanted cash, American dollars, and I'd come prepared. As we finalized the transaction, a cadre of Vietnamese officers snickered behind me.

As quickly as possible, our aircraft, under the call sign of "Repat One," was airborne and on our way to American soil. As we climbed out above Hanoi, I looked down at the city and decided it looked much the same as it had looked to American pilots decades earlier.

"How unfortunate," I told my co-pilot.

As an officer proudly wearing the military uniform of the United States of America, I don't ever want to experience that again. I don't ever want any American man or woman to have to experience that again. To be standing at the site of our most ignoble defeat, forced to grovel in front of people who did not rejoice in liberty and did not respect basic human rights.

To return as the beaten to the setting of a struggle that was, at the outset, just and right. Ultimately, knowing that it was us—the United States of America, not them—who in the end were responsible for our own defeat.

HANOI JOHN & HANOI JANE

When senator and 2004 Democratic presidential candidate John Kerry returned home from his Vietnam service in 1969, he was in much better condition.

He was a decorated veteran, having received the Silver Star, a Bronze Star, and three Purple Hearts for his service as a naval lieutenant junior grade and "Swift Boat" commander patrolling the Mekong Delta region of Vietnam. On the day Kerry returned to the United States, 543,000 American troops were deployed in Southeast Asia and 33,400 had lost their lives for their country.

The vast majority of soldiers, sailors, airmen, and Marines who served in Vietnam returned home safely, were proud to have served, and quietly immersed themselves in the fabric of America. Kerry, though, had ambitions and foresight born of pure political motive.

Prior to his commission and departure to Southeast Asia, Kerry had sought relief from the draft board by petitioning to go to France to study for twelve months. The draft board refused. Idolizing fellow New Englander and former president John F. Kennedy and his naval service during World War II, Kerry joined the Navy.

On December 1, 1968, Lieutenant Kerry was assigned to Coastal Squadron 1, Coastal Division 14, at Cam Ranh Bay, South Vietnam, and command of PCF (Patrol Craft Fast) 44, a "Swift Boat." "I didn't really want to get involved in the war," he would later confess to the *Boston Globe*. "When I signed up for the Swift Boats, they had very little to do with the war. They were engaged in coastal patrolling, and that's what I thought I was going to do."[1]

On December 2, Kerry led his first mission, piloting a small foam-filled "skimmer boat," similar to a Boston whaler, with two enlisted men. Their charter was to interdict possible contraband being trafficked off the peninsula north of Cam Ranh Bay.

At approximately 2:00 a.m., Kerry's crew spotted some people running from a sampan (a flat-bottomed boat), and Kerry authorized his crew to fire. His two crewmen that night, William Zaladonis and Patrick Runyon, did not see the source of the shrapnel that Kerry later claimed lodged in his arm, but Zaladonis said, "I assumed they fired back."[2]

The morning after, Kerry immediately applied for his first Purple Heart. He reported to his immediate superior, Lieutenant Commander Grant Hibbard, holding what appeared to be a fragment from a U.S.-79 grenade, a "squiggly" one-eighth-inch metal shard. Kerry claimed to have received a "stinging piece of heat" in his arm during the interdiction mission. As Hibbard recalls, "People in the office were saying, 'I don't think we got any fire,' and there is a guy holding a little piece of shrapnel in his palm. I've had thorns from a rose that were worse."[3] The boat hadn't taken enemy fire, a prerequisite for a Purple Heart, and Hibbard rejected Kerry's request.

Indeed, Louis Letson, the naval doctor who treated Kerry that day, remembers his encounter with the young lieutenant.

John Kerry was a j.g., the O-in-C or skipper of a Swift Boat, newly arrived in Vietnam. On the night of December 2, he was on patrol north of Cam Ranh, up near Nha Trang area. The next day he came to sick bay, the medical facility, for treatment of a wound that had occurred that night.

The story he told was different from what his crewmen had to say about that night. According to Kerry, they had been engaged in a firefight, receiving small arms fire from the shore. He said that his injury resulted from this enemy action.

Some of his crew confided that they did not receive any fire from the shore, but that Kerry had fired a mortar round at close range to some rocks on shore. The crewman thought that the injury was caused by a fragment ricocheting from that mortar round when it struck the rocks. That seemed to fit the injury which I treated.

What I saw was a small piece of metal sticking very superficially in the skin of Kerry's arm. The metal fragment measured about 1 cm in length and was about 2 or 3 mm in diameter. It certainly did not look like a round from a rifle.

I simply removed the piece of metal by lifting it out of the skin with forceps. I doubt that it penetrated more than 3 or 4 mm. It did not require probing to find it, did not require any anesthesia to remove it, and did not require any sutures to close the wound.[4]

The treatment for Kerry's first war injury consisted solely of the application of bacitracin and a Band-Aid®.

Soon after, Kerry was transferred to another unit, Coastal Division 11 at An Thoi, South Vietnam. Kerry appealed to his new commander to have his Purple Heart request reconsidered. The new supervisor contacted Hibbard and asked for approval. In the process of being reassigned himself, Hibbard thinks he might have approved the award in a hurried process. If so, "it was to my chagrin," Hibbard remembers. "Obviously, he got it, I don't know how."[5]

Kerry would spend only four months "in country." According to his training officer, Lieutenant Kerry accumulated three Purple Hearts in four months without missing a day of duty. B. G. "Jug" Burkett, military historian and author of the acclaimed 1999 book *Stolen Valor: How the Vietnam Generation Was Robbed of Its Heroes and Its History*, describes Kerry's Purple Hearts as "self-reported injuries that were virtually nonexistent." Burkett reports, "He never got a day of treatment, he never spent a day in a medical facility."

Three Purple Hearts and no scars, no limps, no hospital stays. Most of our men serving in much more intense combat tours, engaging the enemy day by day, such as the Navy SEALS and Army Rangers, didn't come home with that kind of medal.

"The idea that John Kerry would have put in for three Purple Hearts during only four months in country is just ridiculous," concludes Mel Howell, a retired Navy officer who flew helicopters in Vietnam. "Most of us came away with all kinds of scratches like the ones Kerry got but never accepted Purple Hearts for them."[6]

On February 28, 1969, now in charge of PCF 94, Kerry came under fire from an enemy location on the shore. The crew's gunner returned fire, hitting and wounding the lone gunman. Kerry directed the boat to charge the enemy position. Beaching his boat, Kerry jumped off, chased the wounded insurgent behind a thatched hutch, and killed him. Beaching the boat was foolish; leaving the boat as the commander was stupid. Killing a wounded man ran counter to the Geneva Conventions and naval regulations. Yet his killing of the wounded man behind the hutch earned Kerry the Silver Star.

With an amazing and unbelievable agenda, Kerry and his crew returned within days, armed with a Super 8 video camera he had purchased at the post exchange at Cam Ranh Bay, and reenacted the skirmish on film. He wanted to document the incident upon which he would stake his military, national security, and political bona fides for years to come. In a bizarre, utterly outlandish sense, he was already running for political office: He was already staging campaign commercials.

In my twenty years of active service, I've never heard of a soldier returning to the scene of a firefight and staging a recreation of the event. I can't even imagine such a thing. It speaks to pompous ego and ambition.

After receiving his third Purple Heart, for a scratch and a bruise, Kerry shrewdly used a little-known loophole in military regulations and requested an early return from the war. Navy Instruction 1300.39, according to the *Boston Globe*, offered the opportunity for a sailor to request a reassignment from his superior officer after receiving three Purple Hearts. The instruction states the reassignment is not automatic but would "be determined after consideration of his physical classification for duty and on an individual basis."

Kerry told fellow officer Lieutenant Junior Grade Jim Galvin, "There's a rule that gets you out of here and I'm getting out. You ought to do the same."[7]

Of the 138 sailors in Kerry's unit, only two others received more than two Purple Hearts. The only other officer to receive three chose to remain in combat with his men. Kerry aggressively worked to come home. Steve Hayes, one of Kerry's fellow Swift Boat commanders, remembers, "There was always something a bit odd about his time with us. . . . I found him a bit aloof and imperious. After a twenty-four-hour patrol, most of us would kick back, get a cold beer, talk, or sleep. After a twenty-four-hour patrol, I remember Kerry would usually be in the squadron office writing. I never knew exactly what he was working on. Notes? Letters? His war diary? But he was always writing." Maybe he was composing his medal citations.

"Kerry could have remained in Vietnam with the rest of us, but he made a formal request to be reassigned to the States," Hayes says, "I recall no one, except Kerry, asking that his tour be cut short and that he be sent home."

After only four months of what was to be a year-long tour, the future senator and presidential nominee returned stateside.

With political aspirations, and sensing that his home state of Massachusetts, the only state that George McGovern would eventually carry in the presidential election of 1972, would not revel in the heroic service of an increasingly unpopular war, Kerry opted for a different route. The former "hawk" would turn "dove." Expediently, he would denounce the war.

On October 15, 1969, Kerry attended the Moratorium March on Washington D.C., an antiwar protest organized by, among others, future president Bill Clinton, and endorsed by Massachusetts senator Ted Kennedy. This mass demonstration had been planned and organized a year earlier by American antiwar leaders and North Vietnamese officials gathering in Communist Cuba. The Vietnam Moratorium Committee was at one time under investigation by the House Internal Security Subcommittee for its involvement with Communists and its backing from Hanoi.

That same month, Kerry piloted a private plane for former Bobby Kennedy speechwriter and Ted Kennedy advisor Adam Walinsky to various locations in New York. Walinsky was delivering speeches against the war.

Lieutenant Kerry was still an active duty member of the Navy receiving a Navy paycheck and presumably carrying a Navy military ID card in his wallet; his participation in antiwar protests was a direct violation of federal law, the Hatch Act, Department of Defense directives, and the Uniform Code of Military Justice. If his attendance and contributions to these causes had come to light, he would have been subject to courts-martial.

Realizing the peace movement could launch his political aspirations, on January 3, 1970, Kerry asked his superior, Rear Admiral Walter F. Schlech Jr., for an early discharge from the Navy so "he could run for Congress on an antiwar platform." The request was approved and Kerry was granted a release six months prior to the expiration of his military commitment.

In May 1970, Kerry went to Paris, France, and met with the enemy with whom we were at war. "I have talked with both delegations at the peace talks, that is to say the Democratic Republic of Vietnam and the Provisional Revolutionary Government," he would later testify. By "both delegations" Kerry did *not* mean delegations from the Communist north and our ally in South Vietnam. He meant two Communist delegations: one from the Communist government of North Vietnam and one from a Communist group based in South Vietnam. Then, as now, U.S. federal law prohibits American citizens from negotiating with foreign governments on matters such as peace treaties. But, needless to say, Kerry was not prosecuted.

Having found an issue, Kerry needed to establish a public identity. The vehicle he chose was the Vietnam Veterans Against the War (VVAW), an extremist group with ties to the Communist Party USA and the Socialist Workers Party.

Here, Kerry associated himself not only with Jane Fonda and Ramsey Clark, but also with radical activist Dick Gregory and Kennedy-assassination conspiracy theorist Mark Lane. Kerry's first protest with the VVAW was at the National Guard Association's annual convention in New York. From September 13 to September 17, 1970, Kerry's group set up picket lines in front of the Americana Hotel and handed out flyers that read, "The National Guard Uses Your Tax Dollar To Support the Military-Industrial Complex, To Honor War Criminals— Westmoreland, Laird, Nixon, Etc., To Applaud Campus Murders by National Guard Units, To Encourage Armed Attacks on Minority Communities." Kerry participated as "NE Rep."—the New England representative—for VVAW.

Also in September 1970, he joined with Jane Fonda, actor Donald Sutherland, Congresswoman Bella Abzug of New York, and self-proclaimed antiwar vets in an eighty-six-mile trek from Morristown,

New Jersey, to Valley Forge, Pennsylvania, in what they coined "Operation RAW," the "rapid American withdrawal" campaign.

Fonda had organized and performed a series of events titled "Fuck the Army" earlier in the year, a perverse USO tour in reverse, performed just outside military bases in the United States. Instead of patriotic entertainers like Bob Hope and Martha Raye, she paraded disgruntled vets. An actress who today performs in such wholesome plays as *The Vagina Monologues*, Fonda was the primary bankroller for VVAW. Her involvement in the antiwar movement began in 1967 after she became convinced from several meetings with Communist activists that America, and not communism, was evil. Speaking at Michigan State University on November 22, 1969, Fonda implored, "I would think that if you understood what communism was, you would hope, you would pray on your knees that we would someday become communist."

In 1972, when more than forty thousand Americans had already been killed on the battlefields of Vietnam and the war was still raging, Fonda made a very visible and highly publicized trip to Hanoi, North Vietnam. Among her many transgressions on that trip was a stunt in which she had her picture taken sitting in a North Vietnamese anti-aircraft gun, wearing a North Vietnamese helmet, vamping to "shoot down" an American jet, "looking for one of those blue-eyed murderers—an American imperialist air raider." She's also pictured with a grin on her face, clapping as she watches a Vietnamese soldier operate the anti-aircraft gun.

The North Vietnamese effectively capitalized on her notoriety. She made radio broadcasts and films from Hanoi specifically designed to break the morale of the U.S. troops and to encourage the Viet Cong to continue their struggle against America.

"I am speaking particularly to the U.S. servicemen," she said in one broadcast. "I don't know what your officers tell you...but [your] weapons are illegal and...the men who are ordering you to use these weapons are war criminals according to international law. In the past, in Germany and Japan, men who committed these kinds of crimes were tried and executed."

She returned home wearing a necklace given to her by the North Vietnamese. It was made from the melted parts of an American B-52 bomber shot down by Hanoi.

She told the media that our prisoners of war were safe and well taken care of—at a time when they were being beaten and tortured.

When our POWs returned home a few years later and offered a dramatically different account, she called them "liars and hypocrites."

Speaking alongside Kerry at the VVAW's "Operation RAW" in Valley Forge, Pennsylvania, on September 7, 1970, she claimed "My Lai was not an isolated incident but rather a way of life of our military," perpetuating a pernicious myth that become a rallying cry for both of them.

From her irresponsible, treasonous actions then to this very day, "Hanoi Jane" is the quintessential lightning rod for veterans of all services, many of whom served in southeast Asia, those tortured as prisoners of war, and for the families of the thousands who died in that conflict.

David Hoffman, a former POW, was shot down flying his F-4 over Vietnam on December 30, 1971. He was tortured by the North Vietnamese for trying to refuse a visit from Fonda.

"When Jane Fonda turned up, she asked that some of us come out and talk with her," Hoffman remembers. "No one wanted to. The guards got very upset, because they sensed the propaganda value of a famous American war protester proving how well they were treating us. A couple of guards came to my cell and ordered me out. I resisted, and they got violently angry. My arm had been broken when I was shot down, and the Vietnamese broke it a second time. It had not healed well, and they knew it caused me great pain. They twisted it. Excruciating pain ripped through my body.

"I was dragged out to see Fonda. When I saw Fonda, and heard her antiwar rhetoric, I was almost sick to my stomach. She called us criminals and murderers. I detested Jane Fonda then and I detest her now, but I would fight to the death to protect her right to say what she thinks. Unfortunately, it was not my right to refuse to be seen with her."

In my twenty years of armed service, I've never heard a fellow veteran utter a single complimentary word about Fonda, though I have seen her likeness and name in many a military urinal around the world.

For millions of veterans, Jane Fonda has become synonymous with treason, with giving comfort and aid to an enemy, and for these reasons many veterans despise her. She continues to participate in politics, contributing to the campaigns of, among others, Senator Hillary Clinton, former senator Max Cleland, Senate Majority Leader Tom Daschle, Senator Maria Cantwell, and ex-Georgia representative Cynthia McKinney, according to a search of federal election commission records.

In his book *Tour of Duty*, Kerry biographer Douglas Brinkley would later write of the Valley Forge event, "Marijuana was in the air, skinny dippers frolicked in the Delaware River.... [The group's] long hair, ripped jeans, army surplus store canteens, and toy guns gave [them] the look of a ragtag band of Haight-Ashbury refugees." Kerry was the keynote speaker. He then immediately and unsuccessfully sought election to Congress in 1970, his campaign lasting less than a month.

His political ambition survived defeat, however. He gave an interview to the *Harvard Crimson*, the campus newspaper, in February 1971. Speaking with Samuel Z. Goldhaber, Kerry offered his views on foreign policy. "I'm an internationalist," Kerry told the *Crimson*. "I'd like to see our troops dispersed through the world only at the directive of the United Nations." On issues of national security and intelligence, Kerry wanted to "almost eliminate CIA activity."

Kerry quickly transformed himself from a little-known former naval lieutenant to the head of the VVAW movement after attending a pivotal event funded by Fonda at a Howard Johnson Comfort

Center motel in Detroit, Michigan. Here, in a second-floor ballroom, Kerry's political ambitions found a catalyst.

From January 31 to February 2, 1971, the VVAW held "The Winter Soldier Investigation." Thomas Paine wrote in 1776, "These are the times that try men's souls. The summer soldier and the sunshine patriot will, in this crisis, shrink from the service of their country; but he that stands it now, deserves the love and thanks of man and woman." Twenty-seven-year-old John Kerry and the VVAW implied that the false and outrageous charges against American servicemen risking their lives in Vietnam were example of patriotism, because their "investigation" was a Kerry-managed pander to the media from more than one hundred "Vietnam veterans." Many of them were actually impostors. These "veterans" testified that American troops routinely committed rape, torture, and murder.

"I swung my machine gun onto this group of peasants and opened fire.... For every ear you cut off someone would buy you two beers.... Our company executed a ten-year-old boy.... The heads of the bodies were cut off and they were placed on stakes.... The major that I worked for had a fantastic capability for stalking prisoners, utilizing a knife that was extremely sharp, and sort of fileting them like a fish.... Prisoners treated like this were executed at the end because there was no way we could take them into any medical aide and say, 'This dude fell down some steps.'"

Kerry recently defended what he heard at Winter Soldier as "highly documented and very disturbing." None of the testimony was ever corroborated, though, and many of the "veterans" were eventually exposed as pretenders and liars.

The Naval Investigative Service eventually concluded that the most grisly and shocking testimony was given by fraudulent "witnesses" who had never served in Vietnam—who had simply lied for effect. Some of these not only lied but also appropriated the names of true veterans. None would sign an affidavit or help the military investigate the atrocity claims.

Burkett is highly critical of Kerry and his opportunistic use of impostors in the antiwar effort. "[Kerry] presented this ragtag bunch of bums as your standard honorably discharged Vietnam vet, and I think nothing could be further from the truth. They weren't."

Nevertheless, in early April of 1971, antiwar senator Mark Hatfield asked for the Winter Soldier transcripts to be entered into the congressional record and called for an official investigation into American war crimes in Vietnam.

A documentary film of the Winter Soldier was produced, winning awards at the Cannes and Berlin film festivals, further perpetuating myths about Vietnam "war crimes," and helping to poison public opinion against a generation of American soldiers.

One of Kerry's colleagues was Al Hubbard, the executive director of VVAW. Hubbard claimed to be an Air Force officer who had spent two years in Vietnam and was wounded in combat. In reality, Hubbard was a fake. While he had served in the military, he was never promoted beyond the rank of staff sergeant, had never served in Vietnam, and was never wounded. Kerry and Hubbard, however, went on NBC's *Meet the Press*, side by side, to denounce the war.

From April 18 to April 23, 1971, more than one thousand "veterans" in shabby, mismatched uniforms "invaded" Washington, D.C. The event was called "Dewey Canyon III," "a limited incursion into the country of Congress." The "vets" marched on the National Mall carrying Viet Cong flags and placards supporting China, Cuba, the Soviet Union, and North Korea, clenched fists raised high into the air. The demonstrators conducted simulated "search and destroy" missions and skits, during which they dramatized the killing of innocent civilians. They splattered red paint, symbolizing blood, on the steps of the Capitol. The brightest star rising above this boorish group was John Forbes Kerry.

"I could not be more proud of the fact that when I came back from that war, having learned what I learned, "said Kerry, "that I led thousands of veterans to Washington, we camped on the Mall underneath the Congress, underneath Richard Nixon's visibility.... We've earned the right to sleep on this Mall and talk to our senators and congressmen."

Actually, while his band of brothers camped out in the park, Kerry enjoyed conditions more in keeping with his silver-spoon lifestyle, staying in a Georgetown townhouse owned by the family of George Butler, a college friend and former veteran. It was there that Kerry worked out the speech of his political lifetime, during which he would revel in his moment in the sun. In this speech, the opportunistic Kerry seized his opportunity to launch a career.

On April 22, 1971, Kerry addressed the Senate Foreign Relations Committee, chaired by Senator J. W. Fulbright and attended by senators Stuart Symington, Claiborne Pell, George Aiken, Clifford Case, and Jacob Javits. Television cameras lined the walls and self-professed veterans of all sizes, shapes, and uniform combinations filled the seats.

Kerry sat at the table across from the congressmen, his long dark hair swept across his forehead, and delivered the speech that would define him. He was dressed in drab olive fatigues displaying his Silver Star and Purple Hearts.

Under oath, Kerry claimed that U.S. soldiers had "personally raped, cut off ears, cut off heads, taped wires from portable telephones to human genitals and turned up the power, cut off limbs, blown up bodies, randomly shot at civilians, razed villages in fashion reminiscent of Genghis Khan, shot cattle and dogs for fun, poisoned food stocks, and generally ravaged the countryside of South Vietnam."

According to Kerry, every day was a My Lai Massacre. Lieutenant William Calley had been prosecuted and sentenced to life imprisonment only three weeks earlier. The press was replete with tales of Calley's atrocities and rampant speculation that more such crimes would soon be exposed.

But as Kerry later admitted, he hadn't actually witnessed any of the events to which he testified. They were based on lies, rumor, and innuendo. "I personally didn't see personal atrocities in the sense I saw somebody cut a head off or something like that," he later said.[8]

Michael Bernique, a decorated naval veteran who served as a Swift Boat commander with Kerry in Vietnam, notes, "I think there was a point in time when John was making it up fast and quick. I think he was saying whatever he needed to say."

Kerry's testimony is repeated in full beginning on page 199.

The U.S. military has a very clear chain of command. One of the most basic military obligations is to inform one's immediate superiors of any violations of the Uniform Code of Military Justice, the laws of war, or the rules of engagement; illegal orders are not to be followed by subordinates and not to be tolerated by superiors. If Kerry had witnessed such crimes, he was under an obligation to inform his commanders, which he never did.

While not observing the atrocities he testified to and perjuring himself, oddly enough, he did confess to his own war crimes. "I did take part in free-fire zones, I did take part in harassment and interdiction fire, I did take part in search-and-destroy missions in which the houses of noncombatants were burned to the ground. And all of these acts, I find out later on, are contrary to the Hague and Geneva conventions and to the laws of warfare. So in that sense, anybody who took part in those, if you carry out the application of the Nuremberg Principles, is in fact guilty."[9]

"We cannot consider ourselves America's 'best men,'" he explained, "when we are ashamed of and hated for what we were called to do." He declared that "war crimes committed in Southeast Asia [are] not isolated incidents but crimes committed on a day-to-day basis with the full awareness of officers at all levels of command." He attested that "two hundred thousand [Vietnamese] a year are murdered by the United States of America."

He characterized the war as the "height of criminal hypocrisy," and offered that perhaps two or three thousand Vietnamese might need to relocate should we withdraw our force from the conflict. He testified that the Communist threat was "bogus, totally artificial. There is no threat."

The nonexistent threat resulted in 750,000 Vietnamese being forced into Communist "reeducation" camps and more than 130,000 Vietnamese becoming "boat people," fleeing the Communist regime. Laos fell to the North Vietnamese Communists, was subjected to a Stalinist government, and has killed an estimated 100,000 Hmong tribesmen (American allies during the war). The Communist Khmer Rouge conquered Cambodia, killing more than two million people in their reign of terror.

As Kerry spoke, the North Vietnamese were torturing American POWs, trying to extort from them the same sorts of statements that Kerry was giving of his own free will. His congressional testimony would eventually be used as an interrogation device by these North Vietnamese guards as a tool for further manipulation.

Retired naval rear admiral Jeremiah Denton was a POW at the time of Kerry's testimony and would later serve in Congress as a senator from Alabama. On July 18, 1965, Denton was leading a group of twenty-eight aircraft from the aircraft carrier USS *Independence* to attack enemy emplacements near Thanh Hoa, North Vietnam. He was shot down, captured, and spent the next seven years and eight months in captivity. Four of those years were spent in solitary confinement.

When the North Vietnamese attempted a propaganda-motivated television interview with their American captives in 1966, millions of Americans watched as Denton, courageously blinking his eyes in Morse code, spelled out the word "torture." It was the first proof for American political leaders and military intelligence that the Communists were torturing American POWs.

Denton now recalls "When Kerry joined me in the Senate, I already knew about his record of defamatory remarks and behavior criticizing U.S. policy in Vietnam and the conduct of our military personnel there. I had learned in North Vietnamese prisons how much harm such statements caused. To me, his remarks and behavior amounted to giving aide and comfort to our Vietnamese and Soviet enemies.... John Kerry is not among the good guys." Commander Denton was the first American POW to step off the plane and onto American soil in Operation Homecoming.

On April 23, 1971, Kerry led members of the VVAW in a protest march to the U.S. Capitol. In a theatrical conclusion to the five-day protest, the veterans and those masquerading as veterans began "returning" their military medals and ribbons to the government by throwing them over a makeshift fence high onto the steps of the Capitol.

Kerry participated as well, throwing what at the time were purported to be his own medals. When questioned later by the *Washington Post*, Kerry said, "They're my medals. I'll do what I want to with them. And there shouldn't be any expectations about them."

In a speech immediately following the event, Kerry said, "The administration forced us to return our medals." "I gave back, I can't remember, six, seven, eight, nine medals," he later said in an interview on a Washington, D.C., news program called *Viewpoints*, which aired on November 6, 1971. When he was asked by the interviewer if he gave back his Bronze Star, Silver Star, and three Purple Hearts, he replied, "Well, and above that, [I] gave back the others."[10]

Kerry later changed his story, explaining that the medals weren't his—even though he'd worn them on his fatigues the day before, when he testified to Congress. He said the medals belonged to a wounded veteran in a VA hospital in New York and a World War II veteran from Lincoln, Massachusetts, but he could not recall these veterans' names.

Ribbons are given along with the award of medals and are in essence the same. Kerry was given a Silver Star ribbon along with his Silver Star medal. The only distinction is this: Medals are worn on the more formal versions of the uniform and ribbons on the blouse of the informal versions. Kerry claims he threw his ribbons away but not his medals. His medals, he avows, are now proudly displayed on his office wall.

The day following Kerry's perjured testimony, more than 250,000 people showed up to join in the protest, and Kerry became a celebrity for the peace movement. Within weeks of his congressional testimony, Kerry was featured in a CBS *60 Minutes* piece and on television's popular *Dick Cavett Show*. He portrayed America's servicemen as unwilling soldiers, morally lacking and haunted by their experiences. He created the illusion that all returning veterans were broken, drug-addicted losers taught to kill at society's expense, "ticking time bombs" ready to come home and explode.

Kerry also wrote a book, *The New Soldier*, published in 1971. It was edited by his former brother-in-law and current campaign advisor, David Thorne, and documentary filmmaker and former Georgetown buddy George Butler.

Try finding a copy. The book has virtually disappeared. Strangely enough, I found a copy at the Air University Library at Maxwell Air Force Base, Alabama, the site for all professional military learning in the Air Force. As the ancient military prophet Sun Tzu once said, "Know your enemy."

On the cover is a picture of Kerry's band of misfits mocking the celebrated World War II monument to the Marine Corps, the raising of the flag at Mount Suribachi on the island of Iwo Jima. The picture on Kerry's book shows his ragtag gang hoisting the American flag upside down.

In the book, Kerry concluded, "We will not quickly join those who march on Veterans' Day waving small flags, calling to memory those thousands who died for the 'greater glory of the United States.' We will not accept the rhetoric. We will not readily join the American Legion and the Veterans of Foreign Wars—in fact, we will find it hard to join anything at all and when we do, we will demand relevancy such as other organizations have recently been unable to provide. We will not take solace from the creation of monuments or the naming of parks after a select few of the thousands of dead Americans and Vietnamese. We will not uphold the traditions which decorously memorialize that which was base and grim.... We are asking America to turn from false glory, hollow victory, fabricated foreign threats, fear which threatens us as a nation, shallow pride which feeds off fear."

Kerry's fantasies of the war and its veterans were adopted as the common view of those on the Left and became a staple of movies and television. But again, Kerry and his radical associates were wrong. A Harris poll in 1980 showed that 91 percent of Vietnam vets were "glad they served their country," that 74 percent "enjoyed their time in the military," and that 89 percent agreed with the statement "Our troops were asked to fight in a war which our political leaders in Washington would not let them win."

In November of 1971, Kerry gave a speech to the students of Bethany College in West Virginia. "Our democracy is a farce," Kerry started. "It is not the best in the world.... There is a disbelief in the American Dream." He concluded his talk by resorting to his common, broad-brushed, and fallacious Vietnam themes. Some veterans, he said "came back with a heroin habit that cost $12 a day in Vietnam. That same habit costs $175 to $250 a day in the U.S." Kerry continued to say that still "other veterans came back with psychological problems, such as those who sleep with knives under their pillows, or those whose wives have to wake them up with code words so they don't get stabbed."[11]

Another myth among Kerry's accusations, and one promulgated by liberals ever since, is that Vietnam was fought by the oppressed, poor, uneducated, and minorities. In his congressional testimony of 1971, Kerry labeled the U.S. military racist, claiming "blacks provided the highest percentage of casualties."

On an April 2000 episode of the PBS *NewsHour with Jim Lehrer*, liberal historians Michael Beschloss and Doris Kearns Goodwin championed this argument. Beschloss stated that Vietnam "was a war that, especially as it went on, was fought by Americans who were poor and African American." Kearns Goodwin fell in lockstep. "I still think that one legacy that's left, however, is that we let the draft go because we didn't want a selective draft, as we had [in Vietnam], because it seemed to weigh so heavily on those who were poor and working-class and the middle-class, better educated kids got out of it."

Several sources, however, reveal a much different reality. Again, B. G. Burkett's authoritative book, *Stolen Valor*, tells a compelling story, as does a review of the facts generated by the "Long Way Home Project" and gathered from the National Archives and the Defense Department.

Of the 2,594,000 men and women who served in Vietnam, only 25 percent (648,500) were draftees. 88.4 percent of the men who served were Caucasian, 10.6 percent were African American, and 1 percent belonged to other races. 86.8 percent of those killed in hostile action were Caucasian, 12.1 percent were African American, and 1.1 percent belonged to other races. Twenty-six percent of combat deaths came from families in the highest third of income levels and 23 percent of all men sent to Vietnam had fathers with professional, managerial, or technical occupations.

Before leaving the VVAW, Kerry attended one last, notoriously memorable meeting in a Mennonite church in Kansas City, Missouri. From November 12 through November 15, 1971, the antiwar organization held steering committee meetings in which a plot to assassinate seven war-supporting senators was discussed. The potential targets included South Carolina Republican Strom Thurmond and Mississippi Democrat John Stennis. According to Thomas Lipscomb of the *New York Sun*, several veterans remember Kerry being present at the meeting when Scott Camil, another member of the VVAW and known as "Scott the Assassin," proposed the plan. They seriously discussed the plot for a day and a half. "My plan was that, on the last day, we would go into the [congressional] offices, we would schedule the most hardcore hawks for last—and we would shoot them all," said Camil.[12]

FBI surveillance of Kerry and his group document and confirm his attendance and the proposed assassination. Kerry reportedly voted against the plan and, from his own account, resigned from his position three days later. He represented the VVAW at a speech at Dartmouth College two months after the "assassination" meeting, though, and on January 26, 1972, he attended a protest meeting in Washington, D.C., where the *New York Times* described him as "a leader of the Vietnam Veterans Against the War." Whatever the case, when future senator Kerry left the "assassination" meeting, he did not call law enforcement.

At first, Kerry's presidential campaign repeatedly stated that he "never, ever" attended a Kansas City meeting of antiwar leaders where an assassination plot aimed at U.S. senators was discussed. When confronted with FBI surveillance files, Kerry's campaign acknowledged his presence as "an historical footnote." Kerry subsequently told a Boston radio host that the story was "such ancient history."

The U.S. military has a code of conduct, a mandate for personal behavior. Developed after POWs during the Korean War were subjected to torture and brainwashing by the enemy, it was approved by President Dwight Eisenhower and in 1955 became the official behavioral benchmark by which all in uniform are expected to abide in peace, in war, and as a POW.

Article VI of the Code of Conduct declares: "I will never forget that I am an American, responsible for my actions, and dedicated to the principles which made my country free. I will trust in my God and in the United States of America."

Aspiring senator Kerry, for personal political gain, chose to heap disrespect on his fellow soldiers. His antiwar remarks were used against those still sitting in the dank and musty cells of the "Hanoi Hilton," who lived by the code Kerry treated with contempt. Kerry has never repudiated his post-Vietnam showmanship of the 1970s. He cannot. It's the reason he is where he is today. Because Kerry so successfully turned antiwar myths into media realities, he handed a propaganda victory to the Communists, undermined America's war effort, and in the words of retired major general George S. Patton III, who commanded troops in Vietnam and is the son of the legendary hero from World War II, "Mr. Kerry probably caused some of my guys to get killed. There is no soap ever invented that can wash that blood off his hands."

Navy Commander Paul Galanti was flying his A-4C Skyhawk over North Vietnam on June 17, 1966. Galanti, a member of Navy Light Jet Attack Squadron 216, was assigned to the aircraft carrier USS *Hancock*. His target this day, he thought, was a series of boxcars on a train track. It was, in fact, a flak trap—North Vietnamese gunners hiding out in bamboo huts fabricated to simulate train cars ripe for aerial attack.

He never saw what hit him. On his ninety-seventh combat mission, Galanti was forced to eject over enemy territory. He spent the next seven years as a prisoner of war. Some of that time was spent at the POW camp at Son Tay. There, the camp commander told Galanti, "We can't beat you on the battlefield, but we can beat you on the streets of New York, Washington, D.C., and San Francisco."

Galanti recalls his captors using "all the news that was fit to print." Stories of Jane Fonda and Ramsey Clark as they protested the war... and the picture of former naval officer, John Kerry, testifying in uniform, with long hair, in front of Congress.

Galanti learned of Kerry's 1971 speech while held captive in the "Hanoi Hilton." "During torture sessions," Galanti said, his captors cited the antiwar speeches as "an example of why we should cross over to [their] side."

When Galanti heard Kerry's testimony, he thought, "That's not right!" His next reaction was: "He's a jerk, an opportunistic SOB. I was just embarrassed he was Navy."

For Galanti and thousands of veterans, "John Kerry was a traitor to the men he served with. The Vietnam Memorial has thousands of additional names due to John Kerry and others like him."

Former Army Green Beret and Vietnam veteran Don Bendell is similarly outraged. Bendell wrote an open letter to Kerry published in several periodicals in February of 2004.

"I was a Green Beret officer who volunteered for duty in Vietnam and fought in the thick of it in 1968 and 1969 on a Special Forces A-team on the Ho Chi Minh Trail, just for starters. We were the elite. We saw the most action. Everybody in the world knows that. But we did not just kill people; we built a church, a school, treated illnesses, passed out soap, food and clothing, and had fun and loving interaction with the indigenous people of Vietnam, just like our boys did in Normandy, Baghdad, Saigon and everywhere American soldiers have ever served. My children and grandchildren could read your words and think those horrendous things about me, Mr. Kerry. You are a bald-faced, unprincipled liar and a disgrace, and you have dishonored me and all my fellow Vietnam veterans.... Your medals and mine are not a free pass for a lifetime, Sen. Kerry, to bypass character, integrity, and morality. I earn my green beret over and over daily in all aspects of my life...Medals don't make a man. Morals do."

On May 4, 2004, Kerry's former Swift Boat mates met in Washington, D.C., held a press conference, and released a letter. The event went largely unnoticed and unreported by elite media. Nineteen of the twenty-three officers who served with Kerry in Vietnam signed the letter, as did nearly every officer who commanded Kerry for any substantial period of time, including retired Coast Guard captain Adrian Lonsdale, retired Navy rear admiral Roy Hoffmann, retired lieutenant commander George Elliot, and retired lieutenant commander Hibbard. More than 90 percent of Kerry's former commanders and squadron mates agreed to sign the letter of condemnation. "It is our collective judgment that, upon your return from Vietnam, you grossly and knowingly distorted the conduct of the American soldiers, Marines, sailors, and airmen of that war," the letter reads. The group's spokesman, John O'Neill, who took over Kerry's PCF 94 when Kerry returned home early, concluded, "We left a lot of friends on the field, and we don't appreciate a guy who lied about it and continues to lie about it right up to the present. We believe, based on our experiences with him, he is totally unfit to be commander in chief."[13]

In a move akin to naming the Libyan delegation to the United Nations to chair the Council on Human Rights, Kerry was selected to chair the Senate Select Committee on POW/MIA Affairs in 1992. The stated goal of the committee was to investigate the reams of evidence of American prisoners not returned from the Vietnam War and reports that some might still be alive and in captivity years after the war's conclusion.

Washington long suspected that Hanoi had not returned all of our war prisoners. The body of evidence was overwhelming. As author Sydney H. Schanberg related the evidence in the *Village Voice* (hardly a conservative forum),

> 1,600 firsthand sightings of live U.S. prisoners; nearly 14,000 secondhand reports; numerous intercepted Communist radio messages from within Vietnam and Laos about American prisoners being moved by their captors from one site to another; a series of satellite photos that continued into the 1990s showing clear prisoner rescue signals carved into the ground in Laos and Vietnam, all labeled inconclusive by the Pentagon; multiple reports about acknowledged prisoners from North Vietnamese informants working for U.S. intelligence agencies, all ignored or declared unreliable; persistent complaints by senior U.S. intelligence officials (some of them made publicly) that live-prisoner evidence was being suppressed; and clear proof that the Pentagon and other keepers of the "secret" destroyed a variety of files over the years to keep the POW/MIA families and the public from finding out and possibly setting off a major public outcry.

The committee met from 1991 to 1993 and got off to an ominous start. Colonel Millard Peck, head of the Pentagon's POW/MIA office, resigned in disgust after only eight months on the job. In his resignation letter, Peck wrote, "The mind-set to 'debunk' is alive and well. It is held at all levels. . . . The sad fact is that . . . a cover up may be in progress. The entire charade does not appear to be an honest effort and may never have been. From what I have witnessed, it appears that any soldier left in Vietnam, even inadvertently, was in fact abandoned years ago, and that the farce that is being played is no more than political legerdemain down with 'smoke and mirrors' to stall the issue until it dies a natural death."

James Schlesinger, who had served as both director of Central Intelligence and secretary of defense, was asked at a committee hearing, "Did we leave some men behind?" He answered, "I think that as of now, I can come to no other conclusion. . . . Some were left behind." Former secretary of defense Melvin Laird and former secretary of state Henry Kissinger also believed men were left behind who might still be alive.

Senator Kerry had another agenda, however. He wanted to clear all the impediments for normalizing relations with Vietnam. The nagging issue of American servicemen not being returned by the Vietnamese, possibly still alive, would have to be silenced for good.

Kerry refused to interview key witnesses and ordered committee staff to shred important intelligence documents. The shredding stopped only when some staffers protested. The committee's final report, issued in January of 1993, officially closed the issue for Congress. It concluded there was "no compelling evidence that proves" that American POWs were still alive in Vietnam. As for what happened to those men who were unaccounted for, the report conceded only that there was "evidence . . . that indicates the possibility of survival, at least for a small number" of prisoners at the end of the war.

Kerry and his committee determined that American POWs were left behind but that none were still alive. They made no attempt to identify those who had been abandoned, how they had died, who killed them, or where their remains might be.

As he had done twenty years earlier, former naval lieutenant Kerry turned his back on those with whom he had served.

With a whimper, the committee buried the POW/MIA issue and opened the door for the normalization of relations between the two countries that Kerry so eagerly sought. Shortly after, Vietnam announced it had granted a large real estate contract to Colliers International, based in Boston. The multimillion-dollar contract was for a massive modernizing of Vietnam's ports, railroads, and other infrastructure.

Colliers International's CEO, C. Stewart Forbes, is John Forbes Kerry's cousin.

Today, Kerry appeals to veterans to support him in his run for the White House and into the position of commander in chief. He should be joking, but, unfortunately, we know he's not. America has already had a draft-dodging president—Bill Clinton—and dishonoring America's veterans hasn't kept John Kerry from a successful political career in Massachusetts.

A soldier knows... and Kerry is not a soldier.

CHAPTER THREE

THE POLITICS OF TREASON II: HILLARY CLINTON AT THE FRONT

"Congressmen who willfully take actions during wartime that damage morale and undermine the military are saboteurs and should be arrested, exiled or hanged."

—President Abraham Lincoln[1]

"**B**roomstick One," as the troops named it, touched down at Kandahar Airport in Afghanistan on November 27, 2003. Off stepped Democratic senator Hillary Clinton of New York, accompanied by her entourage and fellow Democratic senator Jack Reed of Rhode Island.

Senator Clinton was visiting the war zone under the guise of a Thanksgiving "fact-finding" trip to Afghanistan and Iraq, and, ostensibly, to bolster the morale of American troops.

While hundreds of soldiers waited patiently for their opportunity to sit and eat turkey and dressing, Clinton and her clique opted to go directly to the front of the chow line. Perhaps they weren't aware of one of the military's fundamental traditions: Officers (and people pretending to be officers) eat last. But, as is always the case with Hillary, it was all about her.

After finishing her meal, Mrs. Clinton made the rounds with the soldiers, whose commanders had made their attendance mandatory.

Clinton proffered that "the outcome [of the war] is not assured," that "there are many questions at home about the administration's policies," and that "the obstacles and problems are much greater than the administration usually admits to."[2]

Later that day, while dining with soldiers in Baghdad, she charged that President Bush was motivated by his own political concerns in conducting the war on terrorism. The claim that a president would employ the military for political gain is particularly entertaining coming from a former first lady whose husband had a penchant for ordering military action—firing missiles at tents and aspirin factories—to coincide with developments in his impeachment or when his popularity polls needed a bump.

Mrs. Clinton launched into a personal attack on President Bush, these soldiers' commander in chief, claiming he'd been "obsessed with Saddam Hussein for more than a decade." Later, she said that "the Pentagon tried to make do with as few troops as possible...and didn't fully appreciate the conditions we would encounter."[3]

She clearly didn't understand her audience; she and her husband never have when it comes to the military. These young men and women were in this fight together with their commander in chief, after America's second Pearl Harbor—September 11, 2001. They thrive on positive messages, encouragement, motivation, and the knowledge that their sacrifices are recognized and supported at home. Their morale comes from their pride in being America's defenders of freedom. It's part of what keeps them going when the going gets tough, and the primary obligation of leadership is to strengthen that morale.

Instead, Hillary Clinton (a former first lady who really ought to know better) told our troops that they were mismanaged tools of President Bush's obsession with Saddam Hussein. On this day of national thanksgiving, Senator Hillary Rodham Clinton saw her role as that of spreading seeds of doubt to soldiers on battlefields thousands of miles away from homes, spouses, children, and family for purely partisan political gain. "We are fighting an enemy which has a lot of impact by relatively small numbers and we've got to provide security throughout large countries. That's not easy with the force numbers we have."[4]

Senator Reed (a former Army officer who really ought to know better) contributed to the warped picture of dissent back home, saying that the administration's justification for the war was "tenuous at best" and that Americans "could look back and see the decision to attack Iraq was one that ended up being very, very costly."[5] Al-Jazeera, Qatar's television network for jihadists, immediately broadcast Clinton and Reed's remarks in Arabic, providing insurgents everywhere the spark and the fuel to keep going. Essentially, our enemy heard, "You are being effective in spite of your small numbers, support for the war effort from American political leaders is waning, and the United States—especially if the Democrats gain power—does not have the resolve to defeat you."

What our soldiers in combat heard from our senators was that the president was wrong to employ them, that he did so for selfish political gain, that we didn't have enough resources to get the job done so they were wasting their time, and that their buddies' lives that had been lost might have been lost in vain. Being told that you might die for a war that was a mistake must have been a tremendous stimulant for unit morale.

This was politics over country. This was moral and spiritual treason. This was aiding and abetting the enemy. And it serves to materially boost an insurgent enemy fighting from a network of caves and spider holes, hoping that American resolve will again weaken and decide to pull out. That's precisely what happened in Vietnam and Somalia. It's precisely what the insurgents in Afghanistan and Iraq are praying for as well.

This is the Democrats' version of "supporting our troops"—using Afghanistan and Iraq as a platform to criticize the war effort, the Pentagon, and, most importantly, President Bush. Liberals "support our troops" by doing everything they can to politically sabotage their missions, undercut their morale, and, when they have power (as during the Carter and Clinton presidencies) to demoralize them with poor pay, poor equipment, lack of spare parts, and liberal social engineering (co-ed basic training, "dual standards" affirmative action for women in the military, "gays in the military," and so on). Liberals will sell the lives of American servicemen for the opportunity to regain office.

"What I said is what I believe," Mrs. Clinton has said, defending her Thanksgiving Day speeches.

If so, it speaks to the chill in her soul and to her ruthless ambition: politics before the men and women in uniform who are fighting and dying for their country, soldiers whose enemy has just heard a former first lady proclaim that America's war effort is flawed at best, and potentially founded on lies. Will America cut and run if the terrorists ratchet up the violence? Senators Clinton and Reed gave them every reason to think so—and they are merely echoing the usual rhetoric of the John Kerry-Teddy Kennedy-Howard Dean Democratic Party of today.

Hillary, of course, was quick to blame the furor over her remarks as "the latest flaming charge by the right wing." "I think that's reflective of the efforts of this [the Bush] administration to deny and divert attention from what everybody knows. I mean, it's like the old children's story, 'The Emperor Has No Clothes,'" she told Tim Russert on *Meet the Press*.[6] She obviously missed the humor the rest of us saw in her using the image of an unclothed emperor. Her stance was vintage Clintonism: It's always somebody else's fault.

Liberals like Hillary Clinton and the dangerous politics of the Left are poison to the souls of patriotic Americans.

Patriotic Americans don't blame the deaths of our soldiers on our government—they blame them on the enemy who pulled the trigger or ignited the truck bomb.

Patriotic Americans don't criticize the government for "losing the peace" when we are, in fact, winning the war. In the War on Terror, we're not at peace and we're not losing.

Patriotic Americans don't take a noble cause such as defending your country and liberating the oppressed and turn it into a set of talking points aimed solely at the political destruction of a rival.

Patriotic Americans choose their country first. The politics come later.

But for a liberal like Senator John Kerry, the enemy is always America, unless America is led by him: "What we need now is not just regime change in Saddam Hussein and Iraq, but we need regime change in the United States. . . . I don't think [world leaders] are going to trust this president, no matter what. I believe it deeply, that it will take a new president of the United States, declaring a new day for our relationship with the world, to clear the air and turn a new page on American history."[7]

Former vice president Al Gore, with all the emotion he could muster, Dean-screamed, "This nation has never in our two centuries made a worse foreign policy mistake than what George W. Bush made in putting our troops into that quagmire in Iraq. It was a horrible misjudgment."[8]

Would-be Democratic presidential candidate Howard Dean claims that Saudi Arabia tipped off President Bush about the September 11, 2001, attacks and he failed to act, and claimed America is no safer with Saddam Hussein behind bars.

Massachusetts senator Ted Kennedy, speaking to the Center for American Progress, attacked the Bush administration, saying that it had "broken faith with the American people, aided by a congressional majority willing to pursue ideology at any price, even the price of the truth." Kennedy went on, claiming that Bush should not have sent troops "into harm's way in Iraq for ideological reasons and a timetable based on the marketing of a political product."[9] Earlier, Kennedy had called the war in Iraq a fraud "made up in Texas." "There was no imminent danger," he continued, "and we should never have gone to war."[10]

Democratic congressman James McDermott of Washington told a Seattle radio show that he thinks the Army could have caught Saddam at any time and did so only to give President Bush a political boost.

Democratic senator and Senate Minority Leader Tom Daschle of South Dakota claimed, "I am saddened that this president failed so miserably at diplomacy that we're now forced to war."[11]

House Minority Leader Nancy Pelosi shrieked, "I have no regret about my vote on this war. The cost in human lives. The cost to our budget, probably $100 billion. We could have probably brought down that statue for a lot less."[12]

Former Clinton secretary of state Madeleine Albright told journalist Morton Kondracke in a television studio green room that she thinks we've got Osama bin Laden in our sights and will grab him just prior to the 2004 election.

General Wesley Clark, the "Perfumed Prince," campaigning for the Democratic presidential nomination, referred to the war in Iraq as "Not patriotic. Not smart, I don't think it was a patriotic war. I think it was a mistake, a strategic mistake."[13] Clark also called for an impeachment probe of President Bush. "I think this Congress needs to investigate precisely [how the U.S. wound up in a war in Iraq] that was connected to the threat of al-Qaeda," Clark said. "This was an elective war. [Bush] forced us to go to war," he complained.[14] He also charged that Bush "never intended" to capture Osama bin Laden.[15] A clear indication of the extremes the former general was willing to go to for votes was demonstrated with his machismo pose on the cover of *The Advocate* magazine (a national gay and lesbian news source) sporting an open shirt over a v-neck t-shirt for the gay readers.

George Soros, the radical billionaire philanthropist and friend of Bill Clinton who funds groups supporting abortion, atheism, gay marriage, euthanasia, drug legalization, sex education, and other liberal causes, claims, "America, under Bush, is a danger to the world." Soros adds, "I find the foreign policy of the Bush administration exceedingly dangerous." He vowed to do whatever necessary to bring the president down.[16] Soros's brain trust for the effort is Morton Halperin, a former Clinton administration official and liberal mastermind who organized the highly damaging campaign in the 1970s to strip the intelligence gathering capabilities of the FBI and CIA; and John Podesta, former Clinton White House chief of staff.

It would serve well for the Clintons, Kerry, Gore, Kennedy, Pelosi, Daschle, and Clark (who seems to have lost whatever military sense he had when he became a Democratic presidential candidate and tried to get to the left of Howard Dean) to remember this: America's servicemen and women are engaged in combat. Most have written their families a final letter, directing that it be mailed home if they are killed on the battlefield. They have pictures of their wives, husbands, and kids stashed in the webbing of their helmet or in their wallets. They have been ordered into harm's way by their president. They are living to win and come home.

And they think they have accomplished something tremendously significant in defeating the Taliban that harbored al-Qaeda and in toppling Saddam Hussein, who had violated his cease-fire agreement ending the Gulf War, who had routinely fired on British and American aircraft patrolling the "no-fly" zones, who had tried to assassinate former president George H. W. Bush, and who had ordered the killing of more than 300,000 of his own people.

Saddam is behind bars awaiting justice. Uday and Qusay are in "paradise," their murder, torture, and rapes quelled forever. All but nine of the Pentagon's most wanted fifty-two Iraqis have been captured or killed.

The quality of life for Iraq's citizens has similarly been bettered. School attendance for Iraqi children is up by 10 percent over Saddam days. More than 2,500 schools have been renovated by the coalition forces, and the weapons formerly stored there have been removed. Unemployment has been cut in half. Wages are climbing. Public healthcare funding is twenty-five times higher than it was before the war and millions of Iraqi children have been immunized for the first time. The drinkable water supply has doubled. More than 4.5 million Iraqis have clean drinking water for the first time ever. Electrical power is now available to twice as many Iraqis as was so before the war. One hundred percent of Iraq's hospitals are open and functioning, compared to only 35 percent under Saddam. Democratic elections are taking place in every major city.

Since George W. Bush declared his War on Terror, more than three thousand al-Qaeda leaders and foot soldiers have been captured or killed. More than two-thirds of the al-Qaeda leadership have been captured or killed. The State Department's annual report on terrorism notes a 44 percent decrease in "international terrorist" attacks—to their lowest levels since 1969.[17]

Moammar Gadhafi of Libya has voluntarily surrendered his weapons of mass destruction program and has asked to join the community of law-abiding nations. "I will do whatever the Americans want, because I saw what happened in Iraq and was afraid," said Gadhafi to Italian prime minister Silvio Berlusconi.[18]

Pakistan's secret role in passing secrets and technology to terrorist regimes in Libya, Iran, and North Korea has been exposed. Iran has agreed to allow inspections of its nuclear sites. North Korea is considering negotiation and restraint in its nuclear arms development. Syria is openly calculating whether to continue as a rogue state or to follow Gadhafi's example. Hillary Clinton and John Kerry encourage Syria's Ba'athist government to think one way, George W. Bush another.

For the sake of our country, for its safety and security, we need to convince terrorist-supporting states that George W. Bush speaks for America and that the Clinton-Kerry Democrats do not.

THE POLITICS OF TREASON III: THE ONLY SPENDING LIBERALS HATE

"I actually did vote for the $87 billion before I voted against it."

—Senator John Kerry, March 16, 2004[1]

In September of 2003, President George W. Bush addressed the nation regarding the War on Terror. In that speech, the president said, "Our strategy will require new resources. We have conducted a thorough assessment of our military and reconstruction needs in Iraq, and also Afghanistan. I will soon submit to Congress a request for $87 billion."[2]

The Iraq/Afghanistan Supplemental Funding Bill was critical to supporting our troops overseas. It sought to provide $65.6 billion for military "operations and maintenance"—referred to as "O & M" in the defense community—in essence, the funding line that covers the day-to-day operating expenses of the military. Included in the O & M portion of the request was the money necessary to buy body armor for our soldiers and to fund the hazardous duty pay that military members receive when they serve in a war zone. The bill also included a request for $1.3 billion to provide medical care to military families.

John Kerry voted no on the Supplemental Funding Bill. So did fellow liberals Dennis Kucinich and Ted Kennedy; Kucinich called the bill "fraudulent."[3]

Later, in yet another liberal attempt at revisionism, Kerry attacked the Bush administration for not supporting the troops, claiming that it was "shocking" that "tens of thousands of other troops arrived in Iraq to find that—with danger around every corner—there wasn't enough body armor."[4]

The appropriation bill Kerry opposed paid for that armor.

Democratic senator Tom Harkin of Iowa claimed, "This may not be Vietnam, but it sure smells like it. And every time I see those bills coming down for more money, it's costing like Vietnam too."[5]

House Minority Leader Nancy Pelosi offered, "American taxpayers deserve to know how this spending will affect our ability to address the unmet needs in our country."[6] Democratic congressman Henry Waxman of California, not one to hide the checkbook, is now concerned about the "inappropriate" use of taxpayer dollars.

Two points come to mind. First, when did Democrats start caring about America's taxpayers? Second, when did Democrats start worrying about government spending?

In fact, spending on defense might be the only spending liberals hate. Since the 1970s, the Democrats, the party of big spending, have been loath to spend when it comes to our military.

KERRY VOTES NO EVERY TIME

John Kerry's anti-military history and senatorial voting record make him the obvious heir to the George McGovern tradition in the Democratic Party. Not only was Kerry an anti-military voice in the 1970s, but when he ran for and won his Senate seat in 1984, he directly challenged Ronald Reagan's military buildup and modernization that ultimately won the Cold War, as the Soviets couldn't keep stride. Kerry argued instead for a nuclear weapons freeze and for slashing the defense budget, policies that would have put no pressure at all on the Soviet Union. Kerry's 1984 campaign literature claimed, "The Reagan administration has no rational plan for our military. Instead, it acts on misinformed assumptions about the strength of the Soviet military and a presumed 'window of vulnerability,' which we now know not to exist."[7]

Kerry's campaign argued that "The biggest defense buildup since World War II [it wasn't—Korea and Vietnam were larger] has not given us a better defense. Americans feel more threatened by the prospect of war, not less so. And our national priorities become more and more distorted as the share of our country's resources devoted to human needs diminishes."[8]

Kerry was on the board of directors of the radical liberal group Jobs with Peace Campaign, whose charter was to "develop public support for cutting the defense budget." Attacking what he called "the military-industrial corporate welfare complex that has relentlessly chewed up taxpayers' dollars,"[9] Kerry called for cuts totaling $50 billion and voted against the Peacekeeper missile, the B-1 and B-2 bombers, the F-15, F-14A, F-14D, and the AV-8B fighter aircraft, the Aegis air defense cruiser, and the Trident missile during the 1980s.

In 1990, Kerry voted against the B-1 bomber, the B-2 bomber, the F-14, the F-15, the F-16, the Patriot missile, the Aegis air defense cruiser, the Trident missile for naval submarines, the M1 Abrams tank, the Bradley fighting vehicle, and the Tomahawk cruise missile.[10]

In 1995, he voted against the Marine AV-8B Harrier and the AH-64 Apache helicopter. He also tried to delay—which meant a deep cut in deployable numbers—the Air Force F-22 Raptor, the next-generation fighter slated to replace the aging F-15s and F-16s.

In short, Kerry tried to veto nearly the entire military arsenal of the United States. He has even voted twelve times against military pay increases. By comparison, President George Bush has increased military pay by 21 percent. There would be no War on Terror if Kerry had successfully pushed through his anti-military agenda. Hell, there would be no military.

He has repeatedly and consistently opposed the very weapon systems that our men and women in uniform are relying on today to fight and win the war on terrorism. If Kerry had been our president, what would our military have fought with in the first Gulf War, in Afghanistan, and in Iraq? Slingshots and tins cans connected with string?

In 1991, Kerry voted to cut the defense budget by 2 percent. In 1991, he voted to cut $3 billion from defense and shift the funds to social programs in pursuit of the ever-mystical "peace dividend." He proposed his own amendment to the defense budget that year that would have transferred hundreds of millions of dollars directly from U.S. missile defense coffers to "Alcohol and Drug Abuse and Mental Health Services block grants... model projects for pregnant and postpartum women and their infants."[11] In 1992, he voted to cut $6 billion from defense.

In 1993, Kerry voted against a proposed military pay raise at a time when the disparity between military and civilian pay was 13 percent. He voted to reduce overall defense spending by $8.8 billion.[12] He also introduced a plan to cut the number of Navy submarines and their crews, reduce tactical fighter aircraft wings in the Air Force, and cancel the Navy's coastal mine-hunting ship program.

Also, in 1993, he wanted to force the early retirement of 60,000 active duty service members, reduce the number of Army light infantry units to one, reduce the number of Air Force tactical fighter squadrons, and cut the number of Navy submarines and crews.

In February 1994, Kerry proposed trimming $43 billion from defense spending. "What we have offered to the Senate is an opportunity to register our votes for real choices," argued Kerry, "for a set of choices that reflect what the American people would really like to be spending their money on as opposed to being forced to spend it by continuation of programs that the president [Clinton] has asked to have cut."[13]

Kerry couldn't even rally his fellow Democrats for support. Democratic senator Daniel Inouye of Hawaii argued, "We are putting blindfolds over our pilots' eyes."[14] Even Democratic senator Robert Byrd of West Virginia spoke against the proposal. "We have already cut defense spending drastically.... Cutting another $4 billion [for fiscal year 1995] is simply unwise and insupportable."[15]

The Senate rejected Kerry's proposal 75–20.

Kerry voted to freeze defense spending for seven years starting in 1995, and slash $34 billion of projected defense funding, even during the Clinton era of already bare-boned defense spending. In 1996, he proposed a $6.5 billion Department of Defense budget reduction. He again voted for a resolution that would freeze defense spending for an additional seven years, proposing to transfer $34.8 billion from defense coffers to education and job training.[16] That bill was so over the top that he couldn't find a single senator to co-sponsor it with him.

Kerry voted no on the Defend America Act of 1996, which sought to deploy a national missile defense system by 2003. With characteristic shortsightedness, Kerry argued, "The supporters of this bill say that North Korea, Iran, Iraq, or Libya now have or will have shortly, the ability to launch a missile that can reach our shores. That is simply not the case."[17] He also voted no on the American Missile Protection Act of 1998.

In the fall of 1998, North Korea fired its Taepo Dong missile over Japan, on its way to dropping a simulated nuclear warhead off the west coast of the United States. China, using ballistic missile tracking technology obtained from the Clinton administration, has had the ability to reach the U.S. mainland for years.

In summary, in six of the last ten years, Senator Kerry has voted to freeze or reduce the defense budget. He has voted to kill every

military appropriation for the development of major weapon systems since 1988.

The Center for Security Policy analyzed more than seventy-five
Senate votes affecting the military over the last ten years. Kerry gets
one of the lowest rankings of any senator, even lower than peacenik
Democratic congressman Dennis Kucinich.[18]

According to the American Conservative Union, Kerry has a lifetime liberal voting record of 6 percent. Democratic congressman
Dick Gephardt and senators Hillary Clinton and Tom Daschle come
in at 13 percent, Senator John Edwards at 14 percent, Congressman
Dennis Kucinich at 15 percent, and Senator Joe Lieberman at 19
percent. Kerry, in other words, is less than half as conservative as
Hillary Rodham Clinton.

The nonpartisan *National Journal*, in its 2003 rankings of the U.S.
Senate, found that Kerry rated as the single most liberal member in
the Senate. Americans for Democratic Action, the premier liberal rat-
ing organization, puts Kerry's lifetime voting record at 93 percent.
Senator Ted Kennedy has a lifetime rating of 88 percent. Kerry, not
Kennedy, is the liberal senator from Massachusetts.

KERRY'S INTELLIGENCE FOUND MOSTLY LACKING

As most in the military will tell you, intelligence is the key to success or failure. Good, reliable intelligence translates to victories on the
battlefield. Wrong or insufficient intelligence translates into defeat.
Soldiers live or die based on the intelligence they receive.

Kerry's résumé in this regard is equally dismal. In his eight years on
the Senate Intelligence Committee, he voted for cuts to the intelligence
budget three times, never once voting for an increase.

In 1994, just months after the first World Trade Center terrorist
attack, Kerry proposed a bill that would have cut $1 billion from
the budgets for the National Foreign Intelligence Program and the
Tactical Intelligence Program. Even Democratic senator Dennis
DeConcini of Arizona, then the Intelligence Committee chairman,

took Kerry to task. "We no longer seem immune for acts of terrorism in the United States," he said prophetically. It makes no sense for us to close our eyes and ears to developments around the world," DeConcini said.[19]

In 1995, Kerry voted to cut $80 million from the FBI's budget and proposed a bill that would have reduced the overall intelligence budget by $1.5 billion by the year 2000. He offered an amendment that would cut our intelligence agencies by $300 million a year before the USS *Cole* was attacked, $300 million the year before the embassies in Kenya and Tanzania were attacked, and $300 million the year before the Khobar Towers barracks were attacked. Kerry included these proposed cuts in a laundry list of government expenditures that he described as "pointless, wasteful, antiquated, or just plain silly."[20]

Not even liberal senators Kennedy, Patrick Leahy, or Barbara Boxer would get on board. Not a single senator offered to co-sponsor the bill.

In 1997, Kerry asked one of his colleagues, "Now that [the Cold War] struggle is over, why is it that our vast intelligence apparatus continues to grow?"[21]

Soon after the attacks of September 11, 2001, Kerry directed blame at the White House and the intelligence agencies.

"And the tragedy is," Kerry told Bob Schieffer on CBS's *Face the Nation*, following the terrorist attacks, "at the moment, the single most important weapon for the United States of America is intelligence. It's the single most important weapon in this particular war."[22]

How many times during his eight years on the Intelligence Committee did Kerry vote to increase funding for human intelligence or to reform the intelligence community? Zero.

In a time when his country was enduring terrorist attack upon terrorist attack overseas, Kerry voted to cut funding for the FBI by 60 percent, to reduce funding for the CIA by 80 percent, and to slash funding for the National Security Agency by 80 percent. He did vote, however, to increase funding to the United Nations by 800 percent.

Hello. Anybody home?

CHAPTER FIVE

WHERE HAVE ALL THE
FLOWERS GONE?

"'These boat people,' says the government of Hong Kong, 'they all want to go to America.' Well, I swear I don't know why, do you? I mean, take Vietnam. Why would any Vietnamese come to America after what America did to Vietnam? Don't they remember My Lai, napalm, Sylvester Stallone?"

—Liberal commentator Linda Ellerbee

On July 8, 1972, Air Force Captain Steve Ritchie and his formation of four F-4D Phantoms lifted off from the runway at their base in Udorn, Thailand. Ritchie was flying into combat over North Vietnam against MiG-21s, the most advanced Soviet fighters of their time, flown by both North Vietnamese and Russian pilots.

As Ritchie's formation sped east, things were already happening. The shadowboxing was underway. The radios were alive with crisp, staccato transmissions of pilots in aerial engagement. Wingmen were calling out enemy aircraft to their leads. One hundred and fifty miles away, two U.S. RC-121 radar control aircraft, with the call signs of "Disco" and "Red Crown," were monitoring the battle and alerting American pilots as necessary. "Bandit at your three o'clock, level." "Got him." "Oyster flight, multiple bandits in your area. I hold a bandit at zero-two-zero at sixteen. I hold another at three-four-zero at twenty-four."

Ritchie's formation entered the fray. "Two blue bandits," was the radio call from Disco to Ritchie: two MiG-21s just north of his position and heading his way. Ritchie couldn't see them. His eyes searched for fast-moving dots on the horizon—those would be the MiGs.

Air-to-air combat involves flying high-performance aircraft at speeds often reaching five to six hundred miles per hour, the pilots skillfully maneuvering their planes while their bodies, reaching weights several times their normal weight, are shoved deep into their ejection seats with each high-speed turn. The sweat pours off the pilot's head—to the point that his helmet, especially during high-speed maneuvers, can slip forward and block his sight—and his flight suit will be soaked. His adrenaline will be pumping, his reflexes finely honed for air choreography under fire. To the fighter pilot, air-to-air combat is a canvas, each pilot painting aircraft maneuvers with strokes both bold and soft.

"Steve, two miles north of you," came the call from Disco. Ritchie made a hard turn, the engines of his jet pumping smoky exhaust. This information had come at precisely the right time. A few more seconds and Ritchie would have been the hunted, not the hunter. He quickly picked up an enemy aircraft at his ten o'clock position. Dropping his external fuel tanks to lose weight and gain maneuverability, he hit full afterburner. Flames shot out for several feet behind each engine as the aircraft accelerated quickly. The two aircraft passed each other at a distance of only about 350 yards. Ritchie was so close he could see the other pilot in the cockpit. His craft was a bright, spit-polished superb MiG-21, with bright red stars.

Ritchie knew there were two MiGs, though, so he forced himself to wait. Then he saw it, about eight thousand feet off. Ritchie let the MiG pass and kicked his own aircraft into a 6.5 gravity turn, his body weighing six and a half times its normal weight, and pushed the nose of the aircraft toward the ground.

Ritchie and Captain Chuck DeBellevue, his radar intercept officer, picked up the MiGs high and to the left. Out of position, Ritchie executed a "barrel roll." As he rolled out, the target was high in the blue sky, good for a radar lock-on. The MiG's pilot saw Ritchie and DeBellevue and turned down into them. Ritchie squeezed the trigger, firing the missiles hanging from his wings. The first missile hit the center of the MiG's fuselage; the second passed through the resulting fireball.

The second MiG came into view. DeBellevue told Ritchie that he had a lock, and Ritchie pulled the trigger again. The missile flew apparently off-target, then made a dramatic right turn and hit the MiG in the fuselage.

In just eighty-nine seconds, Captain Steve Ritchie and Captain Chuck DeBellevue shot down two of the Communists' most prized fighter aircraft. Not two months later, on his 339th combat mission (he had volunteered for and was serving his second tour of duty in Vietnam), Ritchie shot down his fifth and final MiG. With it, he became the Air Force's only "ace" pilot since the Korean War and the only American pilot to shoot down five MiG-21s.

In another time and another war, Ritchie, a small-town boy and a high school football star, would have been hailed as a hero who represented all that was courageous and good about America. There would have been parades and the keys to the city. This time though, Ritchie's homecoming, like that of hundreds of thousands of his fellow Vietnam-era servicemen, would not be sweet. It was a thankless airplane ride home. "I was spit on in San Francisco, in uniform,"[1] he recalled.

Vietnam. The war liberals love to hate. *Vietnam.* The only war liberals ever won, because America lost. It was a war started by liberals for all the right reasons, and ended by liberals for all the wrong reasons. And it stands today as the Left's raison d'être. Liberals relentlessly use the handy Vietnam analogy to accuse their own country of dishonesty and to joyously predict its defeat. Senator Ted Kennedy, speaking to the Brookings Institution in April 2004, claimed that "Iraq is George Bush's Vietnam" and that President Bush had "created the largest credibility gap since Richard Nixon."[2] Former Democratic senator Max Cleland equated Iraq with Vietnam in an op-ed for the *Atlanta Journal-Constitution*: "Welcome to Vietnam, Mr. President."[3] Howard Dean tells Dan Rather, "We sent troops to Vietnam, without understanding why we were there.... And Iraq is gonna become a disaster under this presidency."[4] Other talking points in the Vietnam tool kit that inevitably roll off liberals' tongues are "quagmire" and "bogged down." Al Gore was already knee-jerkingly referring to George Bush's "quagmire" in Iraq eight days into the lightning-quick military invasion that liberated the country.

A KENNEDY LEGACY

Actually, it was Teddy Kennedy's brother who started the whole mess. Democratic president John F. Kennedy, the last of the strong anti-Communist Democrats, took the initial seven hundred advisors sent to Vietnam under President Dwight Eisenhower and turned them into sixteen thousand. He approved the coup to overthrow South Vietnam's president, Ngo Dinh Diem, who was killed in the process. This Kennedy-approved coup against a pro-Western, anti-Communist ally was one of the greatest early mistakes of the Democrat-run war, embroiling the United States in and further destabilizing South Vietnam's internal politics. Kennedy was assassinated a few weeks later.

Democratic president Lyndon Baines Johnson turned Kennedy's commitment of sixteen thousand into more than 500,000 troops in Vietnam, but he simply had no heart for the war he inherited. LBJ's goals were domestic, creating a mass of new government programs called the Great Society—in fact, he tried to run the war as a huge extension of the welfare state. He micromanaged the war from the Oval Office, even to the point of picking specific targets for his limited bombing campaign—the targets selected not for their strategic military value but always as a mere prod to try to encourage North Vietnam to negotiate for peace.

When the Vietnam War was inherited by Richard Nixon, the Democratic Party turned against it with a vengeance and allowed its ever more stridently emotional opposition to the war to turn into contempt for all things military. Conservative Democratic senator Henry "Scoop" Jackson warned: "I do not want to see the Democratic Party become a party which gives any aid and comfort whatever to people who applaud Vietcong victories or wave Vietcong flags. Our party has room for hawks and doves, but not for mockingbirds who chirp gleefully at those who are shooting our boys."[5]

But "Scoop" Jackson spoke for a wing of the Democratic Party that would soon disappear or become "Reagan Democrats." Though the Vietnam War started as Kennedy and Johnson's war and wound down through Nixon's "peace with honor" strategy (which the Democratic Congress undid, precipitating a Communist victory), the Democrats turned it into "Nixon's war." John Kerry exemplified this Democratic revisionism when he claimed, "I stood up and fought against Richard Nixon's war in Vietnam," after he'd won the Iowa caucuses in February 2004.[6]

THE TURNING POINT

By 1968, the left wing of the Democratic Party—angrier about the "arrogance" of American power than about threats to national security—was taking over. To the Left, American imperialism, not Communism, was the main threat. Even previously anti-Communist liberals began to change their tune after one of the most important events of the Vietnam War.

On January 31, 1968, the eve of Tet, the Vietnamese New Year celebration, North Vietnamese master strategist General Vo Nguyen Giap launched a massive surprise attack—during an agreed truce for Tet festivities—against South Vietnam. North Vietnam was losing the war, and the Communists gambled on a desperate attack of overwhelming scope. Giap sent troops into some seventy cities and towns, attacking thirteen of the sixteen provincial capitals, hoping to generate a popular uprising. In the end, it was a thorough military beating for Giap and the North Vietnamese. The losses were staggering. Approximately thirty-five thousand Communist troops were killed, sixty thousand were wounded, and six thousand were captured. The Viet Cong would never recover militarily from their losses, but they wouldn't have to. American liberals would hand them victory anyway.

This was America's first televised war, and the liberal media cast the results in an entirely different light. In doing so, Giap and the Viet Cong found an unexpected ally. Walter Cronkite, "America's most trusted newsman," was on the scene with fires from enemy action burning in the background, reporting that the war was lost. He characterized the Tet Offensive as a resounding success for the Viet Cong and a disaster for the United States. General William Westmoreland, the commander for U.S. forces in Vietnam, appeared on television and announced a significant military victory, but the American Left proclaimed the "defeat" they had been looking for.

North Vietnamese colonel Bui Tin characterized Tet as "being designed to influence American public opinion." The purpose of the Tet Offensive was "to relieve the pressure General Westmoreland was putting on [North Vietnam] in late 1966 and 1967," said Tin, "and to weaken American resolve during a presidential election year."[7] Giap admitted it had been a military defeat. The American Left turned it into victory. Ho Chi Minh concluded, "We don't need to win military victories, we only need to hit them until they give up and get out."[8]

Cronkite editorialized against the war and talked of the need for negotiation. Aided by antiwar protesters such as Bill and Hillary Clinton, Ted Kennedy, and Jane Fonda, liberal falsehood was accepted as reality, victory became defeat, and the antiwar protesters and liberal media helped the Communists win the Vietnam War. When asked if the American antiwar movement was important to Hanoi's victory, Colonel Tin replied, "It was essential to our strategy.... Visits to Hanoi by people like Jane Fonda and former attorney general Ramsey Clark and ministers gave us confidence that we should hold on.... We were elated when Jane Fonda, wearing a red Vietnamese dress, said at a press conference that she was ashamed of American actions in the war and that she would struggle along with us."[9]

General Giap wrote in his memoirs, published in 1985, that if it weren't for the war protesters and the lack of American resolve, Hanoi would have surrendered to the United States. In other words, the liberals convinced the North Vietnamese that they could win.

Six weeks after the Tet Offensive, President Johnson announced that he would not seek reelection. His job approval numbers had dropped from 80 percent after assuming office to 30 percent after Tet. The Democrats nominated Johnson's vice president, Hubert Humphrey from Minnesota, as their presidential candidate in 1968. He was a liberal, but was also staunchly anti-Communist and pledged strong support for an American military victory in Vietnam. The left wing of the party didn't want him.

As David Horowitz, himself an antiwar radical at the time, notes, "The anti-Humphrey plan was the brainchild of radical leader Tom Hayden, who had met with the Vietnamese Communists in Czechoslovakia the previous year, and gone on to Hanoi to collaborate with the Communist enemy. In the late spring of 1968, Hayden proceeded to plan and then organize a riot at the Democratic Party convention in the full glare of the assembled media. The negative fallout from the chaos in the streets of Chicago and the Democrats' heavy-handed reaction to the 'antiwar' rioters effectively elected the Republican candidate Richard Nixon the following November."[10]

My father, an Air Force pilot like myself, served in the Vietnam War. His chief mission was to interdict Communist supply lines on the Ho Chi Minh Trail in his AC-130 Spectre gunship. As my mother, brother, sister, and I waited for him to serve his twelve months in combat, we watched the CBS evening news and saw the liberal media and liberal Democrats systematically tear down the American military in a bout of leftist hysteria. Antiwar protests swept college campuses, draft cards were burned, ROTC buildings were bombed, and antiwar violence became commonplace. An Air Force recruiter was stabbed to death in his office at the University of California, Berkeley, by a war protester whose legal defense was that the recruiter was sending men to fight an "illegal war." To the Left, anyone in uniform was a war criminal.

Liberals reviled the war and those fighting it. They viewed the military with the same disdain with which they viewed their government. Who else but dupes would fight for their country and against Communism in a war that liberals so despised?

Liberals internalized a gut-level distrust of the military. The soldier became synonymous with American imperialism, big business, and the military-industrial complex. As the war became increasingly unpopular, the academic elite targeted ROTC, the only visible bastion of the armed forces on college campuses. Service in the armed forces was seen as morally suspect and not worthy of a student's consideration. Programs at upper-tier schools such as Stanford, Harvard, Yale, Princeton, Brown, and Columbia, to name a few, were eliminated.

The spirit of the anti-Vietnam, anti-military Democrats thrives among professors and collegiate administrators today. Many colleges and universities continue to ban ROTC and military recruiters from their campuses.

HOW THE DEMOCRATS LOST VIETNAM

In 1972, the Democratic Party nominated an antiwar candidate, the liberal George McGovern. This action affirmed that the Left had taken over the party. McGovern's campaign slogan was "Come Home America;" his policy, peace at any price.

On the battlefield, the war was still winnable. Admiral Thomas Moorer, chairman of the Joint Chiefs of Staff under Nixon, urged the bombing of key strategic sites in and around Hanoi and the mining of

Haiphong Harbor, choosing targets based on their strategic military value and not constrained by political concerns. Nixon agreed to this change from Johnson's policy, and the resulting strategic air campaign worked. Beginning on December 18, 1972, the United States unleashed the greatest aerial assault on an enemy in the history of war. At levels and ferocity not seen again until the Gulf War in 1991, U.S. pilots flew more than four thousand sorties. B-52s launched from Guam flew more than seven hundred bombing missions.

Had this campaign been launched in 1965, the war would have quickly been won, saved untold numbers of lives, and democracy might have taken root in Southeast Asia. In 1972, the bombing campaign forced the North Vietnamese to immediately sue for peace—and they suddenly treated our POWs more humanely.

The Nixon administration delivered peace through strength, and American troops withdrew from South Vietnam. But then, when North Vietnam launched another enormous invasion of South Vietnam in 1975, the Democrats abandoned our ally. As David Horowitz notes, "Following the Watergate scandal and the resignation of Nixon, the newly radicalized Democrats voted to cut off all economic aid to the anti-Communist governments of Cambodia and South Vietnam. Both regimes fell within months of the vote, leading to the mass slaughter in both countries of approximately two and a half million peasants at the hands of their new Communist rulers."[11]

We cut and ran—as Democrats would have us do again and again: in Iran, in Somalia, and today in the war against terrorism. The history of the last forty years shows that only the Republican Party has been willing to enforce peace through strength. For liberals, the war isn't with the enemy; it is with the American military.

MY LAI AND ABU GHRAIB

On March 16, 1968, members of Charlie Company, under the direction of Army Lieutenant William Calley, entered the village of My Lai, in the South Vietnamese district of Son My, and killed at least three hundred innocent men, women, and children. It was a time when a U.S. military unit went well beyond combat engagement, completely over the edge, and established a low mark for America's involvement in the war. Calley was convicted of murder and sentenced to prison. My Lai was a vile war crime, gruesome, and completely indefensible.

Journalist Seymour Hersh "broke" the My Lai story, although the U.S. military had been investigating the incident for months and had already levied charges against Calley. For Kerry, Fonda, and antiwar protesters everywhere, My Lai was held up as the prism through which to view the entire war effort and Vietnam veterans. For liberals, the My Lai massacre demonstrated that America was on the wrong side, in the wrong war, and that American military power was dangerous. It gave the antiwar liberals apparent justification and rhetorical leverage for belittling America's attempt to save South Vietnam from Communism.

In the fall of 2003, a handful of American servicemen and women in the U.S. Army's 372nd Military Police Company guarding detainees and prisoners at Saddam Hussein's infamous Abu Ghraib prison committed pornographic atrocities. Coincidentally, the journalist who "broke" the story was the same Seymour Hersh, although, again, the U.S. military had numerous—and public—investigations under way.

Photographs emerged, showing the world sexual perversion, nudity, and torture supervised by American soldiers. *60 Minutes* aired the photos not once, but twice, and interviews with the soldiers involved, portraying them as victims of the orders they received from their commanding officers.

As with My Lai and Vietnam, Abu Ghraib has become the lens through which liberals and anti-Americans everywhere want to see our involvement in Iraq. Instead of holding the reservist idiots accountable for their actions or at least reserving judgment until the ongoing criminal investigations and court-martials were completed, liberals quickly seized Abu Ghraib for political gain, demanding the necks of Secretary of Defense Donald Rumsfeld and President George W. Bush. For liberals, the war in Iraq is not America's war, it is Bush's war.[12]

Democratic senator Jack Reed of Rhode Island was quick to declare, "For the next fifty years in the Islamic world and many other parts of the world, the image of the United States will be that of an American dragging a prostrate naked Iraqi across the floor on a leash."[13]

Senator Ted Kennedy asserted, "This does not appear to be an isolated incident."[14] He capped that with, "Shamefully, we now learn that Saddam's torture chambers have reopened under new management—U.S. management."[15] Liberals aren't interested in being evenhanded or keeping things in perspective. Saddam Hussein would not have put these soldiers on trial if they had been his; he would have demanded that they do much worse, including mutilation and murder. But liberals don't care that Saddam Hussein was a mass-murdering tyrant and supporter of terror. Instead, they want to use the outrages committed by a handful of soldiers who were caught by the military and are in line to be punished by the military as a means to defeat America's war effort and thereby defeat George W. Bush.

Time magazine ran a cover story featuring one of the photos from Abu Ghraib with the headline "Iraq: How Did It Come to This?" *Newsweek*'s Eleanor Clift reacted to the Abu Ghraib revelations by exclaiming, "If ever there was a moment for John Kerry to come out swinging, this is it. It is the biggest story of the year."[16] The abuse of these prisoners is a bigger story, apparently, than a rebuilt Iraq with a democratic constitution, as planned by George W. Bush. For the media, the prison scandal was far, far bigger than the beheading—under the supervision and possibly hand of Abu Musab al-Zarqawi, a senior al-Qaeda operative—of Nicholas Berg, an American private contractor trying to bring a better life to Iraqis.

Since the media won't give you the bigger picture, I will. The inmates in Cell Block 1A and 1B weren't there for traffic violations or for jaywalking. They were there because they were terrorists, insurgents, and murderers. Any information gleaned from them would translate directly to saving American lives. Some of these men, no doubt, have American blood on their hands. These prisoners were

Saddam Hussein's henchmen, former Ba'ath Party officers who ran Saddam's network of torture and death, and who had joined the insurrection to kill Americans and prevent democracy in Iraq. No matter how shocking the abuses committed by the handful of American servicemen and women, they pale in comparison to the amputations, beheadings, rapes, and gruesome torture that were commonplace in the Abu Ghraib prison under Saddam Hussein.

But of course, for the Democrats, it was all about politics. The Kerry presidential campaign even went so far as to use the pictures and reports from Abu Ghraib for campaign fund-raising. Kerry campaign manager Mary Beth Cahill (on loan from Senator Kennedy's staff) wrote, "Over the past week we have all been shocked by the pictures from the Abu Ghraib prison in Iraq. But we've also been appalled at the slow and inept response by President Bush, which has further undermined America's credibility in the world and created new dangers for Americans in Iraq. George Bush must fire Donald Rumsfeld. . . . Show George Bush and show the media that you support John Kerry's stand: Donald Rumsfeld MUST resign immediately. Keep the ball rolling: Donate Now!"[17]

Abu Ghraib is not the story of the war. It is not even this war's version of My Lai, which was not the story of the Vietnam War. It is an isolated incident of stupidity and abuse committed by a few—who were already in the process of being punished before the liberal media discovered it.

Our soldiers are held to a high standard of behavior, or they are punished. But liberal Democrats can say or do anything, no matter how irresponsible, and no one in the liberal media seems to care.

CHAPTER SIX

WAR TORN: THE LIBERALS' WAR WITH THE U.S. MILITARY

"What you cannot enforce, do not command."

—Sophocles[1]

September 12, 1988: That was the day when Democratic presidential candidate Michael Dukakis pulled on an Army helmet much too big for his head and climbed onto the commander's seat of an M1A1 Abrams tank. It revealed the fundamental disconnect between liberals and the military.

Granted, it was a campaign stunt, but it said so much more. Dukakis looked woefully out of place, dwarfed by both helmet and tank. He was Rocky the Flying Squirrel. He was Snoopy on top of the doghouse, ready to launch after the Red Baron. He was, quite simply, goofy looking. It was at once laughable and yet so telling.

This lone effort to illustrate the comfort and confidence Dukakis would bring to the role of commander in chief morphed into clownish theater and contributed to his loss in the election. It remains his campaign's most memorable image.

Almost overnight, his seventeen-point lead over George H. W. Bush dwindled, and four months later, Dukakis lost the presidential election by 315 electoral votes. The popular vote was Bush 53.4 percent, Dukakis 45.6.

When it comes to matters of national security and the military, liberals have, and have had, the "wrong stuff."

In 1994, one of my C-141 squadron mates based at Travis Air Force Base, California, was flying a "Phoenix Banner mission," Department of Defense priority 1A1. There was none higher. It was White House support; the carrying of President Clinton's limousines and members of the Secret Service on one of the president's many trips.

Clinton, trying to overcome his early stumbling with the military and his image as an ineffectual commander in chief, ordered his personal aide to line up the members of the aircrew in their uniforms for a photograph. As Clinton went down the line shaking hands and smiling for the camera, he extended his hand to my friend, one of the pilots and a lieutenant in the Air Force, single silver bars on his shoulders shining in the sun.

"Howya doin', major?" he asked.

The lieutenant stifled a laugh and the temptation to say, "Not bad, governor." The commander in chief had been in office for more than a year and didn't know the different ranks of his military officers. Excepting the Navy, there are only six who aren't generals.

For a Rhodes Scholar, how hard could it be?

During his two terms, Clinton visited aircraft carriers on five separate occasions, wearing his leather military aviator jacket with the squadron patches, slapping guys on the back, trying to be one of the boys. He always reminded me of a freshman nervously pledging a fraternity.

Unlike Ronald Reagan, Clinton didn't have the military understanding, presence, or credibility to rightfully claim an aviator's jacket as commander in chief. Clinton had never earned an aviator jacket the way pilots do. He was a draft dodger. He offered sloppy salutes, often averting his eyes to the ground, as if ashamed. He had zero moral credibility.

An Air Force lieutenant colonel summed it up this way: "The leftist media's concern over President Bush's carrier landing illustrates they never really understood that while former vice president Al Gore was learning to operate a typewriter in Vietnam, and Bill Clinton was protesting Vietnam as a student in the United Kingdom, President Bush was flying supersonic jet fighters with the Texas Air National Guard."

The Constitution grants the president the legal authority to lead our armed forces. It does not, however, grant him the moral authority to lead. That is something the president—and any commander at any level—is required to earn, by virtue of the nature of leadership. Moral authority cannot be demanded from the top; it must be offered from the bottom. It is the privilege offered by one man to another to command him. Moral authority confers upon the leader the ability to make life and death decisions and order men and women into harm's way. And its existence or absence is found in the character or, lack thereof, of the commander.

Simply put, soldiers, sailors, airmen, and Marines want those who lead them to have an idea, an understanding, of what it's like in the trenches, in the cockpits, or on the ship. You can't bullshit them and you'd better not try, not even once. Credibility is everything. If you can't fly airplanes, you can't command pilots. If you can't shoot a rifle, you can't lead a platoon. If you can't drive a ship, you can't command a cutter. If you lack moral standards, you can't enforce the Uniform Code of Military Justice. If you've committed treason toward your country, you can't be the commander in chief.

When President Bill Clinton came to the United States Air Force Academy to give the commencement address for the graduating class of 1999, I was one of four cadet group commanders. In my position,

I was responsible for the nurturing, military education, and professional mentorship of one thousand cadets. The reaction of the cadets to Clinton's visit was telling, and surprised even me.

It was obvious to the cadets: Clinton had not earned their trust. He didn't have the moral authority to lead them and they weren't giving it to him.

I'd come to this same realization serving Clinton as his Air Force aide, a realization I kept to myself until I retired. I was unsettled, though, to discover the same sentiments reaching all the way down to our service academies, down to the foundations of professional and selfless service.

The outward animosity of the cadets toward their commander in chief was so great that in the days leading up to the most important moment yet of their short careers, we were concerned they wouldn't attend. As one now Air Force lieutenant recalls, "not many of us actually wanted to go. I vividly remember our commanding officers briefing us that we HAD to go. That was unheard of under former presidents and for past graduations.

"What we considered a slap in the face [was that] Clinton never mentioned military service in his almost hour-long speech. It was a campaign speech. He only talked about his policies and accomplishments. We had just graduated from a service academy and, on the most important day of our young lives, our own president didn't even mention the importance of military service. It was all about him and not a word about us."[2]

It was yet another in a number of instances in which this particular commander in chief demonstrated to the military that he didn't get it and didn't care.

Among the New Democrats, it always seems to be about them.

Air Force Captain Hal Cranmer was stationed at Kadena Air Base in Okinawa, Japan. He flew the C-12, a twin-engine propeller-driven aircraft that the Air Force used to ferry dignitaries around the Pacific. One day, Cranmer was asked to fly Massachusetts senator John Kerry and his staff to various locations in Vietnam and Cambodia as part of the POW/MIA discussions. When the Air Force captain introduced himself to Kerry, as was the normal protocol, he noticed the senator wearing a shirt with a picture of his sailboat on it.

"Oh, sir, I have a small twenty-seven footer docked here in Okinawa," Cranmer offered.

"I never sail on anything less than 135 feet," snorted Kerry in response.

Their first stop was Phnom Penh, Cambodia, where Kerry's party was to have lunch with members of the Cambodian government. The crew, meanwhile, had brought along a pizza, purchased at the Kadena Air Base exchange, and stowed it on board for their only meal of what was to be a very long day. Amazingly, without asking, Kerry grabbed the pizza and started passing it around to his party, while the pilots flew the aircraft.

Once in Phnom Penh, Kerry and staff were off for meetings and lunch. The pilots waited in one hundred degree temperatures and 95 percent humidity. The aircraft's engines had to stay off—hence, no air conditioning—to conserve the fuel necessary for the next leg of their mission. Kerry and staff proved to be an hour late. When Kerry finally did arrive, he stepped out of the air-conditioned car onto the aircraft, stuck his head into the cockpit, and told the pilots, "Could you guys get the air conditioning running, I'm a little warm."

The next day, the C-12 crew flew into Noi Bai airfield in Hanoi to pick up Kerry and his staff. As they taxied out, one of the engines indicated a potentially serious malfunction. The pilot taxied to the side of the ramp so that he and the crew could recheck the engine.

According to Cranmer, "Mr. Senator poked his head into the cockpit and says sternly, 'This plane WILL take off. I have a press conference in Bangkok in three hours.'"

The crew fixed the problem and arrived in Bangkok well in time for Kerry's press conference. After Kerry departed the plane, a Navy captain who served as an aide to Kerry approached the pilots, apologized, and said that "he knew Kerry was a jerk, and that we should be glad we don't have to deal with him every day."

The Clinton-Kerry Democrats think of the military as hired help because it's all about them.

NO BALLOTS FOR THOSE WHO RISK BULLETS

I was stationed in Vicenza, Italy, during the presidential election of 2000. As the director of airlift operations for the Bosnia, Kosovo, and Macedonia theaters, I was assigned to NATO's Combined Air Operation Center. Most of the American military in our unit were forced to vote via absentee ballot, as servicemen have done for years. But count on a Democrat to try to deny American servicemen and women their right to vote.

Remember that in the 2000 presidential election Democratic presidential candidate Al Gore tried to disqualify military absentee ballots mailed to Florida. He alleged that the ballots required a postmark—they don't—and wanted to disenfranchise thousands of military personnel stationed overseas. Thanks, Al.

"I think we're pretty disgusted, for the most part," concluded a signals officer in Stuttgart, Germany. "Everybody's talking about it," an Army paratrooper based in Vicenza said. "We got ripped off."[3] An Army officer concluded that Democrats "want to let Florida Democrats vote twice, but they won't let us vote even once."[4]

Most military men and women are conservative and vote Republican. A 1997 study published by Harvard's Olin Institute for Strategic Studies found the ratio of military members describing themselves as conservative versus liberal to be 23 to 1—and growing.[5]

The Triangle Institute for Strategic Studies (TISS), in research conducted during the Clinton administration, discovered that military officers define themselves as Republicans by a margin of 8 to 1, while the public at large is split about evenly over party affiliation. Sixty-six percent of officers believe that the nation's political leadership is "somewhat ignorant" or "very ignorant" about military affairs and the same percentage described themselves as "conservative," compared to 38 percent of the civilian population.[6]

During the Democratic presidential primary season of 2003–04, Stanley Greenberg and James Carville's Democracy Corps surveyed Democratic voters as they left the polls, asking them to rank the campaign's major issues in order of importance. The results were astounding. In Iowa, only 1 percent of those polled were concerned with the War on Terror. Only 2 percent worried about homeland security. In New Hampshire, 2 percent worried about terrorism and 2 percent worried about homeland security.[7]

For liberals, the number one issue was beating George Bush. Even at the expense of ongoing threats to their country. Maybe that's because they think America is the problem. Former UN ambassador (and Democrat turned Republican) Jeane Kirkpatrick addressed the 1984 Republican convention and pointed out that the Democratic Party resorted to "always blaming America first." She rightly concluded that the Democrats are wrong and that "the American people know that it's dangerous to blame ourselves for terrible problems that we did not cause."[8]

At a foreign policy speech to the students of Georgetown University on November 7, 2001, former president Clinton showed that he still blamed America first, even making excuses for the September 11 terrorists. "In the first Crusade, when the Christian soldiers took Jerusalem, they first burned a synagogue. . . . I can tell you that story is still being told today in the Middle East and we're still paying for it. We need to reach out and engage the Muslim world in a debate," he pleaded. As a further dollop of political correctness, he added, "Those of us from various European lineages are not blameless."[9]

Liberals are so inclined to distrust their own country that they're comfortable using military power only when the United Nations gives its approval or can even take command. When Warren Christopher—secretary of state for Bill Clinton and deputy secretary of state for Jimmy Carter—was asked to list the Clinton administration's key foreign policy accomplishments, he took pride in "taking the lead in passing the responsibility to multilateral bodies."[10] Only a liberal could take pride in passing American foreign policy to "multilateral bodies."

For Democrats, it's not national security that's the top concern: it's the environment, domestic welfare programs, and social liberalism. When it comes to national interests and national defense, liberals want to farm that out to "international bodies." And they wouldn't mind if these bodies took over the military as well.

CHAPTER SEVEN

DESERT TORTOISE OR GI JOE?

"In this world of sin and sorrow, if virtue triumphs over vice it is not because it is virtuous, but because it has bigger and better guns; if honesty prevails over double dealing, it is not because it is honest, but because it has a stronger army more ably led; and if good overcomes evil it is not because it is good, but because it has a well-lined purse. It is well to have right on our side, but it is madness to forget that unless we have might as well it will avail us nothing. We must believe that God loves men of good will, but there is no evidence to show that he will save fools from the results of their folly."

—Somerset Maugham, Then As Now, 1948[1]

Environmentalism was discovered by peace activists in the 1960s as a very effective pretext by which to restrict military operations. Now—even while we fight a worldwide war against terrorism—liberals are using the mechanisms of "military encroachment" and "endangered species" designations to curtail the training of America's armed forces. There is no point at which liberals realize that they have reached complete absurdity.

At Fort Bragg, North Carolina, America's largest army base, commanders are told to limit training to preserve the habitat of birds, one red-cockaded woodpecker in particular. Soldiers are told to maintain a 250-foot buffer around trees—all trees, any tree that might possess a bird nest or might someday possess a bird nest. There are 130,000 acres of trees, all potential bird nest sites, on Fort Bragg.

No vehicles are allowed within fifty feet of trees. Soldiers are cautioned to refrain from making sounds that might offend birds. Sounds, obviously, like guns being fired, tanks being operated, and helicopters being flown. Sounds that would be the natural result of our soldiers preparing for combat.

Army units at Fort Bragg are limited to a maximum of two hours while operating in any one area of the reservation. They aren't allowed to dig into the earth and are allowed to fire only small-caliber blank ammunition.

What kind of country doesn't allow its army to dig foxholes or mortar emplacements or shoot bullets? And how many casualties could have been prevented had we been a little less concerned about the life of a woodpecker?

At Fort Hood, Texas, another major center of Army training, only 17 percent of the reservation's 185,000 acres are unaffected by one environmental constraint or another. The Clean Water Act prohibits the digging of foxholes on 70 percent of the area. The Clean Air Act prohibits soldiers from using smoke, flares, or other pyrotechnic devices on 25 percent of the reservation. Soldiers are allowed to use camouflage netting on only one-third of the base's total terrain because of the habitat of two bird species, the golden-cheeked warbler and the black-capped vireo.

At Camp Lejeune, North Carolina, "Marine Corps East," Marines are restricted from using the beaches during the turtle nesting season, making amphibious landing exercises (traditionally the core mission of the USMC) impossible. Their inland training is limited by the ever-present red-cockaded woodpecker, which seems to be thriving at nearby Fort Bragg.

At the Marine Corps Air Station in Yuma, Arizona, at Fort Irwin, California, and at Nellis Air Force Base, Nevada, the liberal eco-concern is for the "desert tortoise." Marines at Yuma are forbidden to train at night for fear they might come across an unsuspecting tortoise in the dark. Most of the fighting occurring in Iraq and Afghanistan happens at night, but liberal environmentalists and their protectors in the Democratic Party don't care. What they do care about is that Marines be trained as "tortoise monitors." So young Marines are instructed to survey the simulated battlefield for tortoises—and notify the training units should they see one. That's a skill that will transfer well in combat if we go to war in, say, the Galapagos Islands.

Vehicles involved in Marine training at Yuma are emblazoned with warning signs instructing the Marines to "notify monitors if you find a tortoise." The Marines are restricted to staying on established roads and paths only and are not allowed to engage in either live or simulated firing.

The desert tortoise and his liberal proponents have made other inroads in seeking to limit military readiness in the $75 million expansion of the Army's National Training Center at Fort Irwin, California. Night training at Fort Irwin is one of the prohibitions—for fear of annoying the tortoise.

At Camp Pendleton, California, the Marines' most important amphibious training base, only one mile of the seventeen miles of beach is available for use, due in part to endangered species limitations. Camp Pendleton has been designated the home for eighteen threatened or endangered species, including the tidewater goby, the gnatcatcher, and the fairy shrimp.

If a Marine landing on Red Beach at Camp Pendleton travels off of one of the three designated roads leaving the beach, he risks a $50,000 fine. Not because he is putting himself or his fellow Marines at risk, but because he might be damaging the nesting ground of the California least tern, a seabird protected by the Endangered Species Act.

During an exercise in March 2001, amphibious training was limited to only five hundred yards of beach because it coincided with the breeding season for the bird: a knotty problem for the officer responsible for scheduling the training, and for the Marines preparing to depart for war. In 2000, the U.S. Fish and Wildlife Service tried to declare 56 percent of Camp Pendleton and 65 percent of nearby Miramar Naval Air Station (former home of "Top Gun") off-limits to training.

But who's encroaching upon whom?

Most military bases were established in remote and undeveloped areas before or during World War II. Because the military needs areas for maneuvers and live firing, most have remained undeveloped. As surrounding properties are developed, the military installations become attractive homes for the displaced flora and fauna.

Commercial construction and development throughout San Diego County have forced the indigenous local species to move to more isolated areas. In San Diego County, that's Camp Pendleton. In another concern, massive development in the area eliminated 90 percent of the "vernal pools" in the county. Of those remaining, 90 percent are located—you got it—on Camp Pendleton.

General James L. Jones, commandant of the Marine Corps, wryly asked a representative of the U.S. Department of Fish and Wildlife if they could list the Marines as an endangered species at Camp Pendleton, "so we would have a chance to survive on our own base."[2]

The Navy has not been immune to ridiculous liberal shackles, either. A suit was filed against the Navy for developing and using an updated version of its surface-towed array sonar system called "Low Frequency Active." Allegedly, it hurt dolphins and whales. But without this upgrade in technology, U.S. Navy ships are vulnerable to the new, ultra-quiet diesel submarines operated by China, North Korea, and Iran. Of the approximately five hundred non-U.S. submarines in the world, about half are operated by non-friendly nations.

The Navy is under a court order to refrain from testing and training with the sonar in spite of a six-year, $10 million study that proved the system could be used with negligible impact to marine mammals. Current legislation prohibits the Navy from operating its new sonar in areas where marine mammals could be "annoyed" or "potentially disturbed." All told, the Navy spends $900 million a year in environmental compliance efforts and programs "in order to ensure we are good stewards of the environment we operate in," said Navy spokesman Lieutenant Doug Spencer.[3]

The Navy also lost its premier military range on the island of Vieques, Puerto Rico. Between 1941 and 1950, the Navy purchased twenty-two thousand acres of this island for $1.5 million. Using only 3 percent of the island, or nine hundred acres, the Navy has long relied on this area as its primary joint combat training ground for units from all the armed services. It was the only area where ships, submarines, fighters, bombers, and amphibious ground forces could train together in realistic terrain using live ammunition.

But in 2003, environmentalists, Puerto Rican protesters, and opportunistic liberals like Jesse Jackson, Al Sharpton (who went on a hunger strike), and Bobby Kennedy Jr., succeeded in pressuring the Navy to pull out from Vieques.

According to Navy Captain James Stark, the commander at the Roosevelt Roads Naval Base in Puerto Rico, Jackson called the naval brass "rapists" and claimed that "the U.S. has no right to own a part of another nation, and it must end its colonial posturing."[4] Apparently, Jackson is unaware that Puerto Rico, like Guam, is a territory of the United States and not "another nation."

The protesters accused the Navy of harming conservation efforts, while the truth was that the Navy had highly developed and extensive programs in place to protect the island's endangered species, including the mangrove forests, sea turtles, brown pelicans, and the West Indies manatees. They even went so far as to build a turtle hatchery in 1991, which incubated eggs collected along the beaches and resulted in the birth of more than twenty-one thousand sea turtles. But the truth didn't matter. The Navy was forced to fragment its training among several locations, where, inevitably, more environmental protests will happen.

On Coronado Island, California, where most of the elite Navy SEAL training is done, training is severely limited for most of the year because of the endangered snowy plover bird. For as many as seven months a year, practice areas for the SEALs can shrink by up to 40 percent.

The examples of environmentalists fencing in our military are endless.

- At Fort Lewis, Washington, 72 percent of the military reservation is labeled a critical habitat for the northern spotted owl, even though none are known to live there.
- The Army's Makua Military Reservation in Hawaii has been closed since 1998 due to environmental lawsuits seeking to protect a tree snail.
- A portion of the Pacific Missile Range in Kauai, Hawaii, has been designated a critical habitat for an endangered species of grass, which Navy officials say could severely compromise ballistic missile defense testing.
- Marine Corps training at San Clemente, California, is restricted because of the presence of a bird called the loggerhead shrike and a creature known as the night lizard.
- The endangered black bear and jay scrub threaten to close the Navy's Pinecastle Bombing Range in Florida. The need to protect the Sonoran pronghorn antelope might lead to closure or severe limitations on Arizona's Barry Goldwater Bombing Range.

All told, military bases, posts, forts, stations, and reservations now provide habitat for more than three hundred federally endangered or threatened species. Which begs the question: Is anybody else in America responsible for environmental protection besides the military?

In 2002, in the wake of the September 11 attacks and our War on Terror, the U.S. House of Representatives voted to relieve the military of some of the silly, yet damaging, environmental restrictions on their training. But when the vote came up in the Senate, Democratic senators Barbara Boxer of California, Joe Lieberman of Connecticut, Bob Graham of Florida, and Harry Reid of Nevada successfully stonewalled the bill's passage. Not a single Democrat, including Hillary Clinton, the Democratic senator from New York, showed for the hearings on the bill. It was her husband's presidency that initiated the closure of the Navy's training facility at Vieques.

For our military, "training like we fight" is the mantra for achieving combat capability and readiness. If constrained from doing so, military units will fail and our men and women will die needlessly. Secretary of Defense Donald Rumsfeld has cautioned that without some relief from environmental laws, "We're going to send men and women into combat without the training they need."[5]

Air Force Vice Chief of Staff Robert "Doc" Foglesong echoed Rumsfeld's concerns. The loss or restricted use of combat training ranges "inhibit our ability to 'train as we fight,' degrade our combat readiness and will eventually limit combat forces to fight only as they have trained," concluded Foglesong.[6]

Deputy Assistant Secretary of the Navy Wayne Arny told Congress, "Before our nation sends its most valuable asset—our men and women, our sons and daughters—into harm's way, we owe it to them and the American public to prepare them as best we can to fight, survive, and win. That starts with realistic and comprehensive training."[7]

In deliberations for the 2004 Defense Authorization Bill, both houses of Congress granted the military some relief from environmental legislation. Environmental groups immediately responded by filing suit. Karen Wyland of the liberal National Resources Defense Council argued, "Exempting the Pentagon from these laws will allow the military to threaten whales, dolphins, and other marine mammals with sonar and underwater explosives, and destroy the habitat of the endangered birds and mammals that live on the 25 million acres it controls across the country—with next to no environmental review."[8] And the lack of realistic military training, ma'am, how many American lives will that endanger, when our armed forces are ordered into action?

Sleep well, America. While American men and women die defending their country in this war against terrorism, the red cockaded-woodpecker, the desert tortoise, whales and dolphins everywhere, and the snowy plover bird are safe.

CHAPTER EIGHT

THE CLINTON CATASTROPHE I: THE ANTI-MILITARY PRESIDENCY

"Where there is no vision, the people will perish."

—Proverbs, 29:18

"I may not have been the greatest president, but I've had the most fun eight years."

—President Bill Clinton[1]

On the afternoon of October 3, 1993, a Somali agent working for the CIA heard that key members of the Somali National Alliance—possibly even its warlord leader, Mohammed Farah Aidid—were to meet at the Olympic Hotel in Mogadishu at 3:00 p.m. Members of Task Force Ranger, the U.S. military contingent tasked by commander in chief Bill Clinton to root out the warlords, and Aidid in particular, sprang into action. Fourteen American helicopters lifted off, their rotors pounding the air with the distinctive "thump, thump, thump." The plan: a "fast rope" lightning-quick "snatch and grab" by the Rangers, who would slide from the helicopters via cables, seize Aidid, and then board a vehicle convoy out of the area.

At 3:40 p.m., the Rangers began securing the area around the hotel, while members of the elite Delta Force stormed the building. Somali clan members and Aideed sympathizers quickly responded. Sporadic gunfire splintered the whitewashed stucco walls; several members of the American team were wounded. The volume of enemy fire increased, with rocket-propelled grenades (RPGs) hitting vehicles in the convoy. It was also directed at the helicopters; the firing tactic of aiming at the helicopters' tail rotors to bring them down had been taught to the Somali insurgents by al-Qaeda. A U.S. MH-60 helicopter, using the call sign "Super 61," was hit and fell violently to the streets of Mogadishu. A second MH-60 hovered over the crash site, preparing to "fast rope" Air Force special operations forces to rescue the seven downed airmen. A flash, another RPG, another wounded helicopter: the MH-60 turned erratically and staggered for safe haven. Minutes later, a third MH-60 was hit, crashing in the distance, two miles away from the Olympic Hotel.

The operation, despite the extreme bravery and skill of the Rangers and other American servicemen, was rapidly turning into a disaster. The Ranger and Delta forces and downed aircrew were stranded, pinned down by intense small-arms fire from seemingly everywhere. It was the firefight from hell and it would last thirteen hours. A last-ditch rescue effort was assembled and finally succeeded; other members of Task Force Ranger used four Pakistani tanks and twenty-four Malaysian armored personnel carriers to recover their fallen and trapped brethren.

Only a month earlier, Major General Thomas Montgomery, the on-scene commander of U.S. forces in Somalia, had requested M1 Abrams tanks, Bradley armored fighting vehicles, and AC-130 Spectre gunships. He needed the extra firepower to execute President Clinton's ever-expanding demands on the task force.

On September 23, 1993, the Clinton administration, through Secretary of Defense Les Aspin, denied the request, despite the fact that it had been seconded by then chairman of the Joint Chiefs of Staff,

General Colin Powell, and by General Joseph Hoar, commander in chief of the U.S. Joint Command, the "theater commander" for Somalia. Aspin denied the request for political reasons, arguing that it would be seen as an escalation of U.S. involvement. It was typical Clintonism: increase the demands on American forces, but deny the troops the equipment they need to properly do the job. Eighteen American soldiers paid the ultimate price for Clintonism during the battle of Mogadishu.

When Bill Clinton assumed the presidency from George H. W. Bush, the American military was already deployed to Somalia under the humanitarian mission banner. We were there to feed and clothe people. In one of his first acts, and soon to be biggest foreign policy gaffes, Clinton reduced the twenty-eight thousand troops deployed under Bush to fewer than five thousand. In an unbelievable lack of foresight, he simultaneously increased the mission scope to one of nation-building and pursuit of the warlord Aidid. As Rich Lowry so accurately portrayed this policy in his book *Legacy: Paying the Price for the Clinton Years*, "This wasn't 'mission creep,' the cliché for gradually widening objectives in a military operation. It was 'mission leap.'"[2]

Now, in the midst of this firefight, the world's only superpower and history's strongest fighting force was relegated to engaging the enemy with borrowed, ill-maintained equipment provided by Third World countries. When the smoke lifted and morning broke, eighteen American servicemen were dead and eighty were wounded. It was an American tragedy and was ultimately symbolic of the Clinton administration's endless foreign policy failures.

The gruesome imagery of savage mobs dragging dead American soldiers through the streets of Mogadishu prompted Clinton to cut and run, pulling American troops out of Somalia. There was no military response to the humiliation. There was no resolve to see the new mission goals to fruition. The only remaining superpower in the world withdrew from Mogadishu with a whimper.

From this debacle, Osama bin Laden learned a lesson he would apply on September 11, 2001: Americans could be attacked with impunity. "We have seen in the last decade the decline of the American government and the weakness of the American soldier," bin Laden told an ABC news reporter. "It also proves they can run in less than twenty-four hours, and this was also repeated in Somalia."[3] Clinton, a decadent president pretending to command a military he would not allow to fight effectively, gave bin Laden every reason to regard the United States with contempt.

DEFENSELESS

In December 2003, Senator Hillary Rodham Clinton appeared on *Meet the Press* to harangue the Bush administration for not supporting our troops with adequate supplies in Iraq and Afghanistan

"We haven't given them enough body armor. We didn't give them enough armored Humvees," she told Tim Russert. "We didn't do what was necessary to give our men and women on the ground the full support that they deserve."

The former first lady—now a voice on the Armed Services Committee—should have a better handle on military affairs. Surely she must remember the savage military budget cuts enacted during her husband's eight years in office and the hollowed military infrastructure their administration handed over to President Bush.

President Clinton and his national security team—comprised largely of retreads from the failed Carter administration, which shared Clinton's animosity to military spending—delivered record numbers of military force and budget reductions and devastated military morale. Clinton's brag about balancing the federal budget came directly at the expense of our men and women in uniform. They took a gradual, measured defense drawdown prudently initiated by the senior President Bush and accelerated it to warp speed.

In 1990, defense spending represented nearly 30 percent of the total annual federal budget. By 2000, this had been chopped to 15 percent. As a percentage of gross domestic product, the defense budget was reduced from 6.2 percent in 1985 to 3 percent in 2000, the lowest level in this country since the Great Depression. In more than 90 percent of the instances in which Clinton exercised his line item veto, he used it to cut defense spending. He slashed 700,000 active duty military members and 293,000 reservists from the payroll (a 40 percent reduction in total force), and reduced the defense budget by approximately $50 billion (in inflation-adjusted dollars). In terms of sheer combat capability, he also reduced the number of Army divisions from eighteen to ten and the number of Air Force active duty fighter aircraft squadrons from twenty-four to twelve.

Vice President Al Gore's "reinventing government" initiative, which he was so proud to trumpet, reduced 305,000 civilian employees from the federal ledger. What he didn't advertise was that 286,000 of these employees, or 90 percent, came from the Department of Defense.

To fully understand Clinton's relative prioritization of military funding, the only domestic programs other than defense to be reduced during his eight years were farm subsidies for wool, honey, and mohair, and water conservation grants in the Interior Department.[4]

The hemorrhaging of the military was obvious. The headlines were screaming. The Navy Times, May 2000: "Band-Aid Navy: How Shortages Are Burning Out Sailors and Wearing Out the Fleet." The New York Times, November 1999: "Army Says Strained Resources Leave Troops Unprepared for War." The Air Force Times, May 2000: "Readiness Hits Lowest Level in 15 Years." The Washington Post, November 1999: "Two Army Divisions Unfit for War: Both Flunk Ratings of Preparedness."[5]

When Clinton left office in 2001, funding for procurement of new weapon systems and the equipment to support our troops topped out at about $40 billion a year. Unfortunately, the requirement established by the Defense Department was $65 to $75 billion a year. Over his eight years, Clinton created a military procurement and modernization shortfall that will take this country, optimistically, a decade from which to recover. He halted or froze development of badly needed defense systems and underfunded other critical programs such as the F-22 advanced tactical fighter aircraft (the eventual replacement for the F-15 and F-16), the C-17 transport aircraft (the backbone of the nation's air mobility assets), missile defense, space assets, and Navy shipbuilding, in essence taking a "procurement holiday" and kicking a can of worms to his successor.

In 2001, the average age of our fighter and attack aircraft topped twenty years. The venerable B-52 bomber was forty years old, older than most pilots flying it, and will now be seventy-five years old when it is ultimately retired. The KC-135 tanker, used to refuel military aircraft in flight, was designed during the Eisenhower presidency. The average age of the amphibious assault vehicles used by the Marines was twenty-eight years old. The design of the CH-46 helicopter, the backbone of the Marine Corps, was forty years old. By 2010, the average Army tank will be twenty-three years old. How many people want to drive a car that is twenty, thirty, or forty years old? And yet we ask our young soldiers to take such vehicles and aircraft into combat where a breakdown isn't merely a headache: It can be lethal.

It takes decades to field a new major weapons system such as the C-17 transport aircraft or F-22 Raptor. It takes twenty years for the Air Force to grow a young pilot into a qualified squadron commander or the Army to develop a young West Point graduate into a battalion commander. The long view was never Clinton's view when it came to defense. But it wasn't just the future he sacrificed. He went after existing military systems as well. More than two thousand Air Force and Navy fighter and attack aircraft, 224 transport and cargo aircraft, and 232 bomber aircraft were retired from the inventory. The Air National Guard lost 350 aircraft. The Navy was reduced from almost six hundred ships to little more than three hundred; four aircraft carriers and 117 surface-combat vessels were retired. And the support, basing, transportation, and logistics required to support these infrastructures were slashed as well. "Operations and maintenance," or O & M—that is, the day-to-day support and lifeblood for our troops—was cut dramatically, meeting only 60 to 70 percent of annual requirements, which meant serious wear and tear on people and equipment.[6]

As the Prussian soldier Carl von Clausewitz, one of history's most revered military thinkers, noted, "The end for which a soldier is recruited, clothed, armed and trained, the whole object of his sleeping, eating, drinking, and marching is simply that he should fight at the right place and the right time."[7] During the Clinton years, the recruiting, clothing, arming, and training of America's soldiers were treated with disdain.

Clinton denied already planned and approved military pay raises and created the "military poor," forcing thirty thousand military families (fifty-five thousand families were eligible) to turn to food stamps and eight thousand to rely on state-funded childcare assistance by 1999. It was "one more sign that Clinton doesn't care," said an Army major.[8]

The gap between military and civilian pay reached 13.5 percent by 1999 (similar to the 14 percent reached under Carter in 1979).[9] In an all-volunteer force, comparable pay is key to attracting and retaining talented, trained, and educated soldiers. When soldiers have families, their salaries and living standards become more important. Yet two-thirds of all military family housing was characterized as "substandard" by the Defense Science Board. Having lived in military housing around the world most of my life, I know that even the "standard" housing doesn't meet civilian standards.

The Clinton administration didn't want soldiers anyway. "Selective early retirement boards" were held for senior officers, while junior troops were just forced out, their jobs eliminated in force reduction cuts. Others "voted with their feet," leaving the services in record numbers at the first possible opportunity.

When the Clintons vacated the White House, military morale was at a historic low as liberal social engineering had been pushed down the services' throats. Clinton set out to dramatically transform military culture by integrating gays into the military, putting women in frontline combat positions, and placing American soldiers, sailors, airmen, and Marines under foreign (United Nations) command. All of this was done with complete disregard for the opinions and concerns of military leadership at the Pentagon and soldiers in the field.

Clinton introduced coed basic training, quotas for women, and "gender-normed" standards. When the Marines became the only service to balk, Assistant Secretary of the Army Sara Lister, a Clinton appointee, called them "extremists" and "dangerous" for not complying with the edict. She then proceeded to make a joke about the Marine uniform.[10] Madeline Morris, a Pentagon consultant for "gender integration" suggested that the military should eliminate "masculinist attitudes," "assertiveness," "aggressiveness," "independence," "self-sufficiency," and "willingness to take risks."[11] More time was spent on "sensitivity" training and lectures on diversity coming directly at the expense of training in the combat specialties.

All the gender-bending led to a spike in sexual harassment charges in the military, and the military responded by court-martialing those convicted and sending them to Fort Leavenworth, the military prison system. Meanwhile, the commander in chief set his own atrocious moral example, one at odds with military law and one of flagrant hypocrisy, given the new "sensitivity" standards he required of the military. He even attempted to invoke the Soldiers and Sailors Relief Act of 1944 as protection from prosecution in the Paula Jones sexual harassment case, based on the fact that he was on "active duty." The Soldiers and Sailors Relief Act was instituted to protect active duty personnel from civil suits, such as divorce, until after their service. He withdrew his petition because veterans groups were outraged and, more important for him, it was legally untenable. The message to the men and women in uniform was received loud and clear. In 1998, almost 80 percent of eligible Air Force pilots declined to extend their commitments.[12]

Clinton took these cuts and implemented his and his wife's liberal agenda while he was deploying the military more than any other president. It was a schizophrenic approach to national security. He dispatched the military overseas forty-four times during his eight years. Our military had been deployed outside our borders only eight times in the previous forty-five years. The American soldier's role changed from homeland defender to nomadic peacekeeper.

Many of these military excursions, this "CNN diplomacy"—foreign policy driven by television news coverage and political polling—were poorly thought out, halfhearted, and silly. Even French president Jacques Chirac condemned Clinton's foreign policies as essentially brain-dead, declaring "that the position of the leader of the free world is vacant."[13]

By example, there were ten so-called "contingencies" to enforce the 1991 "peace" agreement with Iraq as Saddam Hussein consistently thumbed his nose at America and fired on American and British aircraft. Operation Restore Democracy, the Congressional Black Caucus–prompted intervention to reinsert the Marxist defrocked priest Jean-Bertrand Aristide as the ruler in Haiti, a country that has never known democracy in its two hundred years of existence, required five deployments. Other deployments with names such as "Noble Anvil" and "Joint Guardian" were executed in the Balkans, Somalia, Rwanda, Macedonia, Ecuador, East Timor, Kuwait, Liberia, Albania, Congo, Gabon, Sierra Leone, and Sudan.

The combination of massive force cuts and dramatically increased deployments meant that our military was worn to the bone. Training was the first military priority to suffer. Because of the call on its personnel in Haiti, Korea, Somalia, and Bosnia, the Navy was forced to severely limit cockpit training for more than one thousand pilots. The Army had to cease training for two infantry divisions and dramatically reduce tank training to pay for the operations in Rwanda.[14]

You measure a military unit's ability to accomplish its assigned mission in terms of "readiness." Logistics, equipment, the availability of spare parts, training, the number of new recruits, and morale make up the readiness equation. The military Clinton handed to President Bush was the most combat unready since the catastrophe of the Carter years. The Bush administration has moved rapidly to improve readiness and reenergize morale: The military is grateful and America should be.

But in light of the military successes in Iraq and Afghanistan, the former president and first lady have had the gall to claim that our battlefield successes are the result of "their military." Speaking to a Washington think tank, Mrs. Clinton chided President Bush and Vice President Cheney for not thanking her husband for handing the current administration a strong military. "Well, I don't know," she said, "but I don't think any letters have yet arrived on the desks of anyone associated with the Clinton administration."[15]

No, ma'am, and don't hold your breath.

The Clinton Catastrophe II: Corruption, Cowardice, and the Fraud of Richard Clarke

"War should be the only study of a prince. He should consider peace only as a breathing time which gives him leisure to contrive, and furnishes an ability to execute, military plans."

—Niccolò Machiavelli, The Prince[1]

"It is vain, sir, to extenuate the matter. Gentleman may cry, Peace, Peace—but there is no peace. The war is actually begun! The next gale that sweeps from the north will bring to our ears the clash of resounding arms! Our brethren are already in the field! Why stand we here idle? What is it that gentlemen wish? What would they have? Is life so dear, or peace so sweet, as to be purchased at the price of chains and slavery? Forbid it, Almighty God!"

—Patrick Henry, March 23, 1775

On June 12, 1987, President Ronald Reagan stood at the foot of the Brandenburg Gate, the venerable monument to the people of Berlin, Germany, crowned with the horses of the Quadriga. Just around the corner was "Checkpoint Charlie," the symbol of the decades-long Cold War. Reagan gave the speech of the half-century.

"General Secretary Gorbachev, if you seek peace, if you seek prosperity for the Soviet Union and Eastern Europe, if you seek liberalization: Come here to this gate! Mr. Gorbachev, open this gate!

Mr. Gorbachev, tear down this wall!"[2] In a matter of months, the Soviet Union began crashing under its own deadweight. The Cold War was over.

Germans celebrated with singing and sledgehammers as they helped knock down the wall that had divided East and West Germany. *Bier*, Champagne, and Riesling flowed freely as separated family and friends came together again. And the Western world breathed easy: Fifty years of struggle with Communism were ended. But liberals, of course, heard the wrong message. It did not register with them that Ronald Reagan's policy of "peace through strength" had won the Cold War, nor did it register that the world was still a dangerous place. Instead, a Clinton official said early in the administration's first term, "We don't need a strong defense anymore, we don't have any enemies."

The *Oakland Tribune* chimed in, concurring with studies that "see no big security problems arising," and, besides, "no American President is ever again likely to send U.S. troops to fight another insurgency."[3]

But threats to our national security don't disappear, they evolve; power vacuums are always filled. In the collapse of Communism, previously suppressed nationalisms, ethnic rivalries, and radical Islam violently emerged.

Liberal Democrats, however, focused their attention on pork barrel spending—on the "peace dividend." They demanded monies "owed" to them and whined about "guns to butter," "swords to ploughshares," a "farewell to arms," "arms are for hugging," soup kitchens, habitats for the Canadian lynx, art exhibits—anything that restored our "neglected human capital" and cut defense spending.

In the midst of these demands for a "peace dividend," the greatest era of federal social spending in our history, bigger than Franklin Roosevelt's New Deal in the 1930s and Lyndon Johnson's Great Society in the 1960s, in terms of real dollars, was under way. The victims were the Department of Defense and U.S. intelligence agencies.

The beneficiaries of the megabucks bonanza were Medicare, Social Security, and Bill Clinton's political popularity as the man who brought home the bacon. Medicare spending rose by 94 percent and Social Security by 81 percent. Much of the increase in Social Security went to fund disability programs for drug and alcohol addicts and illegal immigrants.

The pork got fatter and the military got thinner. The phrase "the hollow military" was coined by Army Chief of Staff General Edward "Shy" Meyer in 1978 to describe the devastating effects that the Carter administration had on the U.S. defense establishment. The "hollow military" returned during the Clinton administration.

CLINTON'S TUTOR: JIMMY CARTER

Just as Clinton came to power after the end of the Cold War, Carter had come to power after the end of the Vietnam War. Carter also believed in a peace dividend, because he believed it was time for America to get over its "inordinate fear" of Communism. So Carter embarked on massive defense reductions. He offered amnesty to all those who had avoided the Vietnam War draft. He signed a treaty with Panama surrendering the geographically vital Panama Canal. He worked to appease the Soviet Union. He tried to withdraw American troops from South Korea, until even he realized how destabilizing that was to the Pacific Rim. He watched as a Communist government came to power in Nicaragua. Carter's weakness led the Soviets to believe they could invade Afghanistan with impunity. He sold out a longtime American ally, the shah of Iran, leading to the establishment of a powerful radical Islamic state, the rule of the Ayatollah Khomeini, the hostage-taking of American diplomats, and the birth of the Islamic terror network. And Carter so wrecked the American military that Ronald Reagan noted, "When I took office in January 1981, I was appalled by what I found: American planes that could not fly and American ships that could not sail."[4]

You would think that Carter's record would be a warning. For Clinton, it wasn't a warning, it was a model, because Clinton's foreign policy staff came largely from the Carter administration. The

Clinton years were really an extension of the Carter years. The anti-military ideology of McGovern, Carter, and Clinton is simply the standard now for Democrats, including John Kerry, John Edwards, Richard Gephardt, Howard Dean, and Hillary Clinton.

For whatever reason, the Carter-Clinton-Kerry Democrats simply cannot comprehend the most fundamental of facts about the world. A study done by James Dunnigan, a military historian and editor of StrategyPage.com, concludes that of the five thousand years of recorded human existence, only a few hundred have been conflict-free. Depending on how one defines "war," there are *currently* between eighty and 110 armed conflicts being fought around the globe.[5] According to the PBS program *The American Experience*, there have been more than forty-eight U.S. military actions and wars in our 227 years of existence.[6] The Congressional Research Service counted more than 250 foreign deployments of U.S. troops since 1798.[7]

Albert Einstein once noted, "So long as there are men there will be wars." Plato wrote, "Only the dead have seen the last of war." Aristotle concluded, "We fight wars that we may live in peace."

President George H. W. Bush, fresh from the overwhelming victory of Desert Storm and the liberation of Kuwait, handed the Clinton-Gore administration an American military honed to precision after eight years of Ronald Reagan and four years of his own able leadership. Bush, a master foreign policy statesman, handed the incoming Democrats one of the best national security situations ever passed from one administration to the next. U.S. military power and America's international prestige were unparalleled. It would be a tremendous national and international opportunity squandered.

Consider this. In 1992, Russia was an emerging democracy, China was developing a free market, and every tyrant with a Saddam Hussein poster on his wall was peeking at his Swiss bank account and making an evacuation plan in the aftermath of Iraq's embarrassing defeat.

Two Clinton terms later, George W. Bush was handed a mess, not just in terms of vandalized White House computer keyboards, telephones, and a trashed Air Force One, but in a hollowed-out, demoralized military and in a new terrorist threat—al-Qaeda—that the Clinton administration had taught could attack America at will.

After eight years of the Clinton administration, China, using American technology given at Clinton's request, had developed the ability to accurately launch intercontinental ballistic missiles capable of reaching the United States. North Korea, using American technology and taking American financial aid, had developed nuclear weapons and was blackmailing the United States for more money and oil. Russia, China, and Pakistan were colluding with every rogue nation willing to pay for new and more dangerous weaponry. The Ukraine and Pakistan were holding "nuclear bazaars," selling secrets and techniques to anyone who could afford the admission.

Eight separate terrorist attacks targeting American citizens had been met with rhetoric and no effective action by the Clinton administration. American intelligence agencies were emasculated in the Clinton administration's search for "political correctness." General Hugh Shelton, chairman of the Joint Chiefs of Staff, reflecting on Clinton's misuse of the military, confessed, "Our forces are frayed."[8]

CLUELESS

The end of the Cold War was not the end of history.

In his confirmation hearing in 1993, newly appointed director of Central Intelligence James Woolsey warned the Senate Intelligence Committee, "We have slain a large dragon...but we now live in a jungle filled with a bewildering variety of poisonous snakes, and in many ways the dragon was easier to keep track of."[9] The Clinton administration didn't get the memo.

While terrorist threats mounted, Clinton met privately with terrorist Yassir Arafat and intern Monica Lewinsky more often than he met with Woolsey or his successor, George Tenet. In fact, Clinton met more with Arafat than with any other world leader. According to a *USA Today* report, "the head of the CIA got only two private meetings with the president, even after the World Trade Center bombing of February 1993, or the killing of 18 American soldiers in Mogadishu on October 3 of the same year."[10]

The Clinton administration followed its political mantra—"it's the economy, stupid"—and kept the pork barrel rolling, while Clinton's one foreign policy interest was the same as Carter's: cutting a deal with Arafat that would allow the president to claim the mantle of "peacemaker" in the Middle East. Meanwhile, al-Qaeda continued to kill Americans overseas and plotted to attack America at home.

IT'S TERRORISM, STUPID

At 9:49 p.m. on June 25, 1996, in the Saudi Arabian coastal city of Dhahran, a septic tank truck and a car pulled into an area along the north perimeter fence of a U.S. Air Force barracks facility named Khobar Towers. This high-rise complex was home away from home for two thousand American military personnel assigned to the nearby King Abdul Aziz Air Base. It was a sultry evening; the air hung heavy in the night. It was about to get much hotter.

Three sentries posted to an observation point atop the dormitory noticed the truck as it began to back up into the hedges just outside the fence. Suddenly, two men jumped from the truck and into the following car and sped away.

The sentries ran to the barracks, pounding on the doors of the sleeping airmen. They knew this for what it was. Airmen spilled out of their rooms toward the emergency exits.

At 9:55 p.m., the bomb detonated in an explosion so powerful that it left a crater eighty-five feet wide and thirty-five feet deep. The face of the Khobar Towers high-rise was gone. The blast was heard on the island of Bahrain, twenty miles away. Nineteen American Air Force personnel were killed and more than two hundred were wounded.

"The explosion appears to be the work of terrorists, and if that is the case, like all Americans, I am outraged by it," President Clinton remarked. "We will pursue this," he said. "America takes care of our own. The cowards who committed this murderous act must not go unpunished."[11] Nevertheless, the perpetrators of this act of terrorism were never brought to justice.

America's war on terrorism didn't start on September 11, 2001— that was when President Bush decided to fight back. It wasn't begun that night in Dhahran either. It wasn't born in the tragic circumstances of Mogadishu, Somalia, or in the first bombing of the World Trade Center in February 1993. The first shot of this war occurred on January 17, 1979, when the shah of Iran, Mohammed Reza Pahlavi, a longtime ally of the United States and a progressive modern ruler by Islamic standards, was forced to flee his own country.

President Jimmy Carter, who had said in 1977 that "Iran, because of the great leadership of the shah, is an island of stability in the Middle East,"[12] sought to make changes in relations between the countries. With puzzling shortsightedness, Carter began to undermine the shah's regime. Under the guise of a human rights program, he demanded that the shah step down and relinquish power to a cleric in exile in Paris, the Ayatollah Khomeini.

Carter sent Ramsey Clark, the radical former attorney general under Lyndon Johnson, to Paris to meet with Khomeini, a seventy-eight-year-old Shi'ite cleric whose brother had ties to Iranian Communist parties and to Saddam Hussein's Ba'ath National Socialists in Iraq. Khomeini had been exiled from Iran in 1963 for inciting fundamentalist Islamic opposition to the shah.

Carter's United Nations ambassador, Andrew Young, best expressed the administration's thinking at the time, concluding that Khomeini would "eventually be hailed as a saint."[13]

Simultaneously, Carter sent U.S. military officers to Tehran, including Air Force General Robert "Dutch" Huyser, to convince the shah and his top military commanders not to oppose the impending Islamic fundamentalist revolution. The shah was forced to flee his country; within weeks, Khomeini was in power.

In one of his first acts, Iran's new "saint" ordered the execution of 150 of the shah's top military advisors. On November 4, 1979, Islamic fundamentalist radicals stormed the American embassy in Tehran and, with the support of the Iranian government, took sixty-six Americans hostage.

Through selling out an American ally in the shah and supporting the radical Islamic fundamentalist Khomeini, Carter created one of the most militantly anti-American regimes in history and laid the groundwork for the largest state sponsor of radical Islamic terrorism. Of all Carter's catastrophes, this was arguably the worst.[14]

Iran had been a bastion for U.S. interests in the Middle East. It is large, strategically located, and a significant producer of oil. The shah had encouraged the development of a free economy and an increasingly free society. He could have provided a model for a Western-oriented Islam and Middle East. Carter's abandonment of him destabilized the entire region and empowered the fundamentalists. Just five months after Khomeini's ascendancy, the Soviet Union invaded Afghanistan, radicalizing it in the succeeding war and inspiring Osama bin Laden to become a radical Islamic jihadist. The Carter administration's response to the seizure of American diplomats in Iran and the Soviet invasion of Afghanistan was typically inept. Carter broke off diplomatic relations with Iran, embargoed Iranian oil, and ordered the failed rescue attempt at Desert One. Carter's response to the Soviet invasion was to boycott the Olympic Summer Games being held in Moscow. Depriving the Soviets and the world of the presence of our athletes and preventing sixteen-year-old gymnasts from pursuing their lives' ambition was the best he could do.

Carter's ineptitude was Clinton's foreign policy training. Like Carter, Clinton preferred liberal symbolism to substance. He made noise, but did nothing useful, either ignoring terrorism or sending random missile shots that were meant only to "send a message." Osama bin Laden got the message that America wasn't serious.

As President George W. Bush later said, reflecting on September 11, "terrorist attacks are not caused by the use of strength; they are invited by the perception of weakness."[15]

Weakness is what the Carter-Clinton-Kerry Democrats are all about.

THE FRAUD OF RICHARD CLARKE AND THE 9-11 COMMISSION

The Clinton administration never believed that terrorism was a national security threat; it was a matter for law enforcement. Clinton and his appointed counter-terrorism chief, Richard Clarke, never did anything to thwart al-Qaeda. The occasional cruise missile strike was patently pointless. Secret plans to apprehend bin Laden were never carried out. And Clinton did his best to ignore his intelligence chiefs. Rather than thwart al-Qaeda, Clinton and Clarke served only to embolden the terrorists through their inaction.

In 1992, Clarke assumed his position as the counter-terrorism guru in the National Security Council. At the time, terrorism, although growing, was not a serious national security problem due to the diligence of the Reagan and Bush administrations. But when Clarke left the White House in October 2001, after his nine years of oversight, terrorism was the single greatest threat to America.

Only thirty-eight days into Clinton's first term, terrorists working with Ramzi Ahmed Yousef, bin Laden, and al-Qaeda bombed the World Trade Center in New York for the first time. Six people were killed, more than one thousand were injured, and more than $510 million in damage was done. One can only speculate as to what George H. W. Bush's response would have been, but given Ronald Reagan's history of striking back at terrorists militarily—as he did, for instance, after the *Achille Lauro* hijacking of 1985 and the Libyan bombing of a Berlin discotheque in 1986—it is likely that President

Bush would have responded in a similar manner. But President Clinton's reaction was to caution Americans not to overreact. He went on MTV and said that those responsible "did something very stupid."[16] He didn't regard the bombing as anything terribly serious—not as an issue of national security—but as a simple crime investigation for law enforcement to handle. In other words, Clinton, advised by Clarke, did nothing.

In October 1993, the Black Hawk Down debacle occurred in Mogadishu, Somalia, and with it the deaths of eighteen American servicemen. Al-Qaeda was involved. But Clinton, advised by Clarke, did nothing except to announce that America's military presence in Somalia would be withdrawn by March 1994.

As Osama bin Laden recounted, "Our boys . . . went to Somalia and prepared themselves carefully for a long war. Our boys were shocked by the low morale of the American soldier, and they realized that the American soldier was just a paper tiger. He was unable to endure the strikes that were dealt to his army, so he fled, and America had to stop all its bragging."[17]

It was the defining moment for bin Laden in his thinking about America. In bin Laden's mind, as Rich Lowry describes in his book *Legacy*, "Clinton was a weepy, undisciplined, talkative, indecisive, sexually incontinent embodiment of America's alleged weakness and corruption. The Islamists couldn't have created a better symbol of everything that was wrong with America, and why they thought it could be defeated."[18]

In 1994, federal officials in San Francisco, California, arrested Mohammed Jamal Khalifa, Osama bin Laden's brother-in-law and the "money man" for al-Qaeda. Khalifa was, at that time, thought to be in the process of funding Ramzi Ahmed Yousef's "Operation Bojinka," the plot to blow up American commercial airliners. Secretary of State Warren Christopher wrote to Attorney General Janet Reno on January 5, 1995, urging Khalifa's deportation to Jordan. Upon reaching Jordan, Khalifa was set free.[19]

On March 8, 1995, two U.S. diplomats, Jackie Van Landingham and Gary Durrell, were gunned down in Karachi, Pakistan, in retaliation for Yousef's capture. Clinton's response was to send an FBI antiterrorism team to Pakistan to "investigate." Clinton, advised by Clarke, launched no military response against al-Qaeda.

On November 13, 1995, a bomb hidden in a minivan exploded at a U.S. military training center in Riyadh, Saudi Arabia, killing seven, including five Americans, and injuring forty. Clinton's response was, again, to send an FBI anti-terrorism team to "investigate." Clinton, advised by Clarke, took no military response.

On June 25, 1996, the Dhahran military barracks were bombed, killing nineteen American airmen and wounding more than five hundred. Clinton's response was to once again send an FBI anti-terrorism team to Saudi Arabia to "investigate." Clinton, advised by Clarke, ordered no military retaliation.

FBI director Louis Freeh had a fractured relationship with Clinton— Clinton did not speak directly to Freeh for the four years between the Dhahran bombing and the bombing of the USS *Cole*—because Freeh's FBI was also investigating possible campaign fund-raising violations by the Clinton-Gore campaign that went far beyond financial mismanagement to possible violations of national security. The FBI investigation was looking into whether the Communist Chinese government funneled money to the Clinton-Gore campaign. Eventually, twenty-five indictments and nineteen convictions were handed down.[20]

While the FBI investigated the Khobar and Dhahran bombings, Freeh concluded that Sandy Berger, Clinton's national security advisor, was really, in the words of journalist Byron York, "not a national security advisor; he was a public-relations hack, interested in how something would play in the press. After more than two years, [Freeh] had concluded that the administration did not really want to resolve the Khobar bombing."[21]

Similarly, only twice in his two-year service as Clinton's director of Central Intelligence did James Woolsey have a one-on-one meeting with the president. Woolsey would later lament, "I made repeated attempts to see Clinton privately to take up a whole range of issues and was unsuccessful,"[22] and, "It wasn't that I had a bad relationship with the president. It just didn't exist."[23]

On August 7, 1998, al-Qaeda bombed American embassies in Nairobi, Kenya, and Dar es Salaam, Tanzania, killing 224 people, twelve of them Americans. More than five thousand were injured.

Clinton, advised by Clarke, finally retaliated.

On August 20, the president ordered a strike on al-Qaeda for the first and only time in his presidency. With "Operation Infinite Reach," five U.S. warships fired sixty Tomahawk cruise missiles at suspected terrorist camps in Afghanistan and at a pharmaceutical plant in Sudan. The presidential order came only three days after Clinton had appeared before the grand jury investigating the Monica Lewinsky affair. "Infinite Reach" was anything but infinite. The military action was as feckless as it was suspiciously timed. The Pakistanis tipped off bin Laden before the missiles hit, and the presumed chemical weapons plant in Sudan turned out to be an aspirin factory. A nearby candy factory was also hit. The U.S. government paid reparations to the Sudanese government for the miscalculations.

Woolsey later summarized the Clinton "PR-driven" approach to terrorism. "Do something to show you're involved. Launch a few missiles in the desert, bop them on the head, arrest a few people. But just keep kicking the ball down the field."[24]

On October 12, 2000, a small boat loaded with explosives, operated by bin Laden's associates, blasted a huge hole in the side of the USS *Cole*, almost sinking the American warship. Seventeen American sailors were killed and thirty-nine others wounded.

Clinton announced, "If, as it now appears, this was an act of terrorism, it was a despicable and cowardly act. We will find out who was responsible and hold them accountable."[25]

Secretary of State Madeleine Albright added, "If it is a terrorist attack, we obviously will take appropriate steps."[26]

Clinton, advised by Clarke, did nothing.

Richard Miniter, in his excellent book *Losing bin Laden*, systematically documents how Clinton and his administration failed to prosecute a war against terrorism. Among the instances:

- Failing to lock up Khalid Shaikh Mohammed, a key bin Laden lieutenant in Qatar
- Failing to respond militarily to the al-Qaeda bombings of U.S. military installations in Riyadh and Dhahran, Saudi Arabia
- Failing to accept a Sudanese offer to hand over bin Laden into custody
- Failing to agree with Northern Alliance offers to assassinate bin Laden in Afghanistan
- Failing to use special forces to capture bin Laden in Afghanistan
- Tipping off Pakistani officials sympathetic to bin Laden before a planned missile strike on August 20, 1998
- Failing, on three separate occasions, to launch immediate military strikes when intelligence located bin Laden
- Failing to respond militarily when bin Laden bombed the USS *Cole* in 2000

As Clinton's Air Force aide in the summer of 1996, I knew that he was aware of who bin Laden was and of the potential for al-Qaeda attacks on American soil. After the release of my book *Dereliction of Duty* in 2003, Sandy Berger claimed that episodes I discussed that involved him—a missed attempt to support the Kurds in Northern Iraq in 1996 and a missed attempt to attack bin Laden in 1998—"simply are false."[27] But they are true, as I and my fellow military aides witnessed and participated in them. And the indictment can be made more particular.

When TWA Flight 800 crashed into the Atlantic Ocean off the coast of Long Island in July 1996, President Clinton chartered the White House Commission on Aviation Safety and Security and named Vice President Gore as chairman. In September 1996, the commission released its preliminary report. It recommended requiring the airlines to implement counter-terrorism measures. It recommended that aviation security be treated as a national security issue, not just as an airport problem. It recommended that the FAA take on a system of passenger profiling. It recommended that all airline, airport, and screening personnel undergo criminal background checks.[28]

Because the new procedures would be costly and time-consuming, the major airlines, then responsible for airport security, protested. Ten days later, Vice President Gore retreated from the commission's findings and sent a letter to the airlines that promised no loss of revenue. The next day, now-defunct TWA donated $40,000 to the Democratic National Committee (DNC). Within the next two weeks, the DNC received almost $600,000 dollars in campaign contributions from the major airlines.[29]

Following the reelection of Bill Clinton and Al Gore, the White House Commission on Aviation Safety released its final report on February 12, 1997, with watered-down requirements and no deadline for the FAA and the airlines to meet.

With no mechanism to force the FAA to comply, little was done. So when it came to preventing the use of airplanes as missiles, Bill Clinton, Al Gore, and Richard Clarke did less than nothing; the Clinton administration rejected its own commission's findings that might have prevented the September 11, 2001, attacks.

By 1996, the evidence was clear that al-Qaeda was forming plans for an attack on American soil, and the Clinton administration was aware of this. In 1995, Philippine police raided an apartment in Manila, barely missing terrorist suspect Ramzi Yousef but uncovering a treasure trove of al-Qaeda documents. The information was included in a 1996 Presidential Daily Briefing (PDB) given to President Clinton that summer. "Operation Bojinka" involved using hijacked airliners to crash into American targets or to explode them in flight over the Pacific Ocean. One of Yousef's associates, Abdul

Hakim Murad, told Philippine police that he and Yousef had discussed hijacking a commercial jet and flying it into CIA headquarters at Langley.

The 9-11 Commission, more formally known as the "National Commission on Terrorist Attacks upon the United States," chose to focus solely on another PDB, however, one issued on August 6, 2001, by President Bush's National Security Council. It was a historical recounting of terrorist activities under the Clinton administration, with no specific actionable intelligence.

Who deserves the blame for al-Qaeda's September 11, 2001, strike on America? President Clinton, who commanded the world's most powerful military for eight years, who knew al-Qaeda was operating in more than fifty countries and actively running sleeper cells within the United States, who knew it was seeking weapons of mass destruction, and who was president when Osama bin Laden openly declared war on the United States.

Yet the Clinton administration's final policy paper on national security—the document that provided transition guidance to the Bush administration—makes no mention of al-Qaeda anywhere in its 45,000 words. Richard Clarke—who was the chief of counter-terrorism for Clinton—blames the CIA, the FBI, and the Pentagon, anybody but himself and Clinton, for the failure to prevent the terrorist attacks of September 11. His apology before the 9-11 Commission was pure grandstanding before he tried to place the blame elsewhere. According to Clarke, Clinton "identified terrorism as the major post–Cold War threat," but "could not get the CIA, Pentagon, and FBI to act sufficiently to deal with the threat."[30] Who's the president here? Clarkeism is Clintonism: It's somebody else's fault.

Who deserves the blame for the September 11 attacks?

The men who did nothing while al-Qaeda struck at us for eight years.

CHAPTER TEN

WINNING: GEORGE W. BUSH AND THE ART OF COMMAND

"There is a tide in the affairs of men.
  Which, taken at the flood, leads on to fortune;
  Omitted, all the voyage of their life
  Is bound in shallows and in miseries.
  On such a full sea are we now afloat,
  And we must take the current when it serves,
  Or lose our venture."

—William Shakespeare, Julius Caesar,
Act 4, Scene 3, 218–224

The chosen men of the U.S. military's special operations forces knelt on the concrete hangar floor on the barren island of Masirah. It was oppressively hot even as the sun set. Twenty-two years before, this spit of land fifteen miles off the coast of Oman had been the launch site for Desert One, officially known as Operation Eagle Claw, the disastrous attempt under Jimmy Carter to rescue American diplomats kidnapped and held hostage by the radical Islamic Iranian government. Tonight, with renewed vigor, morale, and purpose born under the leadership of President George W. Bush, these elite warriors were preparing to fire the first shot in America's war against terrorism. The lack of vision, leadership, and action in defense of American lives that typified the Clinton administration during eight years of jihad directed against Americans at home and abroad was over. The terrorist group al-Qaeda had brought war to our homeland. These American warriors were about to take it back to the enemy.

Only a month after September 11, 2001, commander in chief Bush was sending a clear message to Osama bin Laden and the Taliban. Clinton was gone: There would be no more hesitation, no more Mogadishus, no more "pinpricks," no more ineffective missile strikes from hundreds of miles away. No. "We will come to you at a time and a place of our choosing, with American military boots on the ground, we will defend the freedom and liberties of our nation, we will find you, and we will kill you" was the message.

The U.S. task force commander, a chiseled, rock-hard, seasoned senior Army officer, stood before his men in the stifling hangar and offered a prayer. "God....as we go into combat this evening, we pray for our hearts to be pure, our decisions to be accurate, and our aim to be true. May we all come home safely."

"On your feet!" he then yelled. "Godspeed," he said as he saluted his troops. It is the loneliest yet most profound moment for a commander, the solitary inhabitant of that outpost called command. He has trained his forces, he has prepared them for fog and friction, and now he must send them into harm's way. He has spent his nights in contemplation. *Is there anything I could have done differently in their training? Do we have the right mix of forces? Is the plan sound? How many will be lost? How and when will this conflict be won?*

The Air Force aircrews, the elite Delta Force, and the Army Rangers silently walked out of the hangar toward their aircraft. In their minds, they reflected and resolved, *There is no more time for good ideas, no more time for planning. We have a great plan and we need to execute it. Just as we have rehearsed it. Just as we've trained for years. Our paced, methodical, and disciplined approach to this air assault will be successful; we'll all come home, if we stick to the script.*

The destinations were Objective Rhino, an isolated airfield in western Afghanistan sixty miles southwest of Kandahar that could be used for future military operations, and Objective Gecko, the Taliban "White House," in Kandahar.

The plan was to launch Air Force Special Operations Command MC-130 Talon IIs loaded with Army Rangers for an airdrop to secure the airfield. MC-130 Talon Is would be used to refuel Army helicopters—MH-47 Chinooks and MH-60 Black Hawks supporting the elite commandos—inflight. AC-130 gunships, with their devastating array of firepower, would protect and cover both "attack packages" from above.

As the sun set, six AC-130 gunships lined abreast and started their engines, sending black exhaust and blowing dust from the propeller wash hundreds of feet into the sky. The sound was at once deafening and reassuring for the warriors. It promised impending death for the enemy.

Each gunship was armed with 105 Howitzer cannons, 40-millimeter or 25-millimeter guns, and state-of-the-art targeting systems. Tonight, each gunship would carry a full combat load of ammunition and thirteen crew members. They would operate high above the objectives, monitoring the action below, supporting the Talons, commandos, and Rangers with overwhelming firepower. Their aircrew's motto: *You can run but you'll only die tired.*

The gunships were ready to taxi in formation to the runway, excepting one, the formation's lead aircraft, tail number 167. Each AC-130 had a name painted on its nose—tail number 167 was named "Azrael," the Angel of Death.

In front of Azrael, a single silhouette, framed by the disappearing sun, touching the nose of the aircraft as one would touch a loved one's face. His head bowed, he prayed. After a minute of conversation with God amid the bittersweet fumes of jet fuel and the numbing noise of twenty-four engines, he found his peace. Then, without hesitation, he quickly raised his head, walked to the aircraft with purpose, and joined his brothers in arms.

The formation leader taxied to the runway for the flight into war. The five other gunships sequenced behind him. Tail number 167 reached takeoff power. Due to the incredible weight of each aircraft and the searing hot temperatures of Oman hampering each engine's effectiveness, he lumbered down the runway, consuming every precious foot of its length before lifting into the darkening sky. His five mates followed in flawlessly timed succession.

Now it was the Talon Is' turn. The Army helicopters they would be refueling had already launched from a floating forward support base at a classified location and were "blacked out"—pilots on night vision goggles and maintaining complete radio silence.

As the Talons taxied, the maintenance teams who had worked countless hours preparing the aircraft for combat stood along the taxiway, in military formation, saluting each machine as it passed.

Each Talon had been christened with hastily applied paint and duct tape on the nose.

"For Our Children," read the first.

"11 September," read the second.

"Fuck Osama," read the third.

"WTC," read the fourth.

The four Talons departed into the night for their rendezvous with the helicopters.

Now, well after sunset, the members of the third and final element of the plan took their place. The young Army warriors were already in their parachutes, quiet, focused, heavily packed and heavily armed. They patiently sat in long parallel lines behind each Talon II aircraft. Their faces were camouflaged, deep in thought or prayer.

The Rangers engage in combat as would a pack of wolves. If the enemy engages one, he engages them all. If the enemy shoots at one, he shoots at them all, and immediately invites a level of ferocity that defies human understanding. The Rangers' attacks are precisely organized and timed to strike with overwhelming speed, surprise, and violence to destroy the enemy.

Tonight, the regimental commander, their leader, equally burdened with equipment, sat on the ramp next to his men, awaiting the direction to board the aircraft. Confident, quiet, and humble, he would lead them into the assault on Objective Rhino. He would ask nothing of his men that he was not willing to do himself.

The Rangers boarded the planes, and the Talon IIs taxied to the runway, illuminated only by a sole position light on the tip of each one's left wing. More than one hundred aircraft maintenance troops, commanded by an Air Force colonel, lined the way, and saluted as each bird passed.

With the moonlight skipping off the calm waters of the Persian Gulf, the Talon IIs were winging toward Afghanistan with their Rangers: lights out, radio silence.

Ten minutes from "time over target," TOT, and the green light to jump, the regimental commander began chanting the Ranger Creed, with his men joining in:

> Energetically will I meet the enemies of my country. I shall defeat them on the field of battle, for I am better trained and will fight with all my might. Surrender is not a Ranger word. I will never leave a fallen comrade to fall into the hands of the enemy and under no circumstances will I ever embarrass my country.... Readily will I display the intestinal fortitude required to fight on to the Ranger objective and complete the mission...though I be the lone survivor.

Then, with the green light, he yelled, "Follow me!"

There is no higher honor.

Most Americans will never know his name or what he and his Rangers would accomplish this night. And that's exactly the way he wanted it.

At Rhino, more than two hundred Rangers parachuted to the isolated runway. Forty Taliban defenders were quickly killed and the airfield seized.

At Gecko, Mullah Mohammed Omar's house was swiftly and effectively seized. As the Rangers searched and secured each room, they propped a New York Fire Department patch on every bed's pillow throughout the complex.

"We remember and we're here," was the message. "We will find you and we will kill you."

Opening night of Operation Enduring Freedom was under way. If Osama bin Laden had expected George W. Bush to behave like Bill Clinton, he had figured wrong. If he'd expected an American leader not to look beyond his ego and poll popularity, he'd miscalculated. If he hadn't known the soul of the American soldier who watched three thousand of his countrymen die on television, he'd soon discover it.

MIDDLE AMERICAN VALUES AND
MILITARY LEADERSHIP

Midland, Texas, is situated on the flat and empty plains of the vast desert expanse between Fort Worth and El Paso. There are few trees, no mountains, and no skyscrapers. The terrain is rugged, mostly sand and shrubs, dotted with oil derricks and windmills. The sky dominates the vista. Midlanders call their city of fewer than 100,000 residents the "Land of the High Sky." The town's motto is "The Sky Is the Limit." The setting is important in understanding the people of Midland and their outlook.

Midland has had its ups and downs. Sitting atop the Permian Basin, the second largest oil reserve in America, it has been home to the booms and the busts of the petroleum industry. Midlanders, in a direct sense, mirror the pioneers that settled America. They are inherently optimistic, having experienced economic prosperity. They are durable and humble, having lived through economic depression. There used to be a military base here; Midland Army Air Field was the largest training base for bombardiers during World War II. Although the airfield is long since closed, residents of Midland still embrace traditional military values. They are conservative, family-oriented, and religious. A sign in a downtown window triumphantly proclaims, "Satan is Defeated." The Boy Scouts are still welcome in Midland.

For all of these reasons and more, the Left is extremely uncomfortable with Midland. The very existence of old-fashioned values challenges the liberal gestalt. Same-sex marriage is not okay in Midland, nor is abortion. Author Michael Lind calls Midland one of the most "reactionary" cities in America. Columnist Molly Ivins echoes Larry L. King's description of Midland as a city of "oilionaires and Neanderthal Republicans with low, sloping foreheads."[1]

"Midland's Rising Son" is President George W. Bush. His family moved there when he was two years old. He grew up in Midland's public schools and he returned as a young oilman in the 1970s. "I would say people—if they want to understand me—need to understand Midland, and the attitude of Midland," Bush told reporters during his first presidential campaign. "The values Midland holds near to its heart are the same ones I hold near to my heart. . . . The slogan 'The Sky's the Limit' was meant for everyone, not just a select few. Midlanders believe if you work hard and believe it will happen, anything can happen. That ethic of hard work and outlook of optimism has stayed with me my whole life."[2]

These values, once so prevalent in the American fabric, still play in Midland. These same values are just as essential to the soul of the soldier and the heart of a military organization as they were fifty years ago; they are the values George W. Bush has brought to the War on Terror and to his obligations as our commander in chief.

The foundations for service in the armed forces have not changed with the liberal agenda. If anything, as American culture has become more culturally liberal, the military has been challenged to ever more insulate itself against popular culture. The military ethic is based on *loyalty to nation, commitment to duty,* and *selfless service,* all alien concepts for the Left.

Here's the real rub for liberals: The art of leadership is the ability to compel people to follow your orders, your direction, because they *want* to. The party of Carter-Clinton-Kerry cannot differentiate between leadership and management. Leadership involves people. Management involves things. Good leadership starts with character. The first requirement for strong leadership is to be a person with honorable character, because honor inspires trust and respect. The U.S. Army Handbook, "Military Leadership," identifies twenty-three traits essential to character. Among these are confidence, courage, integrity, decisiveness, will, compassion, and self-discipline.

George Bush embodies them all. He has engrained his basic nature and personality into his command of the armed forces. Liberal Democrats like Bill and Hillary Clinton and John Kerry are much more "challenged" when it comes to meeting these requirements.

Conservatives see President Bush as a decent, plainspoken, and honest man. The military views him as a commander who makes the difficult decisions, frames the orders clearly and with moral purpose, and then gets out of their way. Ask the soldier in the foxhole, and that's exactly what he wants.

Liberals hate Bush for these very reasons. They see him as stupid and inarticulate. But that is only because the knee-jerk reaction of any liberal is to consider himself more intelligent and more sophisticated than any conservative. But a soldier who has served under the one and under the other knows better. And so do a few Democrats. Georgia senator and former governor Zell Miller, an old-style conservative Democrat, understands the requirements for leadership. "The way I see it," explains Miller, "I don't want to entrust [the future] to any of these folks that are running out there on the Democratic side."[3] Former New York mayor Ed Koch, a lifelong Democrat, agrees. "President Bush has earned my vote because he has shown the resolve and courage necessary to wage the war on terrorism." Democrats, he attests, "inspire no such confidence."[4]

In this time of war, we especially need a commander in chief who understands, respects, and lives the code of the American soldier. No one better summed up the code than Douglas MacArthur:

Duty, Honor, Country—those three hallowed words reverently dictate what you want to be, what you can be, what you will be. They are your rallying point to build courage when courage seems to fail, to regain faith when there seems to be little cause for faith, to create hope when hope becomes forlorn.

The unbelievers will say they are but words, but a slogan, but a flamboyant phrase. Every pedant, every demagogue, every cynic, every hypocrite, every troublemaker, and, I am sorry to say, some others of an entirely different character, will try to downgrade them even to the extent of mockery and ridicule.

But these are some of the things they do . . . they teach you to be proud and unbending in honest failure, but humble and gentle in success; not to substitute words for actions; not to seek the path of comfort, but to face the stress and spur of difficulty and challenge; to learn to stand up in the storm, but to have compassion for those who fall; to master yourself before you seek to master others; to have a heart that is clean, a goal that is high; to learn to laugh, yet never forget how to weep; to reach into the future, yet never neglect the past; to be serious, yet never take yourself too seriously; to be modest so that you will remember the simplicity of true greatness, the open mind of wisdom, the meekness of true strength.[5]

The televised images of President George W. Bush, the Midland man and former Air National Guard officer who flew F-102s, touching down in his U.S. Navy Viking S-3B aboard the aircraft carrier USS *Abraham Lincoln* on May 2, 2003, underscores the extent to which conservatives and Republicans "get it."

Swaggering out of the cockpit in his flight suit, holding his helmet, President Bush was the image of the military aviator. It was obvious he'd worn a flight suit before. He snapped crisp salutes. He walked tall, proud to be among the military, the military proud of its commander in chief. This commander in chief understood the military, understood leadership and what needed to be done.

The sailors on deck were exuberant. They shook hands with the president and he slapped them on the back with warmth and sincerity.

Another defining moment probably lost to most who were watching: The commander in chief spent approximately thirty seconds meeting and greeting the carrier's senior officers; he spent forty-five minutes meeting the young enlisted sailors and their non-commissioned officers who are the heart and soul of any military operation. Intuitively, he knew. Instinctively, he commanded. Quite a change from Bill Clinton . . . or John Kerry.

As I watched the carrier landing take place, I remembered Clinton's visits to naval carriers and military installations. I recalled a much different reaction on the part of our servicemen, a much different atmosphere. Not disrespectful, certainly, but not warm and accommodating either.

I thought back to my time at the White House and tried to imagine President Clinton or Vice President Gore standing in Bush's place. However much Clinton and Gore worshipped the photo op, they couldn't have done it; they couldn't have carried it off. Most of all, they couldn't have begun the rollback of terrorism that was celebrated on the deck of that carrier.

CHAPTER ELEVEN

WHO WOULD OSAMA VOTE FOR?

"The soldier is a man; he expects to be treated as an adult, not a schoolboy. He has rights; they must be made known to him and thereafter respected. He has ambition; it must be stirred. He has a belief in fair play; it must be honored. He has a need of comradeship; it must be supplied. He has imagination; it must be stimulated. He has a sense of personal dignity; it must be sustained. He has pride; it can be satisfied and made the bedrock of character once he has been assured that he is playing a useful and respected role. To give a man this is the acme of inspired leadership. He has become loyal because loyalty was given to him."

—General George C. Marshall, 1944

The Air Force captain climbed into the cockpit of his F-117 stealth fighter. The night was black, the moon hiding behind the layers of clouds that blanketed the airbase at Khamis Mushayt, Saudi Arabia. It was January 17, 1991, and H-hour, the first wave in the aerial assault that was to be Desert Storm, was 3:00 a.m., Baghdad time.

Once on the runway, he checked his instruments and aircraft systems, assuring that all were "in the green" and operating normally. As he did, he pushed the throttles forward for maximum power, released the brakes, accelerated quickly, and climbed into the night.

He would soon be joined by his wingman, just now lifting off behind him for the quiet flight north. Radios were on, but nothing was heard except for the lone call, a position report for the good guys in the night, "Mist 22, Point Alpha."

Nothing to keep him company except the rhythm of his own breathing in his oxygen mask, the stars above him, and the totally unlit desert below, a black nothingness. Occasionally, he'd note the lights of a solitary city.

An hour and a half before, the Navy cruiser USS *San Jacinto*, positioned in the Red Sea, along with the USS *Bunker Hill* and the battleships *Wisconsin* and *Missouri*, had launched the first of what would be a barrage of Tomahawk missiles. The missiles were in flight and would find their mark just after 3:00 a.m.

Before entering Iraqi airspace, the captain and his wingman rendezvoused with an Air Force KC-135 Stratotanker, a gas station in the sky, for the fuel that would get the F-117s into Baghdad and safely out again.

With radios still quiet, the captain moved his black jet from behind and below the tanker, closing to within fifteen feet. Unlike in peacetime, the only lights on the KC-135 were the dim floods lighting the bottom of the wings and small director lights used by the boom operator, one of the enlisted members of the tanker crew, to communicate with the F-117 pilot. The tanker and his receiver were invisible in the desert night.

A long metal boom, a conduit for the fuel, swung down immediately in front of the pilot. The "boomer" flashed the forward light, indicating he was ready for the stealth fighter to approach. The pilot and boom operator coordinated their movements, and, with the refueling done, the F-117s approached the Iraqi border. Game time.

The pilot performed his "FENCE check," a final review of the vital aircraft systems before entering combat:

- F: fuel computations and quantity
- E: engines "in the green" and operating normally
- N: navigational aides programmed or off

- C: communications radios programmed to the proper frequencies and antennas properly retracted beneath the thin radar-absorbent skin of the aircraft
- E: electrics "in the green" with external lights off

His pulse quickened as he approached Baghdad. He could see the city out in front of him for several miles. It wasn't hard. The city was brightly lit. His flight plan had been designed to steer clear of Iraqi air defenses. It had worked. Total surprise had been achieved. Desert Storm, the expulsion of Saddam Hussein's Iraq from Kuwait, was under way.

The next wave of Stealth pilots would see a very different skyline, a town illuminated with thousands of tracers, flashes of antiaircraft fire, and clouds of smoke. To them, it would look like New Year's Eve or the Fourth of July.

The captain knew that his squadron mates were performing their target runs and that the Tomahawks would soon be finding their targets.

He approached his own target. Later, when back at his base and reviewing the mission videotape, he would note his greatly elevated respiration rate and muttered imprecations. As it happened now, he was conscious only of the urgent need to find his target.

His aircraft's infrared sensors were picking up every nuance of the target area, every road, washed-out riverbed, and a few trees here and there. He was looking for a concrete bunker, a square building, an Iraqi military command and control center.

He found it. Maps and satellite photos were right on. The captain moved the crosshairs of the target designator by moving the button on his right throttle, perfectly aligning the cross over his target.

As flak, surface-to-air missiles, and antiaircraft fire from Soviet-provided systems began flying through his altitude, he depressed the red button on his control stick. With a loud clunk, the bomb released from the shackles in the weapons bay. Ignoring everything else, the captain watched his infrared display. In order to have the bomb hit precisely where he wanted, he'd have to maintain the crosshairs on the target until impact. He had to do this despite the turbulence of the exploding shells around him or someone else, one of his buddies, would have to come back and do it again tomorrow night. The pilot's military honor obligated him to achieve a direct hit; he prayed for it to strike.

Finally, he saw what he was looking for at the bottom of the screen: the bomb just before it entered the bunker, just where he'd set the crosshairs. The explosion blew out the doors of the bunker in four directions.

"Bomb on target, we're done. Let's get the hell out of here," he thought.

He rammed his throttles forward and yanked back on the stick, climbing quickly and getting himself out of the "heart of the threat envelope" and into his route out of the target area.

As the throttles hit their forward stops, the reality of the war returned with a thick barrage of enemy fire. A surface-to-air missile exploded so close to his aircraft that he was flash-blinded. After a few seconds—which seemed like an eternity—his vision returned. He recovered his aircraft from a dive and swung it south for home; his wingman, having hit his own target, rejoined him.

Once in Saudi airspace and heading back to Khamis Mushayt, tucked high in the Saudi mountains between Yemen and the Red Sea, they discovered that no American pilots had been shot down on this first run. They said a prayer of thanks but knew that some would not be so lucky.

Once home, they'd have a breakfast of reconstituted eggs—"rubber eggs"—condensed milk, and burned coffee, review the mission tapes, and get some sleep.

Then, they'd get up and do it again.

It is our men and women in uniform who we send into harm's way whenever the president calls. They are entitled to a commander in chief they can trust and respect. They deserve a commander in chief with character, honor, and integrity. George W. Bush has demonstrated these attributes; the Carter-Clinton-Kerry Democrats have not. With an ideology deeply rooted in their antiwar stance during Vietnam, liberal Democrats have not had a national security policy or military strategy worthy of the name in thirty years. As an outgrowth of Vietnam, they are anti-military and unequipped to lead our armed forces at a time when leadership in the War on Terror is critical. The party of McGovern, Kennedy, Carter, Dukakis, Clinton, and Kerry has proven undependable in their stewardship of American fighting men and women.

George W. Bush knows that the military exists to fight wars. The military does not exist to conduct "CNN diplomacy," showing up for photo-op interventions that have no achievable missions for an administration that hasn't got the guts to pursue victory when things get tough. It does not exist to be used with reckless disregard for anything other than America's vital national security interests. It does not exist to become a plaything for favored liberal groups such as feminists and gays and social engineering bureaucrats.

The soldier is no warmonger. As General Douglas MacArthur noted, "On the contrary, the soldier above all other people prays for peace, for he must suffer and bear the deepest wounds and scars of war."[1] But he knows we must be prepared for war and ready to execute it with ferocity, conviction, and courage; with the best equipment; with the best-trained, all-volunteer army in the world; and with numbers and morale sufficient for the job.

Like the military, conservatives view national security as a matter of strategic and moral necessity. Unlike the military, liberals view national security as a means for international social work. For liberals, military interventions in the name of strategic concerns are wrong. In John Kerry's mind, as in Bill Clinton's, terrorism should be handled by law enforcement, not the military. For the Clinton-Kerry Democrats, the United Nations, not the national interest, should determine our foreign policy.

But peace isn't achieved through the United Nations, the International Criminal Court, by protest marches, discussions in liberal academic faculty lounges, or leftist groups that sponsor "human shields" for dictators. When it comes right down to it, peace and America's security are assured only by the combined strength of the United States military.

Former president Jimmy Carter, who continues to be the guiding light of liberal foreign policy, speaks about "respect for international law and alliances that result in wise decisions and mutual restraint." He says that "war can be waged only as a last resort, with all nonviolent options exhausted."[2] While doing so, Carter has consistently coddled America's enemies: terrorist Yassir Arafat, communist Fidel Castro, anti-American despotic ruler Jean-Bertrand Aristide of Haiti, and two generations of tyrants in North Korea.

But where was "international law" when the Communists slaughtered two and a half million peasants after America pulled out of Southeast Asia? How many lives were lost in Rwanda and Bosnia while UN bureaucrats and politicians conducted courtesy calls and "diplomatic pull asides?" How successful were "nonviolent options" while Saddam was murdering 300,000 of his own people?

Moreover, how successful was the foreign policy of Jimmy Carter, which saw the expansion of Communism in Latin America and Afghanistan and saw a pro-Western Iran become the chief radical Islamic terror sponsor against the United States, leaving America looking weak and humiliated? Or how successful were the eight years of Bill Clinton as commander in chief, which saw our military and intelligence capabilities slashed and the threats to our national security from al-Qaeda, Iraq, and North Korea grow without hindrance?

When Democrat Dennis Kucinich announced his run for the presidency, he said his goal was "to enable the goddess of peace to encircle within her arms all the children of this country and all the children of the world. As president, I will work with leaders of the world to make war a thing of the past."[3] That is the liberals' foreign policy. It is a policy of weakness, failure, ineptitude, and contempt for our national defense that we cannot afford. We cannot regress to the policies of Democratic presidents Carter and Clinton, or to the Democratic Party of Kerry, Kucinich, and Dean. They've shown their mettle and they've been proven lacking.

Pacifists didn't turn back German aggression in World War I. Foot soldiers from France, England, and America did.

Peaceniks didn't liberate the Jews from Nazi concentration camps. American, British, and Russian grunts, flyboys, and jarheads did.

The United Nations and their eighteen resolutions aimed at forcing Saddam Hussein to comply with disarmament didn't liberate twenty-five million Iraqis. American and British GIs did.

Future attacks on the citizens of the United States won't be prevented by ethereal calls for world peace or by Democratic Party politicians who blame America first and want to subordinate American foreign policy to the United Nations.

John Kerry recently commented that he didn't "know what it is that all these Republicans who didn't serve in Vietnam or fighting any war have against us who did."[4]

Well, sir, I'll see your four months in Vietnam and raise you the twenty years I spent serving as an Air Force pilot flying in conflicts as far-ranging as Grenada, Somalia, Bosnia, and Haiti.

What I have against you, to be concise, is your post–Vietnam War treason, your complete and demonstrated lack of support for the U.S. military in your nineteen years in the Senate, and my expectation that you will return our national defense to the criminally ineffectual days of the Carter and Clinton administrations.

It is equally important to consider whom our adversaries would want in office.

Al-Jazeera, the Arab news network and the voice of radical Islamic terrorists, is praising Kerry as "a popular mainstream Democrat with liberal tendencies, [who] has been widely seen as a good compromise candidate in a divided party," and noted that Kerry condemned the

Bush administration for stigmatizing "innocent Muslims and Arabs who pose no danger."[5]

The network also carried a "friendship photo" of Kerry meeting with Saudi ambassador Prince Bandar bin Sultan Al Saud, promoting the "history of a long and close friendship between Sen. Kerry and the Saudi kingdom."[6]

The Iranians, according to dissident Ayatollah Mehdi Haeri, "fear Bush." "They think that if Bush is re-elected, they'll be gone. That's why they want to see Kerry elected."[7]

The Egyptians, according to a senior advisor to President Hosni Mubarak, "are certain that a Democratic administration will be more realistic."[8]

North Korea, owing its nuclear program to the beneficence of Presidents Carter and Clinton,[9] has been broadcasting Kerry's speeches and praising his candidacy in glowing terms, hoping for a return to the soft-power politics of the Democrats.

And the French are going wild for Kerry. "He is very much admired in France," says municipal office worker Patrick Forestier. "It seems like he will be more sympathetic to Europe.... And of course anyone who is opposed to Bush will be popular with us."[10]

Recently elected Spanish president and terrorist appeaser José Luis Rodríguez Zapatero, whose first act was to withdraw his troops from the coalition of allies in Iraq, backs Kerry's election as well. "We are aligning ourselves with Kerry. Our alliance will be for peace, against war, no more deaths for oil, and for a dialogue between the government of Spain and the new Kerry administration."[11]

Kerry pledges to abandon the War on Terror, open a dialogue with terrorist regimes, and apologize for the mistakes of the Bush administration. In a speech to the Council on Foreign Relations in December 2003, Kerry called the War on Terror "the most arrogant, inept, reckless, and ideological foreign policy in modern history."[12]

No, that's not the War on Terror, Mr. Kerry. The War on Terror has toppled Saddam Hussein and the Taliban, it has ended Libya's

weapons of mass destruction program and encouraged the cooperation of Pakistan, and it is fighting to secure America from future
attacks. As I've tried to show, if you're looking for "the most arrogant, inept, reckless, and ideological foreign policy" in American history, you have to look at the record of the Democratic Party over the
last forty years. They have treated America's national defense and
America's military defenders with reckless disregard.

As a former Air Force pilot, I don't presume to know the life of the
soldier, the sailor, or the Marine. But I do hope to speak for those who
serve this great nation and go into harm's way. I pray for every air-
man, every soldier, every sailor, every Marine, every Coast Guards-
man. I pray that I do their cause justice because it is America's cause.

Famed World War II correspondent Ernie Pyle wrote a book titled
Brave Men that told, among other stories, the story of Captain
Henry T. Waskow. Before Captain Waskow was killed in action in
Italy in 1943, he wrote a letter to his family:

> If you get to read this, I will have died in defense of my
> country and all that it stands for—the most honorable and
> distinguished death a man can die. It was not because I was
> willing to die for my country...I wanted to live for it....
> To live for one's country is to my mind to live a life of ser-
> vice. To, in a small way, help a fellow man occasionally
> along the way and generally to be useful and serve. It also
> means to me to rise up in all our wrath and with over-
> whelming power to crush any oppressor of human rights.
> That is our job, all of us, as I write this, and I pray to God
> we are wholly successful. I made my choice, dear ones, I
> volunteered in the armed forces because I felt it my duty to
> do so. I thought that I might be able and might do just a
> little bit to help this great country of ours in its hours of
> need—the country that means more to me than life itself.
> If I have done that, then I can rest in peace, for I will have

done my share to make this world a better place in which to live.[13]

That is the soldier's calling.

The words inscribed on the south wall of the Lincoln Memorial say this: "We here highly resolve that these dead shall not have died in vain, that this nation under God shall have a new birth of freedom, and that government of the people, by the people, for the people shall not perish from the earth."

We're in a fight today that requires the same resolve, because the stakes are just as high. The American people have a responsibility to vote to ensure that we have a president worthy of those words and worthy of those who defend them.

Our soldiers have met the call. The question is: Will we?

President George W. Bush's speech to the graduating cadets at West Point on June 1, 2002, has been judged by Yale University professor John Lewis Gaddis as an extremely important document outlining the Bush administration's national security strategy.

REMARKS BY THE PRESIDENT
AT THE 2002 GRADUATION EXERCISES
OF THE UNITED STATES MILITARY ACADEMY
AT WEST POINT, NEW YORK

In every corner of America, the words "West Point" command immediate respect. This place where the Hudson River bends is more than a fine institution of learning. The United States Military Academy is the guardian of values that have shaped the soldiers who have shaped the history of the world.

A few of you have followed in the path of the perfect West Point graduate, Robert E. Lee, who never received a single demerit in four years. Some of you followed in the path of the imperfect graduate, Ulysses S. Grant, who had his fair share of demerits, and said the happiest day of his life was "the day I left West Point." During my college years I guess you could say I was a Grant man.

You walk in the tradition of Eisenhower and MacArthur, Patton and Bradley—the commanders who saved a civilization. And you walk in the tradition of second lieutenants who did the same, by fighting and dying on distant battlefields.

Graduates of this academy have brought creativity and courage to every field of endeavor. West Point produced the chief engineer of the Panama Canal, the mind behind the Manhattan Project, the first American to walk in space. This fine institution gave us the man they say invented baseball, and other young men over the years who perfected the game of football.

You know this, but many in America don't—George C. Marshall, a VMI graduate, is said to have given this order: "I want an officer for a secret and dangerous mission. I want a West Point football player."

As you leave here today, I know there's one thing you'll never miss about this place: Being a plebe. But even a plebe at West Point is made to feel he or she has some standing in the world. I'm told that plebes, when asked whom they outrank, are required to answer this: "Sir, the Superintendent's dog—the Commandant's cat, and all the admirals in the whole damn Navy." I probably won't be sharing that with the Secretary of the Navy.

West Point is guided by tradition, and in honor of the "Golden Children of the Corps," I will observe one of the traditions you cherish most. As the Commander-in-Chief, I hereby grant amnesty to all cadets who are on restriction for minor conduct offenses. Those of you in the end zone might have cheered a little early. Because, you see, I'm going to let General Lennox define exactly what "minor" means.

Every West Point class is commissioned to the Armed Forces. Some West Point classes are also commissioned by history, to take part in a great new calling for their country. Speaking here to the class of 1942—six months after Pearl Harbor—General Marshall said, "We're determined that before the sun sets on this terrible struggle, our flag will be recognized throughout the world as a symbol of freedom on the one hand, and of overwhelming power on the other."

Officers graduating that year helped fulfill that mission, defeating Japan and Germany, and then reconstructing those nations as allies. West Point graduates of the 1940s saw the rise of a deadly new challenge—the challenge of imperial communism—and opposed it from Korea to Berlin, to Vietnam, and in the Cold War, from beginning to end. And as the sun set on their struggle, many of those West Point officers lived to see a world transformed.

History has also issued its call to your generation. In your last year, America was attacked by a ruthless and resourceful enemy. You graduate from this Academy in a time of war, taking your place in an American military that is powerful and is honorable. Our war on terror has only begun, but in Afghanistan it was begun well.

I am proud of the men and women who have fought on my orders. America is profoundly grateful for all who serve the cause of freedom, and for all who have given their lives in its defense. This nation respects and trusts our military, and we are confident in your victories to come.

This war will take many turns we cannot predict. Yet I am certain of this: Wherever we carry it, the American flag will stand not only for our power, but for freedom. Our nation's cause has always been larger than our nation's defense. We fight, as we always fight, for a just peace—a peace that favors human liberty. We will defend the peace against threats from terrorists and tyrants. We will preserve the peace by building good relations among the great powers. And we will extend the peace by encouraging free and open societies on every continent.

Building this just peace is America's opportunity, and America's duty. From this day forward, it is your challenge, as well, and we will meet this challenge together. You will wear the uniform of a great and unique country. America has no empire to extend or utopia to establish. We wish for others only what we wish for ourselves—safety from violence, the rewards of liberty, and the hope for a better life.

In defending the peace, we face a threat with no precedent. Enemies in the past needed great armies and great industrial capabilities to endanger the American people and our nation. The attacks of September the 11th required a few hundred thousand dollars in the hands of a few dozen evil and deluded men. All of the chaos and suffering they caused came at much less than the cost of a single tank. The dangers have not passed. This government and the American people are on watch, we are ready, because we know the terrorists have more money and more men and more plans.

The gravest danger to freedom lies at the perilous crossroads of radicalism and technology. When the spread of chemical and biological and nuclear weapons, along with ballistic missile technology— when that occurs, even weak states and small groups could attain a catastrophic power to strike great nations. Our enemies have declared this very intention, and have been caught seeking these terrible weapons. They want the capability to blackmail us, or to harm us, or to harm our friends—and we will oppose them with all our power.

For much of the last century, America's defense relied on the Cold War doctrines of deterrence and containment. In some cases, those strategies still apply. But new threats also require new thinking. Deterrence—the promise of massive retaliation against nations—means nothing against shadowy terrorist networks with no nation or citizens to defend. Containment is not possible when unbalanced dictators with weapons of mass destruction can deliver those weapons on missiles or secretly provide them to terrorist allies.

We cannot defend America and our friends by hoping for the best. We cannot put our faith in the word of tyrants, who solemnly sign non-proliferation treaties, and then systemically break them. If we wait for threats to fully materialize, we will have waited too long.

Homeland defense and missile defense are part of stronger security, and they're essential priorities for America. Yet the war on terror will not be won on the defensive. We must take the battle to the enemy, disrupt his plans, and confront the worst threats before they emerge. In the world we have entered, the only path to safety is the path of action. And this nation will act.

Our security will require the best intelligence, to reveal threats hidden in caves and growing in laboratories. Our security will require modernizing domestic agencies such as the FBI, so they're prepared to act, and act quickly, against danger. Our security will require transforming the military you will lead—a military that must be ready to strike at a moment's notice in any dark corner of the world. And our security will require all Americans to be forward-looking and resolute, to be ready for preemptive action when necessary to defend our liberty and to defend our lives.

The work ahead is difficult. The choices we will face are complex. We must uncover terror cells in sixty or more countries, using every tool of finance, intelligence and law enforcement. Along with our friends and allies, we must oppose proliferation and confront regimes that sponsor terror, as each case requires. Some nations need military training to fight terror, and we'll provide it. Other nations oppose terror, but tolerate the hatred that leads to terror—and that must change. We will send diplomats where they are needed, and we will send you, our soldiers, where you're needed.

All nations that decide for aggression and terror will pay a price. We will not leave the safety of America and the peace of the planet at the mercy of a few mad terrorists and tyrants. We will lift this dark threat from our country and from the world.

Because the war on terror will require resolve and patience, it will also require firm moral purpose. In this way our struggle is similar to the Cold War. Now, as then, our enemies are totalitarians, holding a creed of power with no place for human dignity. Now, as then, they seek to impose a joyless conformity, to control every life and all of life.

America confronted imperial communism in many different ways—diplomatic, economic, and military. Yet moral clarity was essential to our victory in the Cold War. When leaders like John F. Kennedy and Ronald Reagan refused to gloss over the brutality of tyrants, they gave hope to prisoners and dissidents and exiles, and rallied free nations to a great cause.

Some worry that it is somehow undiplomatic or impolite to speak the language of right and wrong. I disagree. Different circumstances require different methods, but not different moralities. Moral truth is the same in every culture, in every time, and in every place. Targeting innocent civilians for murder is always and everywhere wrong. Brutality against women is always and everywhere wrong. There can be no neutrality between justice and cruelty, between the innocent and the guilty. We are in a conflict between good and evil, and America will call evil by its name. By confronting evil and lawless regimes, we do not create a problem, we reveal a problem. And we will lead the world in opposing it.

As we defend the peace, we also have an historic opportunity to preserve the peace. We have our best chance since the rise of the nation state in the seventeenth century to build a world where the great powers compete in peace instead of prepare for war. The history of the last century, in particular, was dominated by a series of destructive national rivalries that left battlefields and graveyards across the Earth. Germany fought France, the Axis fought the Allies, and then the East fought the West, in proxy wars and tense standoffs, against a backdrop of nuclear Armageddon.

Competition between great nations is inevitable, but armed conflict in our world is not. More and more, civilized nations find ourselves on the same side—united by common dangers of terrorist violence and chaos. America has, and intends to keep, military strengths beyond challenge, thereby making the destabilizing arms races of other eras pointless, and limiting rivalries to trade and other pursuits of peace.

Today the great powers are also increasingly united by common values, instead of divided by conflicting ideologies. The United States, Japan and our Pacific friends, and now all of Europe, share a deep commitment to human freedom, embodied in strong alliances such as NATO. And the tide of liberty is rising in many other nations.

Generations of West Point officers planned and practiced for battles with Soviet Russia. I've just returned from a new Russia, now a country reaching toward democracy, and our partner in the war against terror. Even in China, leaders are discovering that economic freedom is the only lasting source of national wealth. In time, they will find that social and political freedom is the only true source of national greatness.

When the great powers share common values, we are better able to confront serious regional conflicts together, better able to cooperate in preventing the spread of violence or economic chaos. In the past, great power rivals took sides in difficult regional problems, making divisions deeper and more complicated. Today, from the Middle East to South Asia, we are gathering broad international coalitions to increase the pressure for peace. We must build strong and great power relations when times are good, to help manage crisis when times are bad. America needs partners to preserve the peace, and we will work with every nation that shares this noble goal.

And finally, America stands for more than the absence of war. We have a great opportunity to extend a just peace, by replacing poverty, repression, and resentment around the world with hope of a better day. Through most of history, poverty was persistent, inescapable, and almost universal. In the last few decades, we've seen nations from Chile to South Korea build modern economies and freer societies, lifting millions of people out of despair and want. And there's no mystery to this achievement.

The twentieth century ended with a single surviving model of human progress, based on non-negotiable demands of human dignity, the rule of law, limits on the power of the state, respect for women and private property and free speech and equal justice and religious tolerance. America cannot impose this vision—yet we can support and reward governments that make the right choices for their own people. In our development aid, in our diplomatic efforts, in our international broadcasting, and in our educational assistance, the United

States will promote moderation and tolerance and human rights. And we will defend the peace that makes all progress possible.

When it comes to the common rights and needs of men and women, there is no clash of civilizations. The requirements of freedom apply fully to Africa and Latin America and the entire Islamic world. The peoples of the Islamic nations want and deserve the same freedoms and opportunities as people in every nation. And their governments should listen to their hopes.

A truly strong nation will permit legal avenues of dissent for all groups that pursue their aspirations without violence. An advancing nation will pursue economic reform, to unleash the great entrepreneurial energy of its people. A thriving nation will respect the rights of women, because no society can prosper while denying opportunity to half its citizens. Mothers and fathers and children across the Islamic world, and all the world, share the same fears and aspirations. In poverty, they struggle. In tyranny, they suffer. And as we saw in Afghanistan, in liberation they celebrate.

America has a greater objective than controlling threats and containing resentment. We will work for a just and peaceful world beyond the war on terror.

The bicentennial class of West Point now enters this drama. With all in the United States Army, you will stand between your fellow citizens and grave danger. You will help establish a peace that allows millions around the world to live in liberty and to grow in prosperity. You will face times of calm, and times of crisis. And every test will find you prepared—because you're the men and women of West Point. You leave here marked by the character of this Academy, carrying with you the highest ideals of our nation.

Toward the end of his life, Dwight Eisenhower recalled the first day he stood on the plain at West Point. "The feeling came over me," he said, "that the expression 'the United States of America' would now and henceforth mean something different than it had ever before. From here on, it would be the nation I would be serving, not myself."

Today, your last day at West Point, you begin a life of service in a career unlike any other. You've answered a calling to hardship and purpose, to risk and honor. At the end of every day you will know that you have faithfully done your duty. May you always bring to that duty the high standards of this great American institution. May you always be worthy of the long gray line that stretches two centuries behind you.

On behalf of the nation, I congratulate each one of you for the commission you've earned and for the credit you bring to the United States of America. May God bless you all.

The National Security Strategy

of the

United States of America

September 2002

This National Security Strategy laid out by President Bush is a reminder of the serious challenges ahead of us and the president's serious response to them. It is in stark contrast to what we hear from the Democrats.

THE WHITE HOUSE
WASHINGTON

The great struggles of the twentieth century between liberty and totalitarianism ended with a decisive victory for the forces of freedom—and a single sustainable model for national success: freedom, democracy, and free enterprise. In the twenty-first century, only nations that share a commitment to protecting basic human rights and guaranteeing political and economic freedom will be able to unleash the potential of their people and assure their future prosperity. People everywhere want to be able to speak freely; choose who will govern them; worship as they please; educate their children—male and female; own property; and enjoy the benefits of their labor. These values of freedom are right and true for every person, in every society—and the duty of protecting these values against their enemies is the common calling of freedom-loving people across the globe and across the ages.

Today, the United States enjoys a position of unparalleled military strength and great economic and political influence. In keeping with our heritage and principles, we do not use our strength to press for unilateral advantage. We seek instead to create a balance of power that favors human freedom: conditions in which all nations and all societies can choose for themselves the rewards and challenges of political and economic liberty. In a world that is safe, people will be able to make their own lives better. We will defend the peace by fighting terrorists and tyrants. We will preserve the peace by building good relations among the great powers. We will extend the peace by encouraging free and open societies on every continent.

Defending our Nation against its enemies is the first and fundamental commitment of the Federal Government. Today, that task has changed dramatically. Enemies in the past needed great armies and great industrial capabilities to endanger America. Now, shadowy networks of individuals can bring great chaos and suffering to our shores for less than it costs to purchase a single tank. Terrorists are organized to penetrate open societies and to turn the power of modern technologies against us.

To defeat this threat we must make use of every tool in our arsenal—military power, better homeland defenses, law enforcement, intelligence, and vigorous efforts to cut off terrorist financing. The war against terrorists of global reach is a global enterprise of uncertain duration. America will help nations that need our assistance in combating terror. And America will hold to account nations that are compromised by terror, including those who harbor terrorists—because the allies of terror are the enemies of civilization. The United States and countries cooperating with us must not allow the terrorists to develop new home bases. Together, we will seek to deny them sanctuary at every turn.

The gravest danger our Nation faces lies at the crossroads of radicalism and technology. Our enemies have openly declared that they are seeking weapons of mass destruction, and evidence indicates that they are doing so with determination. The United States will not allow these efforts to succeed. We will build defenses against ballistic missiles and other means of delivery. We will cooperate with other nations to deny, contain, and curtail our enemies' efforts to acquire dangerous technologies. And, as a matter of common sense and self-defense, America will act against such emerging threats before they are fully formed. We cannot defend America and our friends by hoping for the best. So we must be prepared to defeat our enemies' plans, using the best intelligence and proceeding with deliberation. History will judge harshly those who saw this coming danger but failed to act. In the new world we have entered, the only path to peace and security is the path of action.

As we defend the peace, we will also take advantage of an historic opportunity to preserve the peace. Today, the international community has the best chance since the rise of the nation-state in the seventeenth century to build a world where great powers compete in peace instead of continually prepare for war. Today, the world's great powers find ourselves on the same side—united by common dangers of terrorist violence and chaos. The United States will build on these common interests to promote global security. We are also increasingly united by common values. Russia is in the midst of a hopeful transition, reaching for its democratic future and a partner in the war on terror. Chinese leaders are discovering that economic freedom is the only source of national wealth. In time, they will find that social and political freedom is the only source of national greatness. America will encourage the advancement of democracy and economic openness in both nations, because these are the best foundations for domestic stability and international order. We will strongly resist aggression from other great powers—even as we welcome their peaceful pursuit of prosperity, trade, and cultural advancement.

Finally, the United States will use this moment of opportunity to extend the benefits of freedom across the globe. We will actively work to bring the hope of democracy, development, free markets, and free trade to every corner of the world. The events of September 11, 2001, taught us that weak states, like Afghanistan, can pose as great a danger to our national interests as strong states. Poverty does not make poor people into terrorists and murderers. Yet poverty, weak institutions, and corruption can make weak states vulnerable to terrorist networks and drug cartels within their borders.

The United States will stand beside any nation determined to build a better future by seeking the rewards of liberty for its people. Free trade and free markets have proven their ability to lift whole societies out of poverty—so the United States will work with individual nations, entire regions, and the entire global trading community to build a world that trades in freedom and therefore grows in prosperity. The United States will deliver greater development assistance through the New Millennium Challenge Account to nations that govern justly, invest in their people, and encourage economic freedom. We will also continue to lead the world in efforts to reduce the terrible toll of HIV/AIDS and other infectious diseases.

In building a balance of power that favors freedom, the United States is guided by the conviction that all nations have important responsibilities. Nations that enjoy freedom must actively fight terror. Nations that depend on international stability must help prevent the spread of weapons of mass destruction. Nations that seek international aid must govern themselves wisely, so that aid is well spent. For freedom to thrive, accountability must be expected and required.

We are also guided by the conviction that no nation can build a safer, better world alone. Alliances and multilateral institutions can multiply the strength of freedom-loving nations. The United States is committed to lasting institutions like the United Nations, the World Trade Organization, the Organization of American States, and NATO as well as other long-standing alliances. Coalitions of the willing can augment these permanent institutions. In all cases, international obligations are to be taken seriously. They are not to be undertaken symbolically to rally support for an ideal without furthering its attainment.

Freedom is the non-negotiable demand of human dignity; the birthright of every person—in every civilization. Throughout history, freedom has been threatened by war and terror; it has been challenged by the clashing wills of powerful states and the evil designs of tyrants; and it has been tested by widespread poverty and disease. Today, humanity holds in its hands the opportunity to further freedom's triumph over all these foes. The United States welcomes our responsibility to lead in this great mission.

THE WHITE HOUSE,
September 17, 2002

TABLE OF CONTENTS

I. Overview of America's International Strategy

"Our Nation's cause has always been larger than our Nation's defense.
We fight, as we always fight, for a just peace—a peace that favors liberty.
We will defend the peace against the threats from terrorists and tyrants.
We will preserve the peace by building good relations among the great powers.
And we will extend the peace by encouraging free and open societies on every continent."

PRESIDENT BUSH
WEST POINT, NEW YORK
JUNE 1, 2002

The United States possesses unprecedented—and unequaled—strength and influence in the world. Sustained by faith in the principles of liberty, and the value of a free society, this position comes with unparalleled responsibilities, obligations, and opportunity. The great strength of this nation must be used to promote a balance of power that favors freedom.

For most of the twentieth century, the world was divided by a great struggle over ideas: destructive totalitarian visions versus freedom and equality.

That great struggle is over. The militant visions of class, nation, and race which promised utopia and delivered misery have been defeated and discredited. America is now threatened less by conquering states than we are by failing ones. We are menaced less by fleets and armies than by catastrophic technologies in the hands of the embittered few. We must defeat these threats to our Nation, allies, and friends.

This is also a time of opportunity for America. We will work to translate this moment of influence into decades of peace, prosperity, and liberty.

The U.S. national security strategy will be based on a distinctly American internationalism that reflects the union of our values and our national interests. The aim of this strategy is to help make the world not just safer but better. Our goals on the path to progress are clear: political and economic freedom, peaceful relations with other states, and respect for human dignity.

And this path is not America's alone. It is open to all.

To achieve these goals, the United States will:

- champion aspirations for human dignity;

- strengthen alliances to defeat global terrorism and work to prevent attacks against us and our friends;

- work with others to defuse regional conflicts;

- prevent our enemies from threatening us, our allies, and our friends, with weapons of mass destruction;

- ignite a new era of global economic growth through free markets and free trade;

- expand the circle of development by opening societies and building the infrastructure of democracy;

- develop agendas for cooperative action with other main centers of global power; and

- transform America's national security institutions to meet the challenges and opportunities of the twenty-first century.

ii. Champion Aspirations for Human Dignity

"Some worry that it is somehow undiplomatic or impolite to speak the language of right and wrong. I disagree. Different circumstances require different methods, but not different moralities."

PRESIDENT BUSH
WEST POINT, NEW YORK
JUNE 1, 2002

In pursuit of our goals, our first imperative is to clarify what we stand for: the United States must defend liberty and justice because these principles are right and true for all people everywhere. No nation owns these aspirations, and no nation is exempt from them. Fathers and mothers in all societies want their children to be educated and to live free from poverty and violence. No people on earth yearn to be oppressed, aspire to servitude, or eagerly await the midnight knock of the secret police.

America must stand firmly for the nonnegotiable demands of human dignity: the rule of law; limits on the absolute power of the state; free speech; freedom of worship; equal justice; respect for women; religious and ethnic tolerance; and respect for private property.

These demands can be met in many ways. America's constitution has served us well. Many other nations, with different histories and cultures, facing different circumstances, have successfully incorporated these core principles into their own systems of governance. History has not been kind to those nations which ignored or flouted the rights and aspirations of their people.

America's experience as a great multi-ethnic democracy affirms our conviction that people of many heritages and faiths can live and prosper in peace. Our own history is a long struggle to live up to our ideals. But even in our worst moments, the principles enshrined in the Declaration of Independence were there to guide us. As a result, America is not just a stronger, but is a freer and more just society.

Today, these ideals are a lifeline to lonely defenders of liberty. And when openings arrive, we can encourage change—as we did in central and eastern Europe between 1989 and 1991, or in Belgrade in 2000. When we see democratic processes take hold among our friends in Taiwan or in the Republic of Korea, and see elected leaders replace generals in Latin America and Africa, we see examples of how authoritarian systems can evolve, marrying local history and traditions with the principles we all cherish.

Embodying lessons from our past and using the opportunity we have today, the national security strategy of the United States must start from these core beliefs and look outward for possibilities to expand liberty.

Our principles will guide our government's decisions about international cooperation, the character of our foreign assistance, and the allocation of resources. They will guide our actions and our words in international bodies.

We will:

- speak out honestly about violations of the nonnegotiable demands of human dignity using our voice and vote in international institutions to advance freedom;

- use our foreign aid to promote freedom and support those who struggle non-violently for it, ensuring that nations moving toward democracy are rewarded for the steps they take;

- make freedom and the development of democratic institutions key themes in our bilateral relations, seeking solidarity and cooperation from other democracies while we press governments that deny human rights to move toward a better future; and

- take special efforts to promote freedom of religion and conscience and defend it from encroachment by repressive governments.

We will champion the cause of human dignity and oppose those who resist it.

III. Strengthen Alliances to Defeat Global Terrorism and Work to Prevent Attacks Against Us and Our Friends

"Just three days removed from these events, Americans do not yet have the distance of history. But our responsibility to history is already clear: to answer these attacks and rid the world of evil. War has been waged against us by stealth and deceit and murder. This nation is peaceful, but fierce when stirred to anger. The conflict was begun on the timing and terms of others. It will end in a way, and at an hour, of our choosing."

President Bush
Washington, D.C. (The National Cathedral)
September 14, 2001

The United States of America is fighting a war against terrorists of global reach. The enemy is not a single political regime or person or religion or ideology. The enemy is terrorism—premeditated, politically motivated violence perpetrated against innocents.

In many regions, legitimate grievances prevent the emergence of a lasting peace. Such grievances deserve to be, and must be, addressed within a political process. But no cause justifies terror. The United States will make no concessions to terrorist demands and strike no deals with them. We make no distinction between terrorists and those who knowingly harbor or provide aid to them.

The struggle against global terrorism is different from any other war in our history. It will be fought on many fronts against a particularly elusive enemy over an extended period of time. Progress will come through the persistent accumulation of successes—some seen, some unseen.

Today our enemies have seen the results of what civilized nations can, and will, do against regimes that harbor, support, and use terrorism to achieve their political goals. Afghanistan has been liberated; coalition forces continue to hunt down the Taliban and al-Qaida. But it is not only this battlefield on which we will engage terrorists. Thousands of trained terrorists remain at large with cells in North America, South America, Europe, Africa, the Middle East, and across Asia.

Our priority will be first to disrupt and destroy terrorist organizations of global reach and attack their leadership; command, control, and communications; material support; and finances. This will have a disabling effect upon the terrorists' ability to plan and operate.

We will continue to encourage our regional partners to take up a coordinated effort that isolates the terrorists. Once the regional campaign localizes the threat to a particular state, we will help ensure the state has the military, law enforcement, political, and financial tools necessary to finish the task.

The United States will continue to work with our allies to disrupt the financing of terrorism. We will identify and block the sources of funding for terrorism, freeze the assets of terrorists and those who support them, deny terrorists access to the international financial system, protect legitimate charities from being abused by terrorists, and prevent the movement of terrorists' assets through alternative financial networks.

However, this campaign need not be sequential to be effective, the cumulative effect across all regions will help achieve the results we seek.

We will disrupt and destroy terrorist organizations by:

- direct and continuous action using all the elements of national and international power. Our immediate focus will be those terrorist organizations of global reach and any terrorist or state sponsor of terrorism which attempts to gain or use weapons of mass destruction (WMD) or their precursors;

- defending the United States, the American people, and our interests at home and abroad by identifying and destroying the threat before it reaches our borders. While the United States will constantly strive to enlist the support of the international community, we will not hesitate to act alone, if necessary, to exercise our right of self-defense by acting preemptively against such terrorists, to prevent them from doing harm against our people and our country; and

- denying further sponsorship, support, and sanctuary to terrorists by convincing or compelling states to accept their sovereign responsibilities.

We will also wage a war of ideas to win the battle against international terrorism. This includes:

- using the full influence of the United States, and working closely with allies and friends, to make clear that all acts of terrorism are illegitimate so that terrorism will be viewed in the same light as slavery, piracy, or genocide: behavior that no respectable government can condone or support and all must oppose;

- supporting moderate and modern government, especially in the Muslim world, to ensure that the conditions and ideologies that promote terrorism do not find fertile ground in any nation;

- diminishing the underlying conditions that spawn terrorism by enlisting the international community to focus its efforts and resources on areas most at risk; and

- using effective public diplomacy to promote the free flow of information and ideas to kindle the hopes and aspirations of freedom of those in societies ruled by the sponsors of global terrorism.

While we recognize that our best defense is a good offense, we are also strengthening America's homeland security to protect against and deter attack.

This Administration has proposed the largest government reorganization since the Truman Administration created the National Security Council and the Department of Defense. Centered on a new Department of Homeland Security and including a new unified military command and a fundamental reordering of the FBI, our comprehensive plan to secure the homeland encompasses every level of government and the cooperation of the public and the private sector.

This strategy will turn adversity into opportunity. For example, emergency management systems will be better able to cope not just with terrorism but with all hazards. Our medical system will be strengthened to manage not just bioterror, but all infectious diseases and mass-casualty dangers. Our border controls will not just stop terrorists, but improve the efficient movement of legitimate traffic.

While our focus is protecting America, we know that to defeat terrorism in today's globalized world we need support from our allies and friends. Wherever possible, the United States will rely on regional organizations and state powers to meet their obligations to fight terrorism. Where governments find the fight against terrorism beyond their capacities, we will match their willpower and their resources with whatever help we and our allies can provide.

As we pursue the terrorists in Afghanistan, we will continue to work with international organizations such as the United Nations, as well as non-governmental organizations, and other countries to provide the humanitarian, political, economic, and security assistance necessary to rebuild Afghanistan so that it will never again abuse its people, threaten its neighbors, and provide a haven for terrorists.

In the war against global terrorism, we will never forget that we are ultimately fighting for our democratic values and way of life. Freedom and fear are at war, and there will be no quick or easy end to this conflict. In leading the campaign against terrorism, we are forging new, productive international relationships and redefining existing ones in ways that meet the challenges of the twenty-first century.

iv. Work with others to Defuse Regional Conflicts

"We build a world of justice, or we will live in a world of coercion.
The magnitude of our shared responsibilities makes our disagreements look so small."

PRESIDENT BUSH
BERLIN, GERMANY
MAY 23, 2002

Concerned nations must remain actively engaged in critical regional disputes to avoid explosive escalation and minimize human suffering. In an increasingly interconnected world, regional crisis can strain our alliances, rekindle rivalries among the major powers, and create horrifying affronts to human dignity. When violence erupts and states falter, the United States will work with friends and partners to alleviate suffering and restore stability.

No doctrine can anticipate every circumstance in which U.S. action—direct or indirect—is warranted. We have finite political, economic, and military resources to meet our global priorities. The United States will approach each case with these strategic principles in mind:

- The United States should invest time and resources into building international relationships and institutions that can help manage local crises when they emerge.

- The United States should be realistic about its ability to help those who are unwilling or unready to help themselves. Where and when people are ready to do their part, we will be willing to move decisively.

The Israeli-Palestinian conflict is critical because of the toll of human suffering, because of America's close relationship with the state of Israel and key Arab states, and because of that region's importance to other global priorities of the United States. There can be no peace for either side without freedom for both sides. America stands committed to an independent and democratic Palestine, living beside Israel in peace and security. Like all other people, Palestinians deserve a government that serves their interests and listens to their voices. The United States will continue to encourage all parties to step up to their responsibilities as we seek a just and comprehensive settlement to the conflict.

The United States, the international donor community, and the World Bank stand ready to work with a reformed Palestinian government on economic development, increased humanitarian assistance, and a program to establish, finance, and monitor a truly independent judiciary. If Palestinians embrace democracy, and the rule of law, confront corruption, and firmly reject terror, they can count on American support for the creation of a Palestinian state.

Israel also has a large stake in the success of a democratic Palestine. Permanent occupation threatens Israel's identity and democracy. So the United States continues to challenge Israeli leaders to take concrete steps to support the emergence of a viable, credible Palestinian state. As there is progress towards security, Israel forces need to withdraw fully to positions they held prior to September 28, 2000. And consistent with the recommendations of the Mitchell Committee, Israeli settlement activity in the occupied territories must stop. As violence subsides, freedom of movement should be restored, permitting innocent Palestinians to resume work and normal life. The United States can play a crucial role but, ultimately, lasting peace can only come when Israelis and Palestinians resolve the issues and end the conflict between them.

In South Asia, the United States has also emphasized the need for India and Pakistan to resolve their disputes. This Administration invested time and resources building strong bilateral relations with India and Pakistan. These strong relations then gave us leverage to play a constructive role when tensions in the region became acute. With Pakistan, our bilateral relations have been bolstered by Pakistan's choice to join the war against terror and move toward building a more open and tolerant society. The Administration sees India's potential to become one of the great democratic powers of the twenty-first century and has worked hard to transform our relationship accordingly. Our involvement in this regional dispute, building on earlier investments in bilateral relations, looks first to concrete steps by India and Pakistan that can help defuse military confrontation.

Indonesia took courageous steps to create a working democracy and respect for the rule of law. By tolerating ethnic minorities, respecting the rule of law, and accepting open markets, Indonesia may be able to employ the engine of opportunity that has helped lift some of its neighbors out of poverty and desperation. It is the initiative by Indonesia that allows U.S. assistance to make a difference.

In the Western Hemisphere we have formed flexible coalitions with countries that share our priorities, particularly Mexico, Brazil, Canada, Chile, and Colombia. Together we will promote a truly democratic hemisphere where our integration advances security, prosperity, opportunity, and hope. We will work with regional institutions, such as the Summit of the Americas process, the Organization of American States (OAS), and the Defense Ministerial of the Americas for the benefit of the entire hemisphere.

Parts of Latin America confront regional conflict, especially arising from the violence of drug cartels and their accomplices. This conflict and unrestrained narcotics trafficking could imperil the health and security of the United States. Therefore we have developed an active strategy to help the Andean nations adjust their economies, enforce their laws, defeat terrorist organizations, and cut off the supply of drugs, while—as important—we work to reduce the demand for drugs in our own country.

In Colombia, we recognize the link between terrorist and extremist groups that challenge the security of the state and drug trafficking activities that help finance the operations of such groups. We are working to help Colombia defend its democratic institutions and defeat illegal armed groups of both the left and right by extending effective sovereignty over the entire national territory and provide basic security to the Colombian people.

In Africa, promise and opportunity sit side by side with disease, war, and desperate poverty. This threatens both a core value of the United States—preserving human dignity—and our strategic priority—combating global terror. American interests and American principles, therefore, lead in the same direction: we will work with others for an African continent that lives in liberty, peace, and growing prosperity. Together with our European allies, we must help strengthen Africa's fragile states, help build indigenous capability to secure porous borders, and help build up the law enforcement and intelligence infrastructure to deny havens for terrorists.

An ever more lethal environment exists in Africa as local civil wars spread beyond borders to create regional war zones. Forming coalitions of the willing and cooperative security arrangements are key to confronting these emerging transnational threats.

Africa's great size and diversity requires a security strategy that focuses on bilateral engagement and builds coalitions of the willing. This Administration will focus on three interlocking strategies for the region:

- countries with major impact on their neighborhood such as South Africa, Nigeria, Kenya, and Ethiopia are anchors for regional engagement and require focused attention;

- coordination with European allies and international institutions is essential for constructive conflict mediation and successful peace operations; and

- Africa's capable reforming states and sub-regional organizations must be strengthened as the primary means to address transnational threats on a sustained basis.

Ultimately the path of political and economic freedom presents the surest route to progress in sub-Saharan Africa, where most wars are conflicts over material resources and political access often tragically waged on the basis of ethnic and religious difference. The transition to the African Union with its stated commitment to good governance and a common responsibility for democratic political systems offers opportunities to strengthen democracy on the continent.

v. Prevent Our Enemies from Threatening Us, Our Allies, and Our Friends with Weapons of Mass Destruction

"The gravest danger to freedom lies at the crossroads of radicalism and technology. When the spread of chemical and biological and nuclear weapons, along with ballistic missile technology—when that occurs, even weak states and small groups could attain a catastrophic power to strike great nations. Our enemies have declared this very intention, and have been caught seeking these terrible weapons. They want the capability to blackmail us, or to harm us, or to harm our friends—and we will oppose them with all our power."

PRESIDENT BUSH
WEST POINT, NEW YORK
JUNE 1, 2002

The nature of the Cold War threat required the United States—with our allies and friends—to emphasize deterrence of the enemy's use of force, producing a grim strategy of mutual assured destruction. With the collapse of the Soviet Union and the end of the Cold War, our security environment has undergone profound transformation.

Having moved from confrontation to cooperation as the hallmark of our relationship with Russia, the dividends are evident: an end to the balance of terror that divided us; an historic reduction in the nuclear arsenals on both sides; and cooperation in areas such as counterterrorism and missile defense that until recently were inconceivable.

But new deadly challenges have emerged from rogue states and terrorists. None of these contemporary threats rival the sheer destructive power that was arrayed against us by the Soviet Union. However, the nature and motivations of these new adversaries, their determination to obtain destructive powers hitherto available only to the world's strongest states, and the greater likelihood that they will use weapons of mass destruction against us, make today's security environment more complex and dangerous.

In the 1990s we witnessed the emergence of a small number of rogue states that, while different in important ways, share a number of attributes. These states:

- brutalize their own people and squander their national resources for the personal gain of the rulers;

- display no regard for international law, threaten their neighbors, and callously violate international treaties to which they are party;

- are determined to acquire weapons of mass destruction, along with other advanced military technology, to be used as threats or offensively to achieve the aggressive designs of these regimes;

- sponsor terrorism around the globe; and

- reject basic human values and hate the United States and everything for which it stands.

At the time of the Gulf War, we acquired irrefutable proof that Iraq's designs were not limited to the chemical weapons it had used against Iran and its own people, but also extended to the acquisition of nuclear weapons and biological agents. In the past decade North Korea has become the world's principal purveyor of ballistic missiles, and has tested increasingly capable missiles while developing its own WMD arsenal. Other rogue regimes seek nuclear, biological, and chemical weapons as well. These states' pursuit of, and global trade in, such weapons has become a looming threat to all nations.

We must be prepared to stop rogue states and their terrorist clients before they are able to threaten or use weapons of mass destruction against the United States and our allies and friends. Our response must take full advantage of strengthened alliances, the establishment of new partnerships with former adversaries, innovation in the use of military forces, modern technologies, including the development of an effective missile defense system, and increased emphasis on intelligence collection and analysis.

Our comprehensive strategy to combat WMD includes:

- *Proactive counterproliferation efforts.* We must deter and defend against the threat before it is unleashed. We must ensure that key capabilities—detection, active and passive defenses, and counterforce capabilities—are integrated into our defense transformation and our homeland security systems. Counterproliferation must also be integrated into the doctrine, training, and equipping of our forces and those of our allies to ensure that we can prevail in any conflict with WMD-armed adversaries.

- *Strengthened nonproliferation efforts to prevent rogue states and terrorists from acquiring the materials, technologies, and expertise necessary for weapons of mass destruction.* We will enhance diplomacy, arms control, multilateral export controls, and threat reduction assistance that impede states and terrorists seeking WMD, and when necessary, interdict enabling technologies and materials. We will continue to build coalitions to support these efforts, encouraging their increased political and financial support for nonproliferation and threat reduction programs. The recent G-8 agreement to commit up to $20 billion to a global partnership against proliferation marks a major step forward.

- *Effective consequence management to respond to the effects of WMD use, whether by terrorists or hostile states.* Minimizing the effects of WMD use against our people will help deter those who possess such weapons and dissuade those who seek to acquire them by persuading enemies that they cannot attain their desired ends. The United States must also be prepared to respond to the effects of WMD use against our forces abroad, and to help friends and allies if they are attacked.

It has taken almost a decade for us to comprehend the true nature of this new threat. Given the goals of rogue states and terrorists, the United States can no longer solely rely on a reactive posture as we have in the past. The inability to deter a potential attacker, the immediacy of today's threats, and the magnitude of potential harm that could be caused by our adversaries' choice of weapons, do not permit that option. We cannot let our enemies strike first.

- In the Cold War, especially following the Cuban missile crisis, we faced a generally status quo, risk-averse adversary. Deterrence was an effective defense. But deterrence based only upon the threat of retaliation is less likely to work against leaders of rogue states more willing to take risks, gambling with the lives of their people, and the wealth of their nations.

- In the Cold War, weapons of mass destruction were considered weapons of last resort whose use risked the destruction of those who used them. Today, our enemies see weapons of mass destruction as weapons of choice. For rogue states these weapons are tools of intimidation and military aggression against their neighbors. These weapons may also allow these states to attempt to blackmail the United States and our allies to prevent us from deterring or repelling the aggressive behavior of rogue states. Such states also see these weapons as their best means of overcoming the conventional superiority of the United States.

- Traditional concepts of deterrence will not work against a terrorist enemy whose avowed tactics are wanton destruction and the targeting of innocents; whose so-called soldiers seek martyrdom in death and whose most potent protection is statelessness. The overlap between states that sponsor terror and those that pursue WMD compels us to action.

For centuries, international law recognized that nations need not suffer an attack before they can lawfully take action to defend themselves against forces that present an imminent danger of attack. Legal scholars and international jurists often conditioned the legitimacy of preemption on the existence of an imminent threat—most often a visible mobilization of armies, navies, and air forces preparing to attack.

We must adapt the concept of imminent threat to the capabilities and objectives of today's adversaries. Rogue states and terrorists do not seek to attack us using conventional means. They know such attacks would fail. Instead, they rely on acts of terror and, potentially, the use of weapons of mass destruction—weapons that can be easily concealed, delivered covertly, and used without warning.

The targets of these attacks are our military forces and our civilian population, in direct violation of one of the principal norms of the law of warfare. As was demonstrated by the losses on September 11, 2001, mass civilian casualties is the specific objective of terrorists and these losses would be exponentially more severe if terrorists acquired and used weapons of mass destruction.

The United States has long maintained the option of preemptive actions to counter a sufficient threat to our national security. The greater the threat, the greater is the risk of inaction— and the more compelling the case for taking anticipatory action to defend ourselves, even if uncertainty remains as to the time and place of the enemy's attack. To forestall or prevent such hostile acts by our adversaries, the United States will, if necessary, act preemptively.

The United States will not use force in all cases to preempt emerging threats, nor should nations use preemption as a pretext for aggression. Yet in an age where the enemies of civilization openly and actively seek the world's most destructive technologies, the United States cannot remain idle while dangers gather.

We will always proceed deliberately, weighing the consequences of our actions. To support preemptive options, we will:

- build better, more integrated intelligence capabilities to provide timely, accurate information on threats, wherever they may emerge;

- coordinate closely with allies to form a common assessment of the most dangerous threats; and

- continue to transform our military forces to ensure our ability to conduct rapid and precise operations to achieve decisive results.

The purpose of our actions will always be to eliminate a specific threat to the United States or our allies and friends. The reasons for our actions will be clear, the force measured, and the cause just.

VI. IGNITE A NEW ERA OF GLOBAL ECONOMIC GROWTH THROUGH FREE MARKETS AND FREE TRADE

"When nations close their markets and opportunity is hoarded by a privileged few, no amount—no amount—of development aid is ever enough. When nations respect their people, open markets, invest in better health and education, every dollar of aid, every dollar of trade revenue and domestic capital is used more effectively."

PRESIDENT BUSH
MONTERREY, MEXICO
MARCH 22, 2002

A strong world economy enhances our national security by advancing prosperity and freedom in the rest of the world. Economic growth supported by free trade and free markets creates new jobs and higher incomes. It allows people to lift their lives out of poverty, spurs economic and legal reform, and the fight against corruption, and it reinforces the habits of liberty.

We will promote economic growth and economic freedom beyond America's shores. All governments are responsible for creating their own economic policies and responding to their own economic challenges. We will use our economic engagement with other countries to underscore the benefits of policies that generate higher productivity and sustained economic growth, including:

- pro-growth legal and regulatory policies to encourage business investment, innovation, and entrepreneurial activity;

- tax policies—particularly lower marginal tax rates—that improve incentives for work and investment;

- rule of law and intolerance of corruption so that people are confident that they will be able to enjoy the fruits of their economic endeavors;

- strong financial systems that allow capital to be put to its most efficient use;

- sound fiscal policies to support business activity;

- investments in health and education that improve the well-being and skills of the labor force and population as a whole; and

- free trade that provides new avenues for growth and fosters the diffusion of technologies and ideas that increase productivity and opportunity.

The lessons of history are clear: market economies, not command-and-control economies with the heavy hand of government, are the best way to promote prosperity and reduce poverty. Policies that further strengthen market incentives and market institutions are relevant for all economies—industrialized countries, emerging markets, and the developing world.

A return to strong economic growth in Europe and Japan is vital to U.S. national security interests. We want our allies to have strong economies for their own sake, for the sake of the global economy, and for the sake of global security. European efforts to remove structural barriers in their economies are particularly important in this regard, as are Japan's efforts to end deflation and address the problems of non-performing loans in the Japanese banking system. We will continue to use our regular consultations with Japan and our European partners—including through the Group of Seven (G-7)—to discuss policies they are adopting to promote growth in their economies and support higher global economic growth.

Improving stability in emerging markets is also key to global economic growth. International flows of investment capital are needed to expand the productive potential of these economies. These flows allow emerging markets and developing countries to make the investments that raise living standards and reduce poverty. Our long-term objective should be a world in which all countries have investment-grade credit ratings that allow them access to international capital markets and to invest in their future.

We are committed to policies that will help emerging markets achieve access to larger capital flows at lower cost. To this end, we will continue to pursue reforms aimed at reducing uncertainty in financial markets. We will work actively with other countries, the International Monetary Fund (IMF), and the private sector to implement the G-7 Action Plan negotiated earlier this year for preventing financial crises and more effectively resolving them when they occur.

The best way to deal with financial crises is to prevent them from occurring, and we have encouraged the IMF to improve its efforts doing so. We will continue to work with the IMF to streamline the policy conditions for its lending and to focus its lending strategy on achieving economic growth through sound fiscal and monetary policy, exchange rate policy, and financial sector policy.

The concept of "free trade" arose as a moral principle even before it became a pillar of economics. If you can make something that others value, you should be able to sell it to them. If others make something that you value, you should be able to buy it. This is real freedom, the freedom for a person—or a nation—to make a living. To promote free trade, the Unites States has developed a comprehensive strategy:

- *Seize the global initiative.* The new global trade negotiations we helped launch at Doha in November 2001 will have an ambitious agenda, especially in agriculture, manufacturing, and services, targeted for completion in 2005. The United States has led the way in completing the accession of China and a democratic Taiwan to the World Trade Organization. We will assist Russia's preparations to join the WTO.

- *Press regional initiatives.* The United States and other democracies in the Western Hemisphere have agreed to create the Free Trade Area of the Americas, targeted for completion in 2005. This year the United States will advocate market-access negotiations with its partners, targeted on agriculture, industrial goods, services, investment, and government procurement. We will also offer more opportunity to the poorest continent, Africa, starting with full use of the preferences allowed in the African Growth and Opportunity Act, and leading to free trade.

- *Move ahead with bilateral free trade agreements.* Building on the free trade agreement with Jordan enacted in 2001, the Administration will work this year to complete free trade agreements with Chile and Singapore. Our aim is to achieve free trade agreements with a mix of developed and developing countries in all regions of the world. Initially, Central America, Southern Africa, Morocco, and Australia will be our principal focal points.

- *Renew the executive-congressional partnership.* Every administration's trade strategy depends on a productive partnership with Congress. After a gap of 8 years, the Administration reestablished majority support in the Congress for trade liberalization by passing Trade Promotion Authority and the other market opening measures for developing countries in the Trade Act of 2002. This Administration will work with Congress to enact new bilateral, regional, and global trade agreements that will be concluded under the recently passed Trade Promotion Authority.

- *Promote the connection between trade and development.* Trade policies can help developing countries strengthen property rights, competition, the rule of law, investment, the spread of knowledge, open societies, the efficient allocation of resources, and regional integration—all leading to growth, opportunity, and confidence in developing countries. The United States is implementing The Africa Growth and Opportunity Act to provide market-access for nearly all goods produced in the 35 countries of sub-Saharan Africa. We will make more use of this act and its equivalent for the Caribbean Basin and continue to work with multilateral and regional institutions to help poorer countries take advantage of these opportunities. Beyond market access, the most important area where trade intersects with poverty is in public health. We will ensure that the WTO intellectual property rules are flexible enough to allow developing nations to gain access to critical medicines for extraordinary dangers like HIV/AIDS, tuberculosis, and malaria.

- *Enforce trade agreements and laws against unfair practices.* Commerce depends on the rule of law; international trade depends on enforceable agreements. Our top priorities are to resolve ongoing disputes with the European Union, Canada, and Mexico and to make a global effort to address new technology, science, and health regulations that needlessly impede farm exports and improved agriculture. Laws against unfair trade practices are often abused, but the international community must be able to address genuine concerns about government subsidies and dumping. International industrial espionage which undermines fair competition must be detected and deterred.

- *Help domestic industries and workers adjust.* There is a sound statutory framework for these transitional safeguards which we have used in the agricultural sector and which we are using this year to help the American steel industry. The benefits of free trade depend upon the enforcement of fair trading practices. These safeguards help ensure that the benefits of free trade do not come at the expense of American workers. Trade adjustment assistance will help workers adapt to the change and dynamism of open markets.

- *Protect the environment and workers.* The United States must foster economic growth in ways that will provide a better life along with widening prosperity. We will incorporate labor and environmental concerns into U.S. trade negotiations, creating a healthy "network" between multilateral environmental agreements with the WTO, and use the International Labor Organization, trade preference programs, and trade talks to improve working conditions in conjunction with freer trade.

- *Enhance energy security.* We will strengthen our own energy security and the shared prosperity of the global economy by working with our allies, trading partners, and energy producers to expand the sources and types of global energy supplied, especially in the Western Hemisphere, Africa, Central Asia, and the Caspian region. We will also continue to work with our partners to develop cleaner and more energy efficient technologies.

Economic growth should be accompanied by global efforts to stabilize greenhouse gas concentrations associated with this growth, containing them at a level that prevents dangerous human interference with the global climate. Our overall objective is to reduce America's greenhouse gas emissions relative to the size of our economy, cutting such emissions per unit of economic activity by 18 percent over the next 10 years, by the year 2012. Our strategies for attaining this goal will be to:

- remain committed to the basic U.N. Framework Convention for international cooperation;

- obtain agreements with key industries to cut emissions of some of the most potent greenhouse gases and give transferable credits to companies that can show real cuts;

- develop improved standards for measuring and registering emission reductions;

- promote renewable energy production and clean coal technology, as well as nuclear power—which produces no greenhouse gas emissions, while also improving fuel economy for U.S. cars and trucks;

- increase spending on research and new conservation technologies, to a total of $4.5 billion—the largest sum being spent on climate change by any country in the world and a $700 million increase over last year's budget; and

- assist developing countries, especially the major greenhouse gas emitters such as China and India, so that they will have the tools and resources to join this effort and be able to grow along a cleaner and better path.

VII. Expand the Circle of Development by Opening Societies and Building the Infrastructure of Democracy

"In World War II we fought to make the world safer, then worked to rebuild it. As we wage war today to keep the world safe from terror, we must also work to make the world a better place for all its citizens."

President Bush
Washington, D.C. (Inter-American Development Bank)
March 14, 2002

A world where some live in comfort and plenty, while half of the human race lives on less than $2 a day, is neither just nor stable. Including all of the world's poor in an expanding circle of development—and opportunity—is a moral imperative and one of the top priorities of U.S. international policy.

Decades of massive development assistance have failed to spur economic growth in the poorest countries. Worse, development aid has often served to prop up failed policies, relieving the pressure for reform and perpetuating misery. Results of aid are typically measured in dollars spent by donors, not in the rates of growth and poverty reduction achieved by recipients. These are the indicators of a failed strategy.

Working with other nations, the United States is confronting this failure. We forged a new consensus at the U.N. Conference on Financing for Development in Monterrey that the objectives of assistance—and the strategies to achieve those objectives—must change.

This Administration's goal is to help unleash the productive potential of individuals in all nations. Sustained growth and poverty reduction is impossible without the right national policies. Where governments have implemented real policy changes, we will provide significant new levels of assistance. The United States and other developed countries should set an ambitious and specific target: to double the size of the world's poorest economies within a decade.

The United States Government will pursue these major strategies to achieve this goal:

- *Provide resources to aid countries that have met the challenge of national reform.* We propose a 50 percent increase in the core development assistance given by the United States. While continuing our present programs, including humanitarian assistance based on need alone, these billions of new dollars will form a new Millennium Challenge Account for projects in countries whose governments rule justly, invest in their people, and encourage economic freedom. Governments must fight corruption, respect basic human rights, embrace the rule of law, invest in health care and education, follow responsible economic policies, and enable entrepreneurship. The Millennium Challenge Account will reward countries that have demonstrated real policy change and challenge those that have not to implement reforms.

- *Improve the effectiveness of the World Bank and other development banks in raising living standards.* The United States is committed to a comprehensive reform agenda for making the World Bank and the other multilateral development banks more effective in improving the lives of the world's poor. We have reversed the downward trend in U.S. contributions and proposed an 18 percent increase in the U.S. contributions to the International Development Association (IDA)—the World Bank's fund for the poorest countries—and the African Development Fund. The key to raising living standards and reducing poverty around the world is increasing productivity growth, especially in the poorest countries. We will continue to press the multilateral development banks to focus on activities that increase economic productivity, such as improvements in education, health, rule of law, and private sector development. Every project, every loan, every grant must be judged by how much it will increase productivity growth in developing countries.

- *Insist upon measurable results to ensure that development assistance is actually making a difference in the lives of the world's poor.* When it comes to economic development, what really matters is that more children are getting a better education, more people have access to health care and clean water, or more workers can find jobs to make a better future for their families. We have a moral

obligation to measure the success of our development assistance by whether it is delivering results. For this reason, we will continue to demand that our own development assistance as well as assistance from the multilateral development banks has measurable goals and concrete benchmarks for achieving those goals. Thanks to U.S. leadership, the recent IDA replenishment agreement will establish a monitoring and evaluation system that measures recipient countries' progress. For the first time, donors can link a portion of their contributions to IDA to the achievement of actual development results, and part of the U.S. contribution is linked in this way. We will strive to make sure that the World Bank and other multilateral development banks build on this progress so that a focus on results is an integral part of everything that these institutions do.

- *Increase the amount of development assistance that is provided in the form of grants instead of loans.* Greater use of results-based grants is the best way to help poor countries make productive investments, particularly in the social sectors, without saddling them with ever-larger debt burdens. As a result of U.S. leadership, the recent IDA agreement provided for significant increases in grant funding for the poorest countries for education, HIV/AIDS, health, nutrition, water, sanitation, and other human needs. Our goal is to build on that progress by increasing the use of grants at the other multilateral development banks. We will also challenge universities, nonprofits, and the private sector to match government efforts by using grants to support development projects that show results.

- *Open societies to commerce and investment.* Trade and investment are the real engines of economic growth. Even if government aid increases, most money for development must come from trade, domestic capital, and foreign investment. An effective strategy must try to expand these flows as well. Free markets and free trade are key priorities of our national security strategy.

- *Secure public health.* The scale of the public health crisis in poor countries is enormous. In countries afflicted by epidemics and pandemics like HIV/AIDS, malaria, and tuberculosis, growth and development will be threatened until these scourges can be contained. Resources from the developed world are necessary but will be effective only with honest governance, which supports prevention programs and provides effective local infrastructure. The United States has strongly backed the new global fund for HIV/AIDS organized by U.N. Secretary General Kofi Annan and its focus on combining prevention with a broad strategy for treatment and care. The United States already contributes more than twice as much money to such efforts as the next largest donor. If the global fund demonstrates its promise, we will be ready to give even more.

- *Emphasize education.* Literacy and learning are the foundation of democracy and development. Only about 7 percent of World Bank resources are devoted to education. This proportion should grow. The United States will increase its own funding for education assistance by at least 20 percent with an emphasis on improving basic education and teacher training in Africa. The United States can also bring information technology to these societies, many of whose education systems have been devastated by HIV/AIDS.

- *Continue to aid agricultural development.* New technologies, including biotechnology, have enormous potential to improve crop yields in developing countries while using fewer pesticides and less water. Using sound science, the United States should help bring these benefits to the 800 million people, including 300 million children, who still suffer from hunger and malnutrition.

VIII. DEVELOP AGENDAS FOR COOPERATIVE ACTION WITH THE OTHER MAIN CENTERS OF GLOBAL POWER

"We have our best chance since the rise of the nation-state in the 17th century to build a world where the great powers compete in peace instead of prepare for war."

PRESIDENT BUSH
WEST POINT, NEW YORK
JUNE 1, 2002

America will implement its strategies by organizing coalitions—as broad as practicable—of states able and willing to promote a balance of power that favors freedom. Effective coalition leadership requires clear priorities, an appreciation of others' interests, and consistent consultations among partners with a spirit of humility.

There is little of lasting consequence that the United States can accomplish in the world without the sustained cooperation of its allies and friends in Canada and Europe. Europe is also the seat of two of the strongest and most able international institutions in the world: the North Atlantic Treaty Organization (NATO), which has, since its inception, been the fulcrum of transatlantic and inter-European security, and the European Union (EU), our partner in opening world trade.

The attacks of September 11 were also an attack on NATO, as NATO itself recognized when it invoked its Article V self-defense clause for the first time. NATO's core mission—collective defense of the transatlantic alliance of democracies—remains, but NATO must develop new structures and capabilities to carry out that mission under new circumstances. NATO must

build a capability to field, at short notice, highly mobile, specially trained forces whenever they are needed to respond to a threat against any member of the alliance.

The alliance must be able to act wherever our interests are threatened, creating coalitions under NATO's own mandate, as well as contributing to mission-based coalitions. To achieve this, we must:

- expand NATO's membership to those democratic nations willing and able to share the burden of defending and advancing our common interests;

- ensure that the military forces of NATO nations have appropriate combat contributions to make in coalition warfare;

- develop planning processes to enable those contributions to become effective multinational fighting forces;

- take advantage of the technological opportunities and economies of scale in our defense spending to transform NATO military forces so that they dominate potential aggressors and diminish our vulnerabilities;

- streamline and increase the flexibility of command structures to meet new operational demands and the associated requirements of training, integrating, and experimenting with new force configurations; and

- maintain the ability to work and fight together as allies even as we take the necessary steps to transform and modernize our forces.

If NATO succeeds in enacting these changes, the rewards will be a partnership as central to the security and interests of its member states as was the case during the Cold War. We will sustain a common perspective on the threats to our societies and improve our ability to take common action in defense of our nations and their interests. At the same time, we welcome our European allies' efforts to forge a greater foreign policy and defense identity with the EU, and commit ourselves to close consultations to ensure that these developments work with NATO. We cannot afford to lose this opportunity to better prepare the family of transatlantic democracies for the challenges to come.

The attacks of September 11 energized America's Asian alliances. Australia invoked the ANZUS Treaty to declare the September 11 was an attack on Australia itself, following that historic decision with the dispatch of some of the world's finest combat forces for Operation Enduring Freedom. Japan and the Republic of Korea provided unprecedented levels of military logistical support within weeks of the terrorist attack. We have deepened cooperation on counterterrorism with our alliance partners in Thailand and the Philippines and received invaluable assistance from close friends like Singapore and New Zealand.

The war against terrorism has proven that America's alliances in Asia not only underpin regional peace and stability, but are flexible and ready to deal with new challenges. To enhance our Asian alliances and friendships, we will:

- look to Japan to continue forging a leading role in regional and global affairs based on our common interests, our common values, and our close defense and diplomatic cooperation;

- work with South Korea to maintain vigilance towards the North while preparing our alliance to make contributions to the broader stability of the region over the longer term;

- build on 50 years of U.S.-Australian alliance cooperation as we continue working together to resolve regional and global problems—as we have so many times from the Battle of the Coral Sea to Tora Bora;

- maintain forces in the region that reflect our commitments to our allies, our requirements, our technological advances, and the strategic environment; and

- build on stability provided by these alliances, as well as with institutions such as ASEAN and the Asia-Pacific Economic Cooperation forum, to develop a mix of regional and bilateral strategies to manage change in this dynamic region.

We are attentive to the possible renewal of old patterns of great power competition. Several potential great powers are now in the midst of internal transition—most importantly Russia, India, and China. In all three cases, recent developments have encouraged our hope that a truly global consensus about basic principles is slowly taking shape.

With Russia, we are already building a new strategic relationship based on a central reality of the twenty-first century: the United States and Russia are no longer strategic adversaries. The Moscow Treaty on Strategic Reductions is emblematic of this new reality and reflects a critical change in Russian thinking that promises to lead to productive, long-term relations with the Euro-Atlantic community and the United States. Russia's top leaders have a realistic assessment of their country's current weakness and the policies—internal and external—needed to reverse those weaknesses. They understand, increasingly, that Cold War approaches do not serve their national interests and that Russian and American strategic interests overlap in many areas.

United States policy seeks to use this turn in Russian thinking to refocus our relationship on emerging and potential common interests and challenges. We are broadening our already extensive cooperation in the global war on terrorism. We are facilitating Russia's entry into the World Trade Organization, without lowering standards for accession, to promote beneficial bilateral trade and investment relations. We have created the NATO-Russia Council with the goal of deepening security cooperation among Russia, our European allies, and ourselves. We will continue to bolster the independence and stability of the states of the former Soviet Union in the belief that a prosperous and stable neighborhood will reinforce Russia's growing commitment to integration into the Euro-Atlantic community.

At the same time, we are realistic about the differences that still divide us from Russia and about the time and effort it will take to build an enduring strategic partnership. Lingering distrust of our motives and policies by key Russian elites slows improvement in our relations. Russia's uneven commitment to the basic values of free-market democracy and dubious record in combating the proliferation of weapons of mass destruction remain matters of great concern. Russia's very weakness limits the opportunities for cooperation. Nevertheless, those opportunities are vastly greater now than in recent years—or even decades.

The United States has undertaken a transformation in its bilateral relationship with India based on a conviction that U.S. interests require a strong relationship with India. We are the two largest democracies, committed to political freedom protected by representative government. India is moving toward greater economic freedom

as well. We have a common interest in the free flow of commerce, including through the vital sea lanes of the Indian Ocean. Finally, we share an interest in fighting terrorism and in creating a strategically stable Asia.

Differences remain, including over the development of India's nuclear and missile programs, and the pace of India's economic reforms. But while in the past these concerns may have dominated our thinking about India, today we start with a view of India as a growing world power with which we have common strategic interests. Through a strong partnership with India, we can best address any differences and shape a dynamic future.

The United States relationship with China is an important part of our strategy to promote a stable, peaceful, and prosperous Asia-Pacific region. We welcome the emergence of a strong, peaceful, and prosperous China. The democratic development of China is crucial to that future. Yet, a quarter century after beginning the process of shedding the worst features of the Communist legacy, China's leaders have not yet made the next series of fundamental choices about the character of their state. In pursuing advanced military capabilities that can threaten its neighbors in the Asia-Pacific region, China is following an outdated path that, in the end, will hamper its own pursuit of national greatness. In time, China will find that social and political freedom is the only source of that greatness.

The United States seeks a constructive relationship with a changing China. We already cooperate well where our interests overlap, including the current war on terrorism and in promoting stability on the Korean peninsula. Likewise, we have coordinated on the future of Afghanistan and have initiated a comprehensive dialogue on counterterrorism and similar transitional concerns. Shared health and environmental threats, such as the spread of HIV/AIDS, challenge us to promote jointly the welfare of our citizens.

Addressing these transnational threats will challenge China to become more open with information, promote the development of civil society, and enhance individual human rights. China has begun to take the road to political openness, permitting many personal freedoms and conducting village-level elections, yet remains strongly committed to national one-party rule by the Communist Party. To make that nation truly accountable to its citizen's needs and aspirations, however, much work remains to be done. Only by allowing the Chinese people to think, assemble, and worship freely can China reach its full potential.

Our important trade relationship will benefit from China's entry into the World Trade Organization, which will create more export opportunities and ultimately more jobs for American farmers, workers, and companies. China is our fourth largest trading partner, with over $100 billion in annual two-way trade. The power of market principles and the WTO's requirements for transparency and accountability will advance openness and the rule of law in China to help establish basic protections for commerce and for citizens. There are, however, other areas in which we have profound disagreements. Our commitment to the self-defense of Taiwan under the Taiwan Relations Act is one. Human rights is another. We expect China to adhere to its nonproliferation commitments. We will work to narrow differences where they exist, but not allow them to preclude cooperation where we agree.

The events of September 11, 2001, fundamentally changed the context for relations between the United States and other main centers of global power, and opened vast, new opportunities. With our long-standing allies in Europe and Asia, and with leaders in Russia, India, and China, we must develop active agendas of cooperation lest these relationships become routine and unproductive.

Every agency of the United States Government shares the challenge. We can build fruitful habits of consultation, quiet argument, sober analysis, and common action. In the long-term, these are the practices that will sustain the supremacy of our common principles and keep open the path of progress.

IX. TRANSFORM AMERICA'S NATIONAL SECURITY INSTITUTIONS TO MEET THE CHALLENGES AND OPPORTUNITIES OF THE TWENTY-FIRST CENTURY

"Terrorists attacked a symbol of American prosperity.
They did not touch its source. America is successful because of the
hard work, creativity, and enterprise of our people."

PRESIDENT BUSH
WASHINGTON, D.C. (JOINT SESSION OF CONGRESS)
SEPTEMBER 20, 2001

The major institutions of American national security were designed in a different era to meet different requirements. All of them must be transformed.

It is time to reaffirm the essential role of American military strength. We must build and maintain our defenses beyond challenge. Our military's highest priority is to defend the United States. To do so effectively, our military must:

- assure our allies and friends;

- dissuade future military competition;

- deter threats against U.S. interests, allies, and friends; and

- decisively defeat any adversary if deterrence fails.

The unparalleled strength of the United States armed forces, and their forward presence, have maintained the peace in some of the world's most strategically vital regions. However, the threats and enemies we must confront have changed, and so must our forces. A military structured to deter massive Cold War-era armies must be transformed to focus more on how an adversary might fight rather than where and when a war might occur. We will channel our energies to overcome a host of operational challenges.

The presence of American forces overseas is one of the most profound symbols of the U.S. commitments to allies and friends. Through our willingness to use force in our own defense and in defense of others, the United States demonstrates its resolve to maintain a balance of power that favors freedom. To contend with uncertainty and to meet the many security challenges we face, the United States will require bases and stations within and beyond Western Europe and Northeast Asia, as well as temporary access arrangements for the long-distance deployment of U.S. forces.

Before the war in Afghanistan, that area was low on the list of major planning contingencies. Yet, in a very short time, we had to operate across the length and breadth of that remote nation, using every branch of the armed forces. We must prepare for more such deployments by developing assets such as advanced remote sensing, long-range precision strike capabilities, and transformed maneuver and expeditionary forces. This broad portfolio of military capabilities must also include the ability to defend the homeland, conduct information operations, ensure U.S. access to distant theaters, and protect critical U.S. infrastructure and assets in outer space.

Innovation within the armed forces will rest on experimentation with new approaches to warfare, strengthening joint operations, exploiting U.S. intelligence advantages, and taking full advantage of science and technology. We must also transform the way the Department of Defense is run, especially in financial management and recruitment and retention. Finally, while maintaining near-term readiness and the ability to fight the war on terrorism, the goal must be to provide the President with a wider range of military options to discourage aggression or any form of coercion against the United States, our allies, and our friends.

We know from history that deterrence can fail; and we know from experience that some enemies cannot be deterred. The United States must and will maintain the capability to defeat any attempt by an enemy—whether a state or non-state actor—to impose its will on the United States, our allies, or our friends. We will maintain the forces sufficient to support our obligations, and to defend freedom. Our forces will be strong enough to dissuade potential adversaries from pursuing a military build-up in hopes of surpassing, or equaling, the power of the United States.

Intelligence—and how we use it—is our first line of defense against terrorists and the threat posed by hostile states. Designed around the priority of gathering enormous information about a massive, fixed object—the Soviet bloc—the intelligence community is coping with the challenge of following a far more complex and elusive set of targets.

We must transform our intelligence capabilities and build new ones to keep pace with the nature of these threats. Intelligence must be appropriately integrated with our defense and law enforcement

systems and coordinated with our allies and friends. We need to protect the capabilities we have so that we do not arm our enemies with the knowledge of how best to surprise us. Those who would harm us also seek the benefit of surprise to limit our prevention and response options and to maximize injury.

We must strengthen intelligence warning and analysis to provide integrated threat assessments for national and homeland security. Since the threats inspired by foreign governments and groups may be conducted inside the United States, we must also ensure the proper fusion of information between intelligence and law enforcement.

Initiatives in this area will include:

- strengthening the authority of the Director of Central Intelligence to lead the development and actions of the Nation's foreign intelligence capabilities;

- establishing a new framework for intelligence warning that provides seamless and integrated warning across the spectrum of threats facing the nation and our allies;

- continuing to develop new methods of collecting information to sustain our intelligence advantage;

- investing in future capabilities while working to protect them through a more vigorous effort to prevent the compromise of intelligence capabilities; and

- collecting intelligence against the terrorist danger across the government with all-source analysis.

As the United States Government relies on the armed forces to defend America's interests, it must rely on diplomacy to interact with other nations. We will ensure that the Department of State receives funding sufficient to ensure the success of American diplomacy. The State Department takes the lead in managing our bilateral relationships with other governments. And in this new era, its people and institutions must be able to interact equally adroitly with non-governmental organizations and international institutions. Officials trained mainly in international politics must also extend their reach to understand complex issues of domestic governance around the world, including public health, education, law enforcement, the judiciary, and public diplomacy.

Our diplomats serve at the front line of complex negotiations, civil wars, and other humanitarian catastrophes. As humanitarian relief requirements are better understood, we must also be able to help build police forces, court systems, and legal codes, local and provincial government institutions, and electoral systems. Effective international cooperation is needed to accomplish these goals, backed by American readiness to play our part.

Just as our diplomatic institutions must adapt so that we can reach out to others, we also need a different and more comprehensive approach to public information efforts that can help people around the world learn about and understand America. The war on terrorism is not a clash of civilizations. It does, however, reveal the clash inside a civilization, a battle for the future of the Muslim world. This is a struggle of ideas and this is an area where America must excel.

We will take the actions necessary to ensure that our efforts to meet our global security commitments and protect Americans are not impaired by the potential for investigations, inquiry, or prosecution by the International Criminal Court (ICC), whose jurisdiction does not extend to Americans and which we do not accept. We will work together with other nations to avoid complications in our military operations and cooperation, through such mechanisms as multilateral and bilateral agreements that will protect U.S. nationals from the ICC. We will implement fully the American Servicemembers Protection Act, whose provisions are intended to ensure and enhance the protection of U.S. personnel and officials.

We will make hard choices in the coming year and beyond to ensure the right level and allocation of government spending on national security. The United States Government must strengthen its defenses to win this war. At home, our most important priority is to protect the homeland for the American people.

Today, the distinction between domestic and foreign affairs is diminishing. In a globalized world, events beyond America's borders have a greater impact inside them. Our society must be open to people, ideas, and goods from across the globe. The characteristics we most cherish—our freedom, our cities, our systems of movement, and modern life—are vulnerable to terrorism. This vulnerability will persist long after we bring to justice those responsible for the September 11 attacks. As time passes, individuals may gain access to means of destruction that until now could be wielded only by armies, fleets, and squadrons. This is a new condition of life. We will adjust to it and thrive—in spite of it.

In exercising our leadership, we will respect the values, judgment, and interests of our friends and partners. Still, we will be prepared to act apart when our interests and unique responsibilities require. When we disagree on particulars, we will explain forthrightly the grounds for our concerns and strive to forge viable alternatives. We will not allow such disagreements to obscure our determination to secure together, with our allies and our friends, our shared fundamental interests and values.

Ultimately, the foundation of American strength is at home. It is in the skills of our people, the dynamism of our economy, and the resilience of our institutions. A diverse, modern society has inherent, ambitious, entrepreneurial energy. Our strength comes from what we do with that energy. That is where our national security begins.

The voice of lies and treason. Here, complete, is John Kerry's infamous testimony before Congress as a recently returned Vietnam veteran.

LEGISLATIVE PROPOSALS RELATING TO THE WAR IN SOUTHEAST ASIA

THURSDAY, APRIL 22, 1971

UNITED STATES SENATE,
COMMITTEE ON FOREIGN RELATIONS,
Washington, D.C.

The committee met, pursuant to notice, at 11:05 a.m., in Room 4221, New Senate Office Building, Senator J. W. Fulbright (Chairman) presiding.

Present: Senators Fulbright, Symington, Pell, Aiken, Case, and Javits.

The CHAIRMAN. The committee will come to order.

OPENING STATEMENT

The committee is continuing this morning its hearings on proposals relating to the ending of the war in Southeast Asia. This morning the committee will hear testimony from Mr. John Kerry and, if he has any associates, we will be glad to hear from them. These are men who have fought in this unfortunate war in Vietnam. I believe they deserve to be heard and listened to by the Congress and by the officials in the executive branch and by the public generally. You have a perspective that those in the Government who make our Nation's policy do not always have and I am sure that your testimony today will be helpful to the committee in its consideration of the proposals before us.

I would like to add simply on my own account that I regret very much the action of the Supreme Court in denying the veterans the right to use the Mall. [Applause.]

I regret that. It seems to me to be but another instance of an insensitivity of our Government to the tragic effects of this war upon our people.

I want also to congratulate Mr. Kerry, you, and your associates upon the restraint that you have shown, certainly in the hearing the other day when there were a great many of your people here. I think you conducted yourselves in a most commendable manner throughout this week. Whenever people gather there is always a tendency for some of the more emotional ones to do things which are even against their own interests. I think you deserve much of the credit because I understand you are one of the leaders of this group.

I have joined with some of my colleagues, specifically Senator Hart, in an effort to try to change the attitude of our Government toward your efforts in bringing to this committee and to the country your views about the war.

(179)

180

I personally don't know of any group which would have both a greater justification for doing it and also a more accurate view of the effect of the war. As you know, there has grown up in this town a feeling that it is extremely difficult to get accurate information about the war and I don't know a better source than you and your associates. So we are very pleased to have you and your associates, Mr. Kerry.

At the beginning if you would give to the reporter your full name and a brief biography so that the record will show who you are.

Senator JAVITS. Mr. Chairman, I was down there to the veterans' camp yesterday and saw the New York group and I would like to say I am very proud of the deportment and general attitude of the group. I hope it continues. I have joined in the Hart resolution, too. As a lawyer I hope you will find it possible to comply with the order even though, like the chairman, I am unhappy about it. I think it is our job to see that you are suitably set up as an alternative so that you can do what you came here to do. I welcome the fact that you came and what you are doing.

[Applause.]

The CHAIRMAN. You may proceed, Mr. Kerry.

STATEMENT OF JOHN KERRY, VIETNAM VETERANS AGAINST THE WAR

Mr. KERRY. Thank you very much, Senator Fulbright, Senator Javits, Senator Symington, Senator Pell. I would like to say for the record, and also for the men behind me who are also wearing the uniforms and their medals, that my sitting here is really symbolic. I am not here as John Kerry. I am here as one member of the group of 1,000, which is a small representation of a very much larger group of veterans in this country, and were it possible for all of them to sit at this table they would be here and have the same kind of testimony.

I would simply like to speak in very general terms. I apologize if my statement is general because I received notification yesterday you would hear me and I am afraid because of the injunction I was up most of the night and haven't had a great deal of chance to prepare.

WINTER SOLDIER INVESTIGATION

I would like to talk, representing all those veterans, and say that several months ago in Detroit, we had an investigation at which over 150 honorably discharged and many very highly decorated veterans testified to war crimes committed in Southeast Asia, not isolated incidents but crimes committed on a day-to-day basis with the full awareness of officers at all levels of command.

It is impossible to describe to you exactly what did happen in Detroit, the emotions in the room, the feelings of the men who were reliving their experiences in Vietnam, but they did. They relived the absolute horror of what this country, in a sense, made them do.

They told the stories at times they had personally raped, cut off ears, cut off heads, taped wires from portable telephones to human genitals and turned up the power, cut off limbs, blown up bodies, randomly shot at civilians, razed villages in fashion reminiscent of Genghis Khan, shot cattle and dogs for fun, poisoned food stocks, and generally ravaged the countryside of South Vietnam in addition to

181

the normal ravage of war, and the normal and very particular ravaging which is done by the applied bombing power of this country.

We call this investigation the "Winter Soldier Investigation." The term "Winter Soldier" is a play on words of Thomas Paine in 1776 when he spoke of the Sunshine Patriot and summertime soldiers who deserted at Valley Forge because the going was rough.

We who have come here to Washington have come here because we feel we have to be winter soldiers now. We could come back to this country; we could be quiet; we could hold our silence; we could not tell what went on in Vietnam, but we feel because of what threatens this country, the fact that the crimes threaten it, not reds, and not redcoats but the crimes which we are committing that threaten it, that we have to speak out.

FEELINGS OF MEN COMING BACK FROM VIETNAM

I would like to talk to you a little bit about what the result is of the feelings these men carry with them after coming back from Vietnam. The country doesn't know it yet, but it has created a monster, a monster in the form of millions of men who have been taught to deal and to trade in violence, and who are given the chance to die for the biggest nothing in history; men who have returned with a sense of anger and a sense of betrayal which no one has yet grasped.

As a veteran and one who feels this anger, I would like to talk about it. We are angry because we feel we have been used in the worst fashion by the administration of this country.

In 1970 at West Point, Vice President Agnew said "some glamorize the criminal misfits of society while our best men die in Asian rice paddies to preserve the freedom which most of those misfits abuse," and this was used as a rallying point for our effort in Vietnam.

But for us, as boys in Asia whom the country was supposed to support, his statement is a terrible distortion from which we can only draw a very deep sense of revulsion. Hence the anger of some of the men who are here in Washington today. It is a distortion because we in no way consider ourselves the best men of this country; because those he calls misfits were standing up for us in a way that nobody else in this country dared to; because so many who have died would have returned to this country to join the misfits in their efforts to ask for an immediate withdrawal from South Vietnam, because so many of those best men have returned as quadriplegics and amputees, and they lie forgotten in Veterans' Administration hospitals in this country which fly the flag which so many have chosen as their own personal symbol. And we cannot consider ourselves America's best men when we are ashamed of and hated what we were called on to do in Southeast Asia.

In our opinion, and from our experience, there is nothing in South Vietnam, nothing which could happen that realistically threatens the United States of America. And to attempt to justify the loss of one American life in Vietnam, Cambodia, or Laos by linking such loss to the preservation of freedom, which those misfits supposedly abuse, is to us the height of criminal hypocrisy, and it is that kind of hypocrisy which we feel has torn this country apart.

We are probably much more angry than that and I don't want to go into the foreign policy aspects because I am outclassed here. I know that all of you talk about every possible alternative of getting out of

182

Vietnam. We understand that. We know you have considered the seriousness of the aspects to the utmost level and I am not going to try to dwell on that, but I want to relate to you the feeling that many of the men who have returned to this country express because we are probably angriest about all that we were told about Vietnam and about the mystical war against communism.

WHAT WAS FOUND AND LEARNED IN VIETNAM

We found that not only was it a civil war, an effort by a people who had for years been seeking their liberation from any colonial influence whatsoever, but also we found that the Vietnamese whom we had enthusiastically molded after our own image were hard put to take up the fight against the threat we were supposedly saving them from.

We found most people didn't even know the difference between communism and democracy. They only wanted to work in rice paddies without helicopters strafing them and bombs with napalm burning their villages and tearing their country apart. They wanted everything to do with the war, particularly with this foreign presence of the United States of America, to leave them alone in peace, and they practiced the art of survival by siding with whichever military force was present at a particular time, be it Vietcong, North Vietnamese, or American.

We found also that all too often American men were dying in those rice paddies for want of support from their allies. We saw first hand how money from American taxes was used for a corrupt dictatorial regime. We saw that many people in this country had a one-sided idea of who was kept free by our flag, as blacks provided the highest percentage of casualties. We saw Vietnam ravaged equally by American bombs as well as by search and destroy missions, as well as by Vietcong terrorism, and yet we listened while this country tried to blame all of the havoc on the Vietcong.

We rationalized destroying villages in order to save them. We saw America lose her sense of morality as she accepted very coolly a My Lai and refused to give up the image of American soldiers who hand out chocolate bars and chewing gum.

We learned the meaning of free fire zones, shooting anything that moves, and we watched while America placed a cheapness on the lives of orientals.

We watched the U.S. falsification of body counts, in fact the glorification of body counts. We listened while month after month we were told the back of the enemy was about to break. We fought using weapons against "oriental human beings," with quotation marks around that. We fought using weapons against those people which I do not believe this country would dream of using were we fighting in the European theater or let us say a non-third-world people theater, and so we watched while men charged up hills because a general said that hill has to be taken, and after losing one platoon or two platoons they marched away to leave the high for the reoccupation by the North Vietnamese because we watched pride allow the most unimportant of battles to be blown into extravaganzas, because we couldn't lose, and we couldn't retreat, and because it didn't matter how many American bodies were lost to prove that point. And so there were Hamburger Hills and Khe Sanhs and Hill 881's and Fire Base 6's and so many others.

183

VIETNAMIZATION

Now we are told that the men who fought there must watch quietly while American lives are lost so that we can exercise the incredible arrogance of Vietnamizing the Vietnamese.

Each day——

[Applause.]

The CHAIRMAN. I hope you won't interrupt. He is making a very significant statement. Let him proceed.

Mr. KERRY. Each day to facilitate the process by which the United States washes her hands of Vietnam someone has to give up his life so that the United States doesn't have to admit something that the entire world already knows, so that we can't say that we have made a mistake. Someone has to die so that President Nixon won't be, and these are his words, "the first President to lose a war."

We are asking Americans to think about that because how do you ask a man to be the last man to die in Vietnam? How do you ask a man to be the last man to die for a mistake? But we are trying to do that, and we are doing it with thousands of rationalizations, and if you read carefully the President's last speech to the people of this country, you can see that he says, and says clearly:

But the issue, gentlemen, the issue is communism, and the question is whether or not we will leave that country to the Communists or whether or not we will try to give it hope to be a free people.

But the point is they are not a free people now under us. They are not a free people, and we cannot fight communism all over the world, and I think we should have learned that lesson by now.

RETURNING VETERANS ARE NOT REALLY WANTED

But the problem of veterans goes beyond this personal problem, because you think about a poster in this country with a picture of Uncle Sam and the picture says "I want you." And a young man comes out of high school and says, "That is fine. I am going to serve my country." And he goes to Vietnam and he shoots and he kills and he does his job or maybe he doesn't kill, maybe he just goes and he comes back, and when he gets back to this country he finds that he isn't really wanted, because the largest unemployment figure in the country—it varies depending on who you get it from, the VA Administration 15 percent, various other sources 22 percent. But the largest corps of unemployed in this country are veterans of this war, and of those veterans 33 percent of the unemployed are black. That means 1 out of every 10 of the Nation's unemployed is a veteran of Vietnam.

The hospitals across the country won't, or can't meet their demands. It is not a question of not trying. They don't have the appropriations. A man recently died after he had a tracheotomy in California, not because of the operation but because there weren't enough personnel to clean the mucous out of his tube and he suffocated to death.

Another young man just died in a New York VA hospital the other day. A friend of mine was lying in a bed two beds away and tried to help him, but he couldn't. He rang a bell and there was nobody there to service that man and so he died of convulsions.

I understand 57 percent of all those entering the VA hospitals talk about suicide. Some 27 percent have tried, and they try because they-

184

come back to this country and they have to face what they did in Vietnam, and then they come back and find the indifference of a country that doesn't really care, that doesn't really care.

LACK OF MORAL INDIGNATION IN UNITED STATES

Suddenly we are faced with a very sickening situation in this country, because there is no moral indignation and, if there is, it comes from people who are almost exhausted by their past indignations, and I know that many of them are sitting in front of me. The country seems to have lain down and shrugged off something as serious as Laos, just as we calmly shrugged off the loss of 700,000 lives in Pakistan, the so-called greatest disaster of all times.

But we are here as veterans to say we think we are in the midst of the greatest disaster of all times now because they are still dying over there, and not just Americans, Vietnamese, and we are rationalizing leaving that country so that those people can go on killing each other for years to come.

Americans seem to have accepted the idea that the war is winding down, at least for Americans, and they have also allowed the bodies which were once used by a President for statistics to prove that we were winning that war, to be used as evidence against a man who followed orders and who interpreted those orders no differently than hundreds of other men in Vietnam.

We veterans can only look with amazement on the fact that this country has been unable to see there is absolutely no difference between ground troops and a helicopter crew, and yet people have accepted a differentiation fed them by the administration.

No ground troops are in Laos, so it is all right to kill Laotians by remote control. But believe me the helicopter crews fill the same body bags and they wreak the same kind of damage on the Vietnamese and Laotian countryside as anybody else, and the President is talking about allowing that to go on for many years to come. One can only ask if we will really be satisfied only when the troops march into Hanoi.

REQUEST FOR ACTION BY CONGRESS

We are asking here in Washington for some action, action from the Congress of the United States of America which has the power to raise and maintain armies, and which by the Constitution also has the power to declare war.

We have come here, not to the President, because we believe that this body can be responsive to the will of the people, and we believe that the will of the people says that we should be out of Vietnam now.

EXTENT OF PROBLEM OF VIETNAM WAR

We are here in Washington also to say that the problem of this war is not just a question of war and diplomacy. It is part and parcel of everything that we are trying as human beings to communicate to people in this country, the question of racism, which is rampant in the military, and so many other questions also, the use of weapons, the hypocrisy in our taking umbrage in the Geneva Conventions and using that as justification for a continuation of this war, when we

185

are more guilty than any other body of violations of those Geneva Conventions, in the use of free fire zones, harassment interdiction fire, search and destroy missions, the bombings, the torture of prisoners, the killing of prisoners, accepted policy by many units in South Vietnam. That is what we are trying to say. It is part and parcel of everything.

An American Indian friend of mine who lives in the Indian Nation of Alcatraz put it to me very succinctly. He told me how as a boy on an Indian reservation he had watched television and he used to cheer the cowboys when they came in and shot the Indians, and then suddenly one day he stopped in Vietnam and he said "My God, I am doing to these people the very same thing that was done to my people." And he stopped. And that is what we are trying to say, that we think this thing has to end.

WHERE IS THE LEADERSHIP?

We are also here to ask, and we are here to ask vehemently, where are the leaders of our country? Where is the leadership? We are here to ask where are McNamara, Rostow, Bundy, Gilpatric and so many others. Where are they now that we, the men whom they sent off to war, have returned? These are commanders who have deserted their troops, and there is no more serious crime in the law of war. The Army says they never leave their wounded.

The Marines say they never leave even their dead. These men have left all the casualties and retreated behind a pious shield of public rectitude. They have left the real stuff of their reputations bleaching behind them in the sun in this country.

ADMINISTRATION'S ATTEMPT TO DISOWN VETERANS

Finally, this administration has done us the ultimate dishonor. They have attempted to disown us and the sacrifice we made for this country. In their blindness and fear they have tried to deny that we are veterans or that we served in Nam. We do not need their testimony. Our own scars and stumps of limbs are witnesses enough for others and for ourselves.

We wish that a merciful God could wipe away our own memories of that service as easily as this administration has wiped their memories of us. But all that they have done and all that they can do by this denial is to make more clear than ever our own determination to undertake one last mission, to search out and destroy the last vestige of this barbaric war, to pacify our own hearts, to conquer the hate and the fear that have driven this country these last 10 years and more, and so when, in 30 years from now, our brothers go down the street without a leg, without an arm, or a face, and small boys ask why, we will be able to say "Vietnam" and not mean a desert, not a filthy obscene memory but mean instead the place where America finally turned and where soldiers like us helped it in the turning.

Thank you. [Applause.]

The CHAIRMAN. Mr. Kerry, it is quite evident from that demonstration that you are speaking not only for yourself but for all your associates, as you properly said in the beginning.

186

COMMENDATION OF WITNESS

You said you wished to communicate. I can't imagine anyone communicating more eloquently than you did. I think it is extremely helpful and beneficial to the committee and the country to have you make such a statement.

You said you had been awake all night. I can see that you spent that time very well indeed. [Laughter.]

Perhaps that was the better part, better that you should be awake than otherwise.

PROPOSALS BEFORE COMMITTEE

You have said that the question before this committee and the Congress is really how to end the war. The resolutions about which we have been hearing testimony during the past several days, the sponsors of which are some members of this committee, are seeking the most practical way that we can find and, I believe, to do it at the earliest opportunity that we can. That is the purpose of these hearings and that is why you were brought here.

You have been very eloquent about the reasons why we should proceed as quickly as possible. Are you familiar with some of the proposals before this committee?

Mr. KERRY. Yes, I am, Senator.

The CHAIRMAN. Do you support or do you have any particular views about any one of them you wish to give the committee?

Mr. KERRY. My feeling, Senator, is undoubtedly this Congress, and I don't mean to sound pessimistic, but I do not believe that this Congress will, in fact, end the war as we would like to, which is immediately and unilaterally and, therefore, if I were to speak I would say we would set a date and the date obviously would be the earliest possible date. But I would like to say, in answering that, that I do not believe it is necessary to stall any longer. I have been to Paris. I have talked with both delegations at the peace talks, that is to say the Democratic Republic of Vietnam and the Provisional Revolutionary Government and of all eight of Madam Binh's points it has been stated time and time again, and was stated by Senator Vance Hartke when he returned from Paris, and it has been stated by many other officials of this Government, if the United States were to set a date for withdrawal the prisoners of war would be returned.

I think this negates very clearly the argument of the President that we have to maintain a presence in Vietnam, to use as a negotiating block for the return of those prisoners. The setting of a date will accomplish that.

As to the argument concerning the danger to our troops were we to withdraw or state that we would, they have also said many times in conjunction with that statement that all of our troops, the moment we set a date, will be given safe conduct out of Vietnam. The only other important point is that we allow the South Vietnamese people to determine their own future and that ostensibly is what we have been fighting for anyway.

I would, therefore, submit that the most expedient means of getting out of South Vietnam would be for the President of the United States to declare a cease-fire, to stop this blind commitment to a dictatorial regime, the Thieu-Ky-Khiem regime, accept a coalition regime which

187

would represent all the political forces of the country which is in fact what a representative government is supposed to do and which is in fact what this Government here in this country purports to do, and pull the troops out without losing one more American, and still further without losing the South Vietnamese.

DESIRE TO DISENGAGE FROM VIETNAM

The CHAIRMAN. You seem to feel that there is still some doubt about the desire to disengage. I don't believe that is true. I believe there has been a tremendous change in the attitude of the people. As reflected in the Congress, they do wish to disengage and to bring the war to an end as soon as we can.

QUESTION IS HOW TO DISENGAGE

The question before us is how to do it. What is the best means that is most effective, taking into consideration the circumstances with which all governments are burdened? We have a precedent in this same country. The French had an experience, perhaps not traumatic as ours has been, but nevertheless they did make up their minds in the spring of 1954 and within a few weeks did bring it to a close. Some of us have thought that this is a precedent, from which we could learn, for ending such a war. I have personally advocated that this is the best procedure. It is a traditional rather classic procedure of how to end a war that could be called a stalemate, that neither side apparently has the capacity to end by military victory, and which apparently is going to go on for a long time. Speaking only for myself, this seems the more reasonable procedure.

I realize you want it immediately, but I think that procedure was about as immediate as any by which a country has ever succeeded in ending such a conflict or a similar conflict. Would that not appeal to you?

Mr. KERRY. Well, Senator, frankly it does not appeal to me if American men have to continue to die when they don't have to, particularly when it seems the Government of this country is more concerned with the legality of where men sleep than it is with the legality of where they drop bombs. [Applause.]

The CHAIRMAN. In the case of the French when they made up their mind to take the matter up at the conference in Geneva, they did. The first thing they did was to arrange a ceasefire and the killing did cease. Then it took only, I think, two or three weeks to tidy up all the details regarding the withdrawal. Actually when they made up their mind to stop the war, they did have a ceasefire which is what you are recommending as the first step.

Mr. KERRY. Yes, sir; that is correct.

The CHAIRMAN. It did not drag on. They didn't continue to fight. They stopped the fighting by agreement when they went to Geneva and all the countries then directly involved participated in that agreement.

I don't wish to press you on the details. It is for the committee to determine the best means, but you have given most eloquently the reasons why we should proceed as early as we can. That is, of course, the purpose of the hearing.

188

Mr. Kerry. Senator, if I may interject, I think that what we are trying to say is we do have a method. We believe we do have a plan, and that plan is that if this body were by some means either to permit a special referendum in this country so that the country itself might decide and therefore avoid this recrimination which people constantly refer to or if they couldn't do that, at least do it through immediate legislation which would state there would be an immediate ceasefire and we would be willing to undertake negotiations for a coalition government. But at the present moment that is not going to happen, so we are talking about men continuing to die for nothing and I think there is a tremendous moral question here which the Congress of the United States is ignoring.

The Chairman. The Congress cannot directly under our system negotiate a cease-fire or anything of this kind. Under our constitutional system we can advise the President. We have to persuade the President of the urgency of taking this action. Now we have certain ways in which to proceed. We can, of course, express ourselves in a resolution or we can pass an act which directly affects appropriations which is the most concrete positive way the Congress can express itself.

But Congress has no capacity under our system to go out and negotiate a cease-fire. We have to persuade the Executive to do this for the country.

EXTRAORDINARY RESPONSE DEMANDED BY EXTRAORDINARY QUESTION

Mr. Kerry. Mr. Chairman, I realize that full well as a study of political science. I realize that we cannot negotiate treaties and I realize that even my visits in Paris, precedents had been set by Senator McCarthy and others, in a sense are on the borderline of private individuals negotiating, et cetera. I understand these things. But what I am saying is that I believe that there is a mood in this country which I know you are aware of and you have been one of the strongest critics of this war for the longest time. But I think if we can talk in this legislative body about filibustering for porkbarrel programs, then we should start now to talk about filibustering for the saving of lives and of our country. [Applause.]

And this, Mr. Chairman, is what we are trying to convey.

I understand. I really am aware that there are a tremendous number of difficulties in trying to persuade the Executive to move at this time. I believe they are committed. I don't believe we can. But I hope that we are not going to have to wait until 1972 to have this decision made. And what I am suggesting is that I think this is an extraordinary enough question so that it demands an extraordinary response, and if we can't respond extraordinarily to this problem then I doubt very seriously as men on each that we will be able to respond to the other serious questions which face us. I think we have to start to consider that. This is what I am trying to say.

If this body could perhaps call for a referendum in the country or if we could perhaps move now for a vote in 3 weeks, I think the people of this country would rise up and back that. I am not saying a vote nationwide. I am talking about a vote here in Congress to cut off the funds, and a vote to perhaps pass a resolution calling on the Supreme Court to rule on the constitutionality of the war, and to do

189

the things that uphold those things which we pretend to be. That is what we are asking. I don't think we can turn our backs on that any longer, Senator.

The CHAIRMAN. Senator Symington?

WITNESS' SERVICE DECORATIONS

Senator SYMINGTON. Thank you, Mr. Chairman.

Mr. Kerry, please move your microphone. You have a Silver Star; have you not?

Mr. KERRY. Yes, I do.

Senator SYMINGTON. And a Purple Heart?

Mr. KERRY. Yes, I do.

Senator SYMINGTON. How many clusters?

Mr. KERRY. Two clusters.

Senator SYMINGTON. So you have been wounded three times.

Mr. KERRY. Yes, sir.

Senator SYMINGTON. I have no further questions, Mr. Chairman.

The CHAIRMAN. Senator Aiken. [Applause.]

NORTH VIETNAMESE AND VC ATTITUDE TOWARD DEFINITE WITHDRAWAL DATE

Senator AIKEN. Mr. Kerry, the Defense Department seems to feel that if we set a definite date for withdrawal when our forces get down to a certain level, they would be seriously in danger by the North Vietnamese and the Vietcong. Do you believe that the North Vietnamese would undertake to prevent our withdrawal from the country and attack the troops that remain there?

Mr. KERRY. Well, Senator, if I may answer you directly, I believe we are running that danger with the present course of withdrawal because the President has neglected to state to this country exactly what his response will be when we have reached the point that we do have, let us say, 50,000 support troops in Vietnam.

Senator AIKEN. I am not telling you what I think. I am telling you what the Department says.

Mr. KERRY. Yes, sir; I understand that.

Senator AIKEN. Do you believe the North Vietnamese would seriously undertake to impede our complete withdrawal?

Mr. KERRY. No, I do not believe that the North Vietnamese would and it has been clearly indicated at the Paris peace talks they would not.

Senator AIKEN. Do you think they might help carry the bags for us? [Laughter.]

Mr. KERRY. I would say they would be more prone to do that than the Army of the South Vietnamese. [Laughter.] [Applause.]

Senator AIKEN. I think your answer is ahead of my question. [Laughter.]

SAIGON GOVERNMENT'S ATTITUDE TOWARD COMPLETE WITHDRAWAL DATE

I was going to ask you next what the attitude of the Saigon government would be if we announced that we were going to withdraw our troops, say, by October 1st, and be completely out of there—air, sea, land—leaving them on their own. What do you think would be the attitude of the Saigon government under those circumstances?

190

Mr. KERRY. Well, I think if we were to replace the Thieu-Ky-Khiem regime and offer these men sanctuary somewhere, which I think this Government has an obligation to do since we created that government and supported it all along. I think there would not be any problems. The number two man at the Saigon talks to Ambassador Lam was asked by the Concerned Laymen, who visited with them in Paris last month, how long they felt they could survive if the United States would pull out and his answer was 1 week. So I think clearly we do have to face this question. But I think, having done what we have done to that country, we have an obligation to offer sanctuary to the perhaps 2,000, 3,000 people who might face, and obviously they would, we understand that, might face political assassination or something else. But my feeling is that those 3,000 who may have to leave that country——

ATTITUDE OF SOUTH VIETNAMESE ARMY AND PEOPLE TOWARD WITHDRAWAL

Senator AIKEN. I think your 3,000 estimate might be a little low because we had to help 800,000 find sanctuary from North Vietnam after the French lost at Dienbienphu. But assuming that we resettle the members of the Saigon government, who would undoubtedly be in danger, in some other area, what do you think would be the attitude of the large, well-armed South Vietnamese army and the South Vietnamese people? Would they be happy to have us withdraw or what?

Mr. KERRY. Well, Senator, this obviously is the most difficult question of all, but I think that at this point the United States is not really in a position to consider the happiness of those people as pertains to the army in our withdrawal. We have to consider the happiness of the people as pertains to the life which they will be able to lead in the next few years.

If we don't withdraw, if we maintain a Korean-type presence in South Vietnam, say 50,000 troops or something, with strategic bombing raids from Guam and from Japan and from Thailand dropping these 15,000 pound fragmentation bombs on them, et cetera, in the next few years, then what you will have is a people who are continually oppressed, who are continually at warfare, and whose problems will not at all be solved because they will not have any kind of representation.

The war will continue. So what I am saying is that yes, there will be some recrimination but far, far less than the 200,000 a year who are murdered by the United States of America, and we can't go around—President Kennedy said this, many times. He said that the United States simply can't right every wrong, that we can't solve the problems of the other 94 percent of mankind. We didn't go into East Pakistan; we didn't go into Czechoslovakia. Why then should we feel that we now have the power to solve the internal political struggles of this country?

We have to let them solve their problems while we solve ours and help other people in an altruistic fashion commensurate with our capacity. But we have extended that capacity; we have exhausted that capacity, Senator. So I think the question is really moot.

Senator AIKEN. I might say I asked those questions several years ago, rather ineffectively. But what I would like to know now is if we, as we complete our withdrawal and, say, get down to 10,000, 20,000,

191

30,000 or even 50,000 troops there, would there be any effort on the part of the South Vietnamese government or the South Vietnamese army, in your opinion, to impede their withdrawal?

Mr. KERRY. No; I don't think so, Senator.

Senator AIKEN. I don't see why North Vietnam should object.

Mr. KERRY. I don't for the simple reason, I used to talk with officers about their—we asked them, and one officer took great pleasure in playing with me in the sense that he would say, "Well, you know you Americans, you come over here for 1 year and you can afford, you know, you go to Hong Kong for R. & R. and if you are a good boy you get another R. & R. or something you know. You can afford to charge bunkers, but I have to try and be here for 30 years and stay alive." And I think that that really is the governing principle by which those people are now living and have been allowed to live because of our mistake. So that when we in fact state, let us say, that we will have a ceasefire or have a coalition government, most of the 2 million men you often hear quoted under arms, most of whom are regional popular reconnaissance forces, which is to say militia, and a very poor militia at that, will simply lay down their arms, if they haven't done so already, and not fight. And I think you will find they will respond to whatever government evolves which answers their needs, and those needs quite simply are to be fed, to bury their dead in plots where their ancestors lived, to be allowed to extend their culture, to try and exist as human beings. And I think that is what will happen.

I can cite many, many instances, sir, as in combat when these men refused to fight with us, when they shot with their guns over tin this area like this and their heads turned facing the other way. When we were taken under fire we Americans, supposedly fighting with them, and pinned down in a ditch, and I was in the Navy and this was pretty unconventional, but when we were pinned down in a ditch recovering bodies or something and they refused to come in and help us, point blank refused. I don't believe they want to fight, sir.

OBLIGATION TO FURNISH ECONOMIC ASSISTANCE

Senator AIKEN. Do you think we are under obligation to furnish them with extensive economic assistance?

Mr. KERRY. Yes, sir. I think we have a very definite obligation to make extensive reparations to the people of Indochina.

Senator AIKEN. I think that is all.

The CHAIRMAN. Senator Pell.

Senator PELL. Thank you, Mr. Chairman.

As the witness knows, I have a very high personal regard for him and hope before his life ends he will be a colleague of ours in this body.

GROWTH OF OPPOSITION TO WAR

This war was really just as wrong, immoral, and unrelated to our national interests 5 years ago as it is today, and I must say I agree with you. I think it is rather poor taste for the architects of this war to now be sitting as they are in quite sacrosanct intellectual glass houses.

192

I think that this committee, and particularly Chairman Fulbright, deserve a huge debt of gratitude from you and everyone of your men who are here because when he conducted hearings some years ago when we were fighting in Vietnam. At that time the word "peace" was a dirty word. It was tied in with "appeasement" and Nervous Nellies and that sort of thing. Chairman Fulbright and this committee really took public opinion at that time and turned it around and made "peace" a respectable word and produced the climate that produced President Johnson's abdication.

The problem is that the majority of the people in the Congress still don't agree with the view that you and we have. As the chairman pointed out, and as you know as a student of political science, whenever we wanted to end this war, we could have ended this war if the majority of us had used the power of the purse strings. That was just as true 5 years ago as it is today.

I don't think it is a question of guts. We didn't have the desire to do that and I am not sure the majority has the desire to do that yet. Whenever we want to as a Congress, we could do it. We can't start an action, but we can force an action with the purse strings.

I think it is wonderful you veterans have come down here as a cutting edge of public opinion because you again make this have more respect and I hope you succeed and prevail on the majority of the Congress.

VOTING OF VETERANS AND NONVETERANS CONCERNING VIETNAM WAR

It is interesting, speaking of veterans and speaking of statistics, that the press has never picked up and concentrated on quite interesting votes in the past. In those votes you find the majority of hawks were usually nonveterans and the majority of doves were usually veterans. Specifically, of those who voted in favor of the Hatfield-McGovern end-the-war amendment in the last session of the Congress 79 percent were veterans with actual military service. Of those voting against the amendment, only 36 percent were veterans.

Now on the sponsors of the Cooper-Church amendment you will find very much the same statistics. Eighty-two percent were veterans as compared to 71 percent of the Senate as a whole being veterans. So I would hope what you are doing will have an effect on the Congress.

OBLIGATION TO SOUTH VIETNAMESE ALLIES

I have two questions I would like to ask you. First, I was very much struck by your concern with asylum because now I see public opinion starting to swing and Congress passing legislation. Before they wouldn't get out at all; now they are talking about getting out yesterday. When it comes to looking after the people who would be killed if we left or badly ruined, I would hope you would develop your thinking at little bit to make sure that American public opinion, which now wants to get out, also bears in mind that when we depart we have an obligation to these people. I hope you will keep to that point.

193

ACTIONS OF LIEUTENANT CALLEY

Finally, in connection with Lieutenant Calley, which is a very emotional issue in this country, I was struck by your passing reference to that incident.

Wouldn't you agree with me though that what he did in herding old men, women and children into a trench and then shooting them was a little bit beyond the perimeter of even what has been going on in this war and that that action should be discouraged. There are other actions not that extreme that have gone on and have been permitted. If we had not taken action or cognizance of it, it would have been even worse. It would have indicated we encouraged this kind of action.

Mr. KERRY. My feeling, Senator, on Lieutenant Calley is what he did quite obviously was a horrible, horrible, horrible thing and I have no bone to pick with the fact that he was prosecuted. But I think that in this question you have to separate guilt from responsibility, and I think clearly the responsibiilty for what has happened there lies elsewhere.

I think it lies with the men who designed free fire zones. I think it lies with the men who encouraged body counts. I think it lies in large part with this country, which allows a young child before he reaches the age of 14 to see 12,500 deaths on television, which glorifies the John Wayne syndrome, which puts out fighting man comic books on the stands, which allows us in training to do calisthenics to four counts, on the fourth count of which we stand up and shout "kill" in unison, which has posters in barracks in this country with a crucified Vietnamese, blood on him, and underneath it says "kill the gook," and I think that clearly the responsibility for all of this is what has produced this horrible abberation.

Now, I think if you are going to try Lieutenant Calley then you must at the same time, if this country is going to demand respect for the law, you must at the same time try all those other people who have responsibility, and any aversion that we may have to the verdict as veterans is not to say that Calley should be freed, not to say that he is innocent, but to say that you can't just take him alone, and that would be my response to that.

Senator PELL. I agree with you. The guilt is shared by many, many, many of us, including the leaders of the get-out-now school. But in this regard if we had not tried him, I think we would be much more criticized and should be criticized. I would think the same fate would probably befall him as befell either Sergeant or Lieutenant Schwarz of West Virginia who was tried for life for the same offense and is out on a 9 months commuted sentence. By the same token I would hope the quality of mercy would be exercised in this regard for a young man who was not equipped for the job and ran amuck. But I think public opinion should think this through. We who have taken this position find ourselves very much in the minority.

Mr. KERRY. I understand that, Senator, but I think it is a very difficult thing for the public to think through faced with the facts. The fact that 18 other people indicted for the very same crime were freed

194

and the fact among those were generals and colonels. I mean this simply is not justice. That is all. It is just not justice.

Senator PELL. I guess it is the old revolutionary adage. When you see the whites of their eyes you are more guilty. This seems to be our morality as has been pointed out. If you drop a bomb from a plane, you don't see the whites of their eyes.

I agree with you with the body count. It is like a Scottish nobleman saying, "How many grouse were caught on the moor." Four or five years ago those of us who criticized were more criticized.

Thank you for being here and I wish you all success. [Applause.]

The CHAIRMAN. Senator from New Jersey.

Senator CASE. Thank you, Mr. Chairman.

STRATEGIC IMPLICATIONS OF VIETNAM WAR

Mr. Kerry, thank you too for coming. You have made more than clear something that I think always has been true: that the war never had any justification in terms of Indochina itself. I wish you would take this question a little further and touch on the larger strategic implications. It is in these larger strategic implications, if anywhere, that may be found justification for our involvement. As you know, the President said the other day that it is easy to get out and to end the war immediately.

The question is to get out and leave a reasonable chance for lasting peace. We have to look at this because the American people are going to see the issue in the terms he has defined it. I would be glad to have your comment on this matter, although I won't press you to discuss it because in a sense you have already said this is not your area.

Mr. KERRY. I do want to. I want to very much.

Senator CASE. And I would be very glad to have you do it.

Mr. KERRY. Thank you, sir. I would like to very much.

In my opinion, what we are trying to do, as the President talks about getting out with a semblance of honor is simply whitewashing ourselves. On the question of getting out with some semblance of peace, as a man who has fought there, I am trying to say that this policy has no chance for peace. You don't have a chance for peace when you arm the people of another country and tell them they can fight a war. That is not peace; that is fighting a war; that is continuing a war. That is even criminal in the sense that this country, if we are really worried about recrimination, is going to have to some day face up to the fact that we convinced a certain number of people, perhaps hundreds of thousands, perhaps there will be several million, that they could stand up to something which they couldn't and ultimately will face the recrimination of the fact that their lives in addition to all the lives at this point, will be on our conscience. I don't think it is a question of peace at all. What we are doing is very, very hypocritical in our withdrawal, and we really should face up to that.

Senator CASE. May I press you just a little further or at least raise the question on which I would ask you to comment.

Mr. KERRY. I wish you would, please.

195

INDOCHINA AND QUESTION OF WORLD PEACE

Senator CASE. I think your answer was related still to the question of Indochina, but I think the President has tried to tie in Indochina with the question of world peace.

Mr. KERRY. I would like to discuss that.

It is my opinion that the United States is still reacting in very much the 1945 mood and postwar cold-war period when we reacted to the forces which were at work in World War II and came out of it with this paranoia about the Russians and how the world was going to be divided up between the super powers, and the foreign policy of John Foster Dulles which was responsible for the creation of the SEATO treaty, which was, in fact, a direct reaction to this so-called Communist monolith. And I think we are reacting under cold-war precepts which are no longer applicable.

I say that because so long as we have the kind of strike force we have, and I am not party to the secret statistics which you gentlemen have here, but as long as we have the ones which we of the public know we have, I think we have a strike force of such capability and I think we have a strike force simply in our Polaris submarines, in the 62 or some Polaris submarines, which are constantly roaming around under the sea. And I know as a Navy man that underwater detection is the hardest kind in the world, and they have not perfected it, that we have the ability to destroy the human race. Why do we have to, therefore, consider and keep considering threats?

At any time that an actual threat is posed to this country or to the security and freedom I will be one of the first people to pick up a gun and defend it, but right now we are reacting with paranoia to this question of peace and the people taking over the world. I think if we are ever going to get down to the question of dropping those bombs most of us in my generation simply don't want to be alive afterwards because of the kind of world that it would be with mutations and the genetic probabilities of freaks and everything else.

Therefore, I think it is ridiculous to assume we have to play this power game based on total warfare. I think there will be guerrilla wars and I think we must have a capability to fight those. And we may have to fight them somewhere based on legitimate threats, but we must learn, in this country, how to define those threats and that is what I would say to this question of world peace. I think it is bogus, totally artificial. There is no threat. The Communists are not about to take over our McDonald hamburger stands. [Laughter.]

Senator, I will say this. I think that politically, historically, the one thing that people try to do, that society is structured on as a whole, is an attempt to satisfy their felt needs; and you can satisfy those needs with almost any kind of political structure, giving it one name or the other. In this name it is democratic; in others it is communism; in others it is benevolent dictatorship. As long as those needs are satisfied, that structure will exist.

But when you start to neglect those needs, people will start to demand a new structure, and that, to me, is the only threat that this country faces now, because we are not responding to the needs and we are not responding to them because we work on these old cold-war precepts and because we have not woken up to realizing what is happening in the United States of America.

Senator CASE. I thank you very much. I wanted you to have a chance to respond to the question of Indochina in a large context.

Mr. Chairman, I have just one further thing to do. Senator Javits had to go to the floor on important business, and he asked me to express his regret that he couldn't stay and also that if he had stayed he would have limited his participation to agreement with everything Senator Symington said. [Applause.]

BACKGROUND OF VIETNAM WAR

The CHAIRMAN. Mr. Kerry, I have one other aspect of this I would like to explore for a moment. I recognize you and your associates, putting it on a personal point of view, feeling the seriousness and the tragedy of the experience in Vietnam. But I am disturbed very much by the possibility that your generation may become or is perhaps already in the process of becoming disillusioned with our whole country, with our system of government. There was much said about it. You didn't say it, but others have said this. I wonder if we could explore for a moment the background of this war.

It has seemed to me that its origin was essentially a mistake in judgment, beginning with our support of the French as a colonial power, which, I believe, is the only time our country has ever done that. Always our sympathies has been with the colony. If you will recall, we urged the British to get out of Egypt and India, and we urged, many thought too vigorously, the Dutch prematurely to get out of Indonesia. I think there was much criticism that we acted prematurely in urging the Belgians to get out of the Congo. In any case, the support of the French to maintain their power was a departure from our traditional attitude toward colonial powers because of our own history.

It started in a relatively small way by our support of the French. Then one thing led to another. But these were not decisions, I believe, that involved evil motives. They were political judgments which at that time were justified by the conditions in the world. You have already referred to the fact that after World War II there was great apprehension, and I think properly. The apprehension was justified by the events, especially from Stalin's regime. There was apprehension that he would be able, and if he could he would, impose his regime by force on all of Western Europe, which could have created an extremely difficult situation which would amount to what you said a moment ago. You said if our country was really threatened, you would have no hesitancy in taking up a gun. So I think, in trying to evaluate the course of our involvement in this war, we have to take all of this into consideration. It was not a sign of any moral degradation or of bad motives. They were simply political judgments as to where our interest really was.

In retrospect I think we can say that our interest was not in supporting the French, that it was not in intervening, and it was not in undoing the Geneva Accords by the creation of SEATO, but that is all history. I am not saying this in order to try to lay the blame on anyone, but to get a perspective of our present situation, and hopefully to help, if I

197

can, you and others not to be too disillusioned and not to lose faith in the capacity of our institutions to respond to the public welfare. I believe what you and your associates are doing today certainly contributes to that, by the fact that you have taken the trouble to think these things through, and to come here. I know it is not very pleasant to do the things you have done.

While I wouldn't presume to compare my own experience, I have taken a great deal of criticism since I myself in 1965 took issue with the then President Johnson over his policies. I did what I could within my particular role in the Government to persuade both President Johnson and subsequent political leaders that this was not in the interests of our country. I did this, not because I thought they were evil men inherently or they were morally misguided, but their political judgment was wrong. All of us, of course, know that as fallible human beings we all make errors of judgment.

POSSIBILITY OF MAKING U.S. INSTITUTIONS WORK EFFECTIVELY

I think it is helpful to try to put it in perspective and not lose confidence in the basically good motives and purposes of this country. I believe in the possibility of making our institutions work effectively. I think they can be made responsive to the welfare of the people and to proper judgments. I only throw this out because I have a feeling that because of the unusual horror that has developed from this war too many people may lose confidence in our system as a whole. I know of no better system for a country as large as this, with 200-plus millions of people. No other country comparable to it in history has ever made a democratic system work.

They have all become dictatorships when they have achieved the size and complexity of this country. Only smaller countries really have made a democratic system work at all.

So I only wish to throw it out hopefully that, in spite of the tragic experiences of you and so many other people and the deaths of so many people, this system is not beyond recall and with the assistance of people like yourself and the younger generation we can get back on the track, and can make this system operate effectively.

I know that the idea of working within the system has been used so much, and many people have lost confidence that it can be done. They wish to destroy the system, to start all over, but I don't think in the history of human experience that those destructions of systems work. They usually destroy everything good as well as bad, and you have an awful lot of doing to recreate the good part and to get started again.

So I am very hopeful that the younger generation—and I am certainly getting at the end of my generation because I have been here an awfully long time—but that you younger people can find it possible to accept the system and try to make it work because I can't at the moment think of a better one given the conditions that we have in this country and the great complexity and diversity.

I really believe if we can stop this war—I certainly expect to do everything I can. I have done all I can with all my limitations. I am sure many people have thought I could do better, but I did all that I was capable of doing and what wisdom I may have has been applied

198

to it. I hope that you and your colleagues will feel the same way or at least you will accept the structure of the system and try to make it work. I can see no better alternative to offer in its place.

If I thought there was one, I would certainly propose it or try.

CAN BASIC SYSTEM BE MADE TO WORK?

Have you yourself arrived at the point where you believe that basic structural changes must be brought about in our system or do you believe it can be made to work?

Mr. KERRY. I don't think I would be here if I didn't believe that it can be made to work, but I would have to say, and one of the traits of my generation now is that people don't pretend to speak for other people in it, and I can only speak as an individual about it, but I would say that I have certainly been frustrated in the past months, very, very seriously frustrated. I have gone to businessmen all over this country asking for money for fees, and met with a varying range of comments, ranging from "You can't sell war crimes" to, "War crimes are a glut on the market" or to "well, you know we are tired now, we have tried, we can't do anything." So I have seen unresponsiveness on the racial question in this country. I see an unwillingness on the part of too many of the members of this body to respond, to take gutsy stands, to face questions other than their own reelection, to make a profile of courage, and I am—although still with faith—very, very, very full of doubt, and I am not going to quit. But I think that unless we can respond on as a great a question as the war, I seriously question how we are going to find the kind of response needed to meet questions such as poverty and hunger and questions such as birth control and so many of the things that face our society today from low income housing to schooling, to recent reaction to the Supreme Court's decision on busing.

But I will say that I think we are going to keep trying. I also agree with you, Senator. I don't see another system other than democracy, but democracy has to remain responsive. When it does not, you create the possibilities for all kinds of other systems to supplant it, and that very possibility, I think, is beginning to exist in this country.

The CHAIRMAN. That is why I ask you that. The feeling that it cannot be made responsive comes not so much from what you have said but from many different sources. I can assure you I have been frustrated too. We have lost most of our major efforts. That is we have not succeeded in getting enough votes, but there has been a very marked increase, I think, in the realization of the seriousness of the war. I think you have to keep in perspective, as I say, the size and complexity of the country itself and the difficulties of communication. This war is so far removed. The very fact, as you have said, you do not believe what happens there to be in the vital interests of this country, has from the beginning caused many people to think it wasn't so important.

GRADUAL DEVELOPMENT OF CONCERN ABOUT VIETNAM WAR

In the beginning, back in the times that I mentioned when we first supported the French and throughout the 1950's up until the 1960's, this whole matter was not very much on the minds of anybody in the Congress. We were more preoccupied with what was going on in West-

199

ern Europe, the fear, particularly during Stalin's time, that he might be able to subjugate all of Western Europe, which would have been a very serious challenge to us. This grew up almost as a peripheral matter without anyone taking too much notice until the 1960's. The major time when the Congress, I think, really became concerned about the significance of the war was really not before 1965, the big escalation. It was a very minor sideshow in all the things in which this country was involved until February of 1965. That was when it became a matter that, you might say, warranted and compelled the attention of the country. It has been a gradual development of our realization of just what we were into.

As I said before, I think this came about not because of bad motives but by very serious errors in political judgment as to where our interest lies and what should be done about it.

I am only saying this hopefully to at least try to enlist your consideration, of the view that in a country of this kind I don't believe there is a better alternative from a structural point of view. I think the structure of our Government is sound.

To go back to my own State certainly, leaving out now the war, its affairs are being well managed. The people are, as you may say, maybe too indifferent to this.

Mr. Kerry. As it does in Massachusetts, too.

The Chairman. I have often thought they were too indifferent to it, but they have responded to the arguments as to where our interest lies quite well, at least from my personal experience. Otherwise I would not be here. But I think there is a gradual recognition of this.

WAR'S INTERFERENCE WITH DEALING WITH OTHER PROBLEMS

I also feel that if we could finish the war completely within the reasonably near future, as some of the proposals before this committee are designed to do if we can pass them, I think the country can right itself and get back on the track, in a reasonably quick time, dealing with the problems you mentioned. We are aware and conscious of all of them.

The thing that has inhibited us in doing things about what you mention has been the war. It has been the principal obstacle to dealing with these other problems with which you are very concerned, as, I think, the Congress is. Always we are faced with the demands of the war itself. Do you realize that this country has put well over $1,000 billion into miltary affairs since World War II?

I think it now approaches $1,500 billion. It is a sum so large no one can comprehend it, but I don't think outside of this war issue there is anything fundamentally wrong with the system that cannot be righted.

If we can give our resources to those developments, I don't have any doubt myself that it can be done. Whether it will be done or not is a matter of will. It is a matter of conviction of the various people who are involved, including the younger generation.

In that connection, I may say, the recent enactment of the right of all people from 18 years up to vote is at least a step in the direction where you and your generation can have an effect.

I hope that you won't lose faith in it. I hope you will use your talents after the war is over, and it surely will be over, to then attack these other problems and to make the system work.

200

I believe it can be made to work.

Do you have anything else you would like to say?

Mr. KERRY. Would you like me to respond at all, sir?

The CHAIRMAN. If you care to.

Mr. KERRY. Well, my feeling is that if you are talking about the ideal structure of this country as it is written down in the Constitution, then you or I would not differ at all. Yes, that is an ideal structure.

DEVELOPMENTS IN UNITED STATES REQUIRING FUNDAMENTAL CHANGES

What has developed in this country, however, at this point is something quite different and that does require some fundamental changes.

I do agree with you that what happened in Vietnam was not the product of evil men seeking evil goals. It was misguided principles and judgments and other things.

However, at some point you have to stop playing the game. At some point you have to say, "All right we did make a mistake." At some point the basic human values have to come back into this system and at this moment we are so built up within it by these outside structures, other interests, for instance, government by vested power which, in fact, you and I really know it is. When a minority body comes down here to Washington with a bill, those bodies which have the funds and the ability to lobby are those which generally get it passed. If you wanted to pass a health care medical bill, which we have finally perhaps gotten to this year, we may, but in past years the AMA has been able to come down here and squash them. The American Legion has successfully prevented people like Vietnam Veterans against the War from getting their programs through the Veterans' Administration. Those bodies in existence have tremendous power.

There is one other body that has tremendous power in this country, which is a favorite topic of Vice President Agnew and I would take some agreement with him. That would be the fourth estate. The press. I think the very reason that we veterans are here today is the result partially of our inability to get our story out through the legitimate channels.

That is to say, for instance, I held a press conference here in Washington, D.C., some weeks ago with General Shoup, with General Hester, with the mother of a prisoner of war, the wife of a man who was killed, the mother of a soldier who was killed, and with a bilateral amputee, all representing the so-called silent majority, the silent so-called majority which the President used to perpetuate the war, and because it was a press conference and an antiwar conference and people simply exposing ideas we had no electronic media there.

I called the media afterward and asked them why and the answer was, from one of the networks, it doesn't have to be identified, "because, sir, news business is really partly entertainment business visually, you see, and a press conference like that is not visual."

Of course, we don't have the position of power to get our ideas out. I said, "If I take some crippled veterans down to the White House and we chain ourselves to the gates, will we get coverage?" "Oh, yes, we will cover that."

So you are reduced to a position where the only way you can get your ideas out is to stage events, because had we not staged the events, with all due respect, Senator, and I really appreciate the fact that I

201

am here obviously, and I know you are committed to this, but with all due respect I probably wouldn't be sitting at this table. You see this is the problem.

It goes beyond that. We really have a constitutional crisis in this country right now. The Constitution under test, and we are failing. We are failing clearly because the power of the Executive has become exorbitant, because Congress has not wanted to exercise its own power, and so that is going to require some very fundamental changes.

So the system itself on paper, no, it is a question of making it work, and in that I would agree with you, and I think that things are changing in a sense. I think the victory of the ABM was a tremendous boost.

The CHAIRMAN. SST.

Mr. KERRY. SST, excuse me.

The CHAIRMAN. I hope the ABM.

[Applause.]

Mr. KERRY. Wrong system.

I think the fact that certain individuals are in Congress today, particularly in the House, who several years ago could never have been. I would cite Representative Dellums and Congresswoman Abzug and Congressman Drinan and people like this. I think this is a terribly encouraging sign, and I think if nothing more, and this is really sad poetic justice, if nothing more, this war when it is over, will ultimately probably have done more to awaken the conscience of this country than any other similar thing. It may in fact be the thing that will set us on the right road.

I earnestly hope so and I join you in that.

But meanwhile, I think we still need that extraordinary response to the problem that exists and I hope that we will get it.

IMPACT OF VIETNAM WAR AND OTHERS ON CONSTITUTIONAL BALANCE

The CHAIRMAN. I am glad to hear you say that. I have the same feeling. But you must remember we have been through nearly 30 years of warfare or cold war or crises which I think have upset the balance, as you say, in our constitutional system. Senator Javits has introduced a bill with regard to the war powers in an effort to reestablish what we believe to be the constitutional system in which you say you have confidence. I introduced and we passed a commitments resolution. There are a number of others. I won't relate them all, but they are all designed to try to bring back into proper relationship the various elements in our Government. This effort is being made.

I think the culprit is the war itself. The fact we had been at war, not just the Vietnam war but others too, diverted the attention of our people from our domestic concerns and certainly eroded the role of the Congress. Under the impact of this and other wars we have allowed this distortion to develop. If we can end the war, there is no good reason why it cannot be corrected.

REPRESENTATION OF CONSTITUENCIES

You mentioned some new faces in the Congress. After all, all these people get here because of the support back home, as you know. They are simply representative of their constituents. You do accept that, I believe.

Mr. KERRY. Partially, not totally.

202

The CHAIRMAN. Why not?

Mr. KERRY. As someone who ran for office for 3½ weeks, I am aware of many of the problems involved, and in many places, you can take certain districts in New York City, the structure is such that people can't really run and represent necessarily the people. People often don't care. The apathy is so great that they believe they are being represented when in fact they are not. I think that you and I could run through a list of people in this body itself and find many who are there through the powers of the office itself as opposed to the fact they are truly representing the people. It is very easy to give the illusion of representing the people through the frank privileges which allow you to send back what you are doing here in Congress. Congressman insert so often.

You know, they gave a speech for the Polish and they gave a speech for the Irish and they gave a speech for this, and actually handed the paper in to the clerk and the clerk submits it for the record and a copy of the record goes home and people say, "Hey, he really is doing something for me." But he isn't.

The CHAIRMAN. Well——

Mr. KERRY. Senator, we also know prior to this past year the House used to meet in the Committee of the Whole and the Committee of the Whole would make the votes, and votes not of record and people would file through, and important legislation was decided then, and after the vote came out and after people made their hacks and cuts, and the porkbarrel came out, the vote was reported and gave them an easy out and they could say "Well, I voted against this." And actually they voted for it all the time in the committee.

Some of us know that this is going on. So I would say there are problems with it. Again I come back and say they are not insoluble. They can be solved, but they can only be solved by demanding leadership, the same kind of leadership that we have seen in some countries during war time. That seems to be the few times we get it. If we could get that kind because I think we are in a constant war against ourselves and I would like to see that come—they should demand it of each other if we can demand it of people.

The CHAIRMAN. Take the two cases of what goes on in the House about the secret votes. That is not a structural aspect of our Government. That is a regulation or whatever you call it of the procedures in the House itself.

NECESSITY OF INFORMED ELECTORATE

Fundamentally you said that the people can bamboozle their constituents; they can fool them. Of course, that is quite true of any system of a representative nature. The solution to that is to inform the electorate itself to the extent that they recognize a fraud or a phony when they have one. This is not easy to do, but it is fundamental in a democracy. If you believe in a democratic system, the electorate who elect the representatives have to have sufficient capacity for discrimination. They have to be able to tell the difference between a phony, someone who simply puts pieces in the record, and someone who actually does something, so that they can recognize it in an election, if they are interested.

203

Now if they are apathetic, as you say they are apathetic, and don't care, then democracy cannot work if they continue to be apathetic and don't care who represents them. This comes back to a fundamental question of education through all different resources, not only the formal education but the use of the media and other means to educate them. Our Founding Fathers recognized that you couldn't have a democracy without an informed electorate. It comes back to the informing of the electorate; doesn't it? That is not a structural deficiency in our system. You are dealing now with the deficiencies of human nature, the failure of their education and their capacity for discrimination in the selection of their representatives.

I recognize this is difficult. All countries have had this same problem and so long as they have a representative system this has to be met. But there is no reason why it cannot be met.

A structural change does not affect the capacity of the electorate to choose good representatives; does it?

COST OF ELECTION CAMPAIGNS

Mr. KERRY. Well, no, sir; except for the fact that to run for representative in any populated area costs about $50,000. Many people simply don't have that available, and in order to get it inevitably wind up with their hands tied.

The CHAIRMAN. That is a common statement, but we had an example during this last year of a man being elected because he walked through Florida with a minimum of money. As he became attractive to the people he may have received more, but he started without money. You are familiar with Mr. Chiles.

Mr. KERRY. Yes, I am familiar. I understand it.

The CHAIRMAN. I know in my own state, our Governor started without any money or with just himself and came from nowhere and defeated a Rockefeller. So it is not true that you have to have a lot of money to get elected. If you have the other things that it takes, personality, the determination and the intelligence, it is still possible. There were other examples, but those are well known. I don't think it is correct to say you have to have a lot of money. It helps, of course. It makes it easier and all that, but it isn't essential. I think you can cite many examples where that is true.

ESSENTIAL QUESTION WILL BE RESPONSE TO VIETNAM ISSUE

Mr. KERRY. Senator, I would basically agree with what you are saying and obviously we could find exceptions to parts of everything everywhere and I understand really the essential question is going to be the response to the issue of Vietnam.

The CHAIRMAN. I agree with that. I can assure you that this committee and, certainly, I are going to do everything we can. That is what these hearings are about. It is just by coincidence you came to Washington in the very midst of them. We only opened these hearings on Tuesday of this week. I personally believe that the great majority of all the people of this country are in accord with your desire, and certainly mine, to get the war over at the earliest possible moment. All we are concerned with at the moment is the best procedure to bring that

204

about, the procedure to persuade the President to take the steps that will bring that about. I for one have more hope now than I had at any time in the last 6 years because of several things you have mentioned. I think there is a very good chance that it will be brought about in the reasonably near future.

COMMENDATION OF VIETNAM VETERANS AGAINST THE WAR

I think you and your associates have contributed a great deal in the actions you have taken. As I said in the beginning, the fact that you have shown both great conviction and patience about this matter and at the same time conducted yourself in the most commendable manner has been the most effective demonstration, if I may use that word. Although you have demonstrated in the sense that has become disapproved of in some circles, I think you have demonstrated in the most proper way and the most effective way to bring about the results that you wish and I believe you have made a great contribution.

I apologize. I am not trying to lecture you about our Government. I have just been disturbed, not so much by you as by other things that have happened, that the younger generation has lost faith in our system. I don't think it is correct. I think the paranoia to which you referred has been true. It arose at a time when there was reason for it perhaps, but we have long since gone out of that time, and I think your idea of timing is correct. But I congratulate you and thank you very much for coming. [Applause.]

Senator Symington would like to ask a question.

Senator SYMINGTON. Yes. Mr. Kerry, I had to leave because we are marking up the selective service bill in the Armed Services Committee. But I will read the record.

ATTITUDE OF SERVICEMEN TOWARD CONGRESSIONAL OPPOSITION TO WAR

The staff has a group of questions here, four of which I would ask. Over the years members of this committee who spoke out in opposition to the war were often accused of stabbing our boys in the back. What, in your opinion, is the attitude of servicemen in Vietnam about congressional opposition to the war?

Mr. KERRY. If I could answer that, it is very difficult, Senator, because I just know, I don't want to get into the game of saying I represent everybody over there, but let me try to say as straightforwardly as I can, we had an advertisement, ran full page, to show you what the troops read. It ran in Playboy and the response to it within two and a half weeks from Vietnam was 1,200 members. We received initially about 50 to 80 letters a day from troops there. We now receive about 20 letters a day from troops arriving at our New York office. Some of these letters—and I wanted to bring some down, I didn't know we were going to be testifying here and I can make them available to you—are very, very moving, some of them written by hospital corpsmen on things, on casualty report sheets which say, you know, "Get us out of here." "You are the only hope we have got." "You have got to get us back; it is crazy." We received recently 80 members of the 101st Airborne signed up in one letter. Forty members from a helicopter assault squadron, crash and rescue mission signed up in another one.

I think they are expressing, some of these troops, solidarity with us,

205

right now by wearing black arm bands and Vietnam Veterans Against the War buttons. They want to come out and I think they are looking at the people who want to try to get them out as a help.

However, I do recognize there are some men who are in the military for life. The job in the military is to fight wars. When they have a war to fight, they are just as happy in a sense, and I am sure that these men feel they are being stabbed in the back. But, at the same time, I think to most of them the realization of the emptiness, the hollowness, the absurdity of Vietnam has finally hit home, and I feel if they did come home the recrimination would certainly not come from the right, from the military. I don't think there would be that problem.

Senator SYMINGTON. Thank you.

Has the fact Congress has never passed a declaration of war undermined the morale of U.S. servicemen in Vietnam, to the best of your knowledge?

Mr. KERRY. Yes; it has clearly and to a great, great extent.

USE OF DRUGS BY U.S. SERVICEMEN IN VIETNAM

Senator SYMINGTON. There have been many reports of widespread use of drugs by U.S. servicemen in Vietnam. I might add I was in Europe last week and the growth of that problem was confirmed on direct questioning of people in the military. How serious is the problem and to what do you attribute it?

Mr. KERRY. The problem is extremely serious. It is serious in very many different ways. I believe two Congressmen today broke a story. I can't remember their names. There were 35,000 or some men, heroin addicts that were back.

The problem exists for a number of reasons, not the least of which is the emptiness. It is the only way to get through it. A lot of guys, 60, 80 percent stay stoned 24 hours a day just to get through the Vietnam——

Senator SYMINGTON. You say 60 to 80 percent.

Mr. KERRY. Sixty to 80 percent is the figure used that try something, let's say, at one point. Of that, I couldn't give you a figure of habitual smokers, let's say, of pot, and I certainly couldn't begin to say how many are hard drug addicts, but I do know that the problem for the returning veteran is acute because we have, let's say, a veteran picks up a $12 habit in Saigon. He comes back to this country and the moment he steps off an airplane that same habit costs him some $90 to support. With the state of the economy, he can't get a job. He doesn't earn money. He turns criminal or just finds his normal sources and in a sense drops out.

The alienation of the war, the emptiness of back and forth, all combined adds to this. There is no real drug rehabilitation program. I know the VA hospital in New York City has 20 beds allocated for drug addicts; 168 men are on the waiting list, and I really don't know what a drug addict does on the waiting list.

And just recently the same hospital gave three wards to New York University for research purposes.

It is very, very widespread. It is a very serious problem. I think that this Congress should undertake to investigate the sources because I heard many implications of Madam Ky and others being involved in the traffic and I think there are some very serious things here at stake.

206

Senator SYMINGTON. In the press there was a woman reporter. I think her name was Emerson. In any case she stated she bought drugs six or nine times openly, heroin, in a 15-mile walk from Saigon. The article had a picture of a child with a parasol and a parrot. She said this child was one of the people from whom she had bought, herself, these drugs; and that the cost of the heroin was from $3 to $6.

If we are over there, in effect, protecting the Thieu-Ky government, why is it that this type and character of sale of drugs to anybody, including our own servicemen, can't be controlled?

Mr. KERRY. It is not controllable in this country. Why should it be controllable in that country?

Senator SYMINGTON. It isn't quite that open in this country; do you think?

Mr. KERRY. It depends on where you are. [Applause.]

Senator SYMINGTON. We are talking about heroin, not pot, or LSD.

Mr. KERRY. I understand that, but if you walk up 116th Street in Harlem I am sure somebody can help you out pretty fast. [Laughter.]

ACCURACY OF INFORMATION THROUGH OFFICIAL MILITARY CHANNELS

Senator SYMINGTON. Mr. Kerry, from your experience in Vietnam do you think it is possible for the President or Congress to get accurate and undistorted information through official military channels.

(Shouts of "No" from the audience.)

Mr. KERRY. I don't know——

Senator SYMINGTON. I am beginning to think you have some supporters here.

Mr. KERRY. I don't know where they came from, sir, maybe Vietnam.

I had direct experience with that. Senator, I had direct experience with that and I can recall often sending in the spot reports which we made after each mission, and including the GDA, gunfire damage assessments, in which we would say, maybe 15 sampans sunk or whatever it was. And I often read about my own missions in the Stars and Stripes and the very mission we had been on had been doubled in figures and tripled in figures.

The intelligence missions themselves are based on very, very flimsy information. Several friends of mine were intelligence officers and I think you should have them in sometime to testify. Once in Saigon I was visiting this friend of mine and he gave me a complete rundown on how the entire intelligence system should be re-set up on all of its problems, namely, that you give a young guy a certain amount of money, he goes out, sets up his own contacts under the table, gets intelligence, comes in. It is not reliable; everybody is feeding each other double intelligence, and I think that is what comes back to this country.

I also think men in the military, sir, as do men in many other things, have a tendency to report what they want to report and see what they want to see. And this is a very serious thing because I know on several visits—Secretary Laird came to Vietnam once and they staged an entire invasion for him. When the initial force at Dang Tam, it was the 9th Infantry when it was still there—when the initial recon platoon went out and met with resistance, they changed the entire operation the night before and sent them down into the South China Seas so they would not run into resistance and the Secretary would have a chance to see how smoothly the war was going.

207

I know General Wheeler came over at one point and a major in Saigon escorted him around. General Wheeler went out to the field and saw 12 pacification leaders and asked about 10 of them how things were going and they all said, "It is really going pretty badly." The 11th one said, "It couldn't be better, General. We are really doing the thing here to win the war." And the General said, "I am finally glad to find somebody who knows what he is talking about." (Laughter.)

This is the kind of problem that you have. I think that the intelligence which finally reaches the White House does have serious problems with it in that I think you know full well, I know certainly from my experience, I served as aide to an admiral in my last days in the Navy before I was discharged, and I have seen exactly what the response is up the echelon, the chain of command, and how things get distorted and people say to the man above him what is needed to be said, to keep everybody happy, and so I don't—I think the entire thing is distorted.

It is just a rambling answer.

Senator SYMINGTON. How do you think this could be changed?

Mr. KERRY. I have never really given that spect of it all that much thought. I wish I had this intelligence officer with me. He is a very intelligent young man.

REPORTING OF VIETNAM WAR IN THE PRESS

Senator SYMINGTON. There has been considerable criticism of the war's reporting by the press and news media. What are your thoughts on that?

Mr. KERRY. On that I could definitely comment. I think the press has been extremely negligent in reporting. At one point and at the same time they have not been able to report because the Government of this country has not allowed them to. I went to Saigon to try to report. We were running missions in the Mekong Delta. We were running raids through these rivers on an operation called Sealord and we thought it was absurd.

We didn't have helicopter cover often. We seldom had jet aircraft cover. We were out of artillery range. We would go in with two quarter-inch aluminum hull boats and get shot at and never secure territory or anything except to quote Admiral Zumwalt to show the American flag and prove to the Vietcong they don't own the rivers. We found they did own them with 60 percent casualties and we thought this was absurd.

I went to Saigon and told this to a member of the news bureau there and I said, "Look, you have got to tell the American people this story." The response was, "Well, I can't write that kind of thing. I can't criticize that much because if I do I would lose my accreditation, and we have to be very careful about just how much we say and when."

We are holding a press conference today, as a matter of fact, at the National Press Building—it might be going on at this minute—in which public information officers who are members of our group, and former Army reporters, are going to testify to direct orders of censorship in which they had to take out certain pictures, phrases they couldn't use and so on down the line and, in fact, the information they gave newsmen and directions they gave newsmen when an operation was going on when the military didn't want the press informed

208

on what was going on they would offer them transportation to go
someplace else, there is something else happened and they would fly a
guy 55 miles from where the operation was. So the war has not been
reported correctly.

I know from a reporter of Time—showed the massacre of 150 Cam-
bodians, these were South Vietnamese troops that did it, but there
were American advisers present and he couldn't even get other newsmen to get it out let alone his own magazine, which doesn't need to be
named here. So it is a terrible problem, and I think that really it
is a question of the Government allowing free ideas to be exchanged
and if it is going to fight a war then fight it correctly. The only people
who can prevent My Lais are the press and if there is something to
hide perhaps we shouldn't be there in the first place.

Senator SYMINGTON. Thank you, Mr. Chairman.

[Applause.]

REQUEST FOR LETTERS SENT TO VIETNAM VETERANS AGAINST WAR

The CHAIRMAN. With regard to the letters you have mentioned, I
wondered about them. I have received a great many letters, but usually
particularly in those from Vietnam, the men would say that they
would not like me to use them or use their names for fear of retaliation. Of course, I respected their request. If you have those letters, it
might be interesting, if you would like to, and if the writer has no
objection, to submit them for the record which would be for the information of the committee.

CHANGING MOOD OF TROOPS IN VIETNAM

Mr. KERRY. Senator, I would like to add a comment on that. You
see the mood is changing over there and a search and destroy mission
is a search and avoid mission, and troops don't—you know, like that
revolt that took place that was mentioned in the New York Times
when they refused to go in after a piece of dead machinery, because
it didn't have any value. They are making their own judgments.

There is a GI movement in this country now as well as over there,
and soon these people, these men, who are prescribing wars for these
young men to fight are going to find out they are going to have to find
some other men to fight them because we are going to change prescrip-
tions. They are going to have to change doctors, because we are not
going to fight for them. That is what they are going to realize. There
is now a more militant attitude even within the military itself, among
these soldiers evidenced by the advertisements recently in the New
York Times in which members of the First Air Cavalry publicly
signed up and said, "We would march on the 24th if we could be there,
but we can't because we are in Vietnam." Those men are subject obviously to some kind of discipline, but people are beginning to be willing to submit to that. And I would just say, yes, I would like to enter
the letters in testimony when I can get hold of them and I think you
are going to see this will be a continuing thing.

(As of the date of publication the information referred to had not
been received.)

The CHAIRMAN. If you would like to we can incorporate some of
them in the record.

209

DOCUMENTARY ENTITLED "THE SELLING OF THE PENTAGON"

This is inspired by your reply to the Senator from Missouri's question. Did you happen to see a documentary called, "The Selling of the Pentagon"?

Mr. KERRY. Yes, I did. I thought it was the most powerful and persuasive and helpful documentary in recent years.

The CHAIRMAN. But you know what happened to CBS? They have been pilloried by the——

Mr. KERRY. They are doing all right.

The CHAIRMAN. You think they can defend themselves?

Mr. KERRY. I think they have; yes, sir. I think the public opinion in this country believes that, "The Selling of the Pentagon." I was a public information officer before I went to Vietnam, and I know that those things were just the way they said because I conducted several of those tours on a ship, and I have seen my own men wait hours until people got away, and I have seen cooks put on special uniforms for them.

I have seen good food come out for the visitors and everything else. It really happens.

The CHAIRMAN. The Senator from New York has returned. Would he care to ask a question?

RESOLUTION CONCERNING VIETNAM VETERANS' ENCAMPMENT

Senator JAVITS. I don't want to delay either the witness or the committee. Senator Case was tied up on the floor on your resolution on the encampment and the expected occurred, of course. It has gone to the calendar.

Senator SYMINGTON. If you will yield, Senator. I have to preside at 1 o'clock. I thank you for your testimony.

Mr. KERRY. Thank you, Senator. [Applause.]

Senator JAVITS. It has gone to the calendar but I think the point has been very well made by, I think, the total number of sponsors. There were some 27 Senators.

WITNESS' CREDENTIALS

Senator Case was kind enough to express my view. I wish to associate myself with the statement Senator Symington made when I was here as to your credentials. That is what we always think about with a witness and your credentials couldn't be higher.

The moral and morale issues you have raised will have to be finally acted upon by the committee. I think it always fires us to a deeper sense of emergency and dedication when we hear from a young man like yourself in what we know to be the reflection of the attitude of so many others who have served in a way which the American people so clearly understand. It is not as effective unless you have those credentials. The kind you have.

The only other thing I would like to add is this:

210

EVALUATION OF TESTIMONY

I hope you will understand me and I think you will agree with me. Your testimony about what you know and what you see, how you feel and how your colleagues feel, is entitled to the highest standing and priority. When it comes to the bits and pieces of information, you know, like you heard that Madam Ky is associated with the sale of narcotics or some other guy got a good meal, I hope you will understand as Senators and evaluators of testimony we have to take that in the context of many other things, but I couldnt think of anybody whose testimony I would rather have and act on from the point of view of what this is doing to our young men we are sending over there, how they feel about it, what the impact is on the conscience of a country, what the impact is on even the future of the military services from the point of view of the men who served, than your own.

Thank you very much.

Mr. KERRY. Thank you, Senator. [Applause.]

The CHAIRMAN. Mr. Kerry, I am sure you can sense the committee members appreciate very much your coming. Do you have anything further to say before we recess?

EXPRESSION OF APPRECIATION

Mr. KERRY. No, sir; I would just like to say on behalf of the Vietnam Veterans Against the War that we do appreciate the efforts made by the Senators to put that resolution on the floor, to help us, help us in their offices in the event we were arrested and particularly for the chance to express the thoughts that I have put forward today. I appreciate it.

The CHAIRMAN. You have certainly done a remarkable job of it. I can't imagine their having selected a better representative or spokesman.

Thank you very much. [Applause.]

(Whereupon, at 1 p.m. the committee was adjourned subject to the call of the Chair.)

ACKNOWLEDGMENTS

I'm tremendously blessed to be associated with Eagle and Regnery Publishing. I stumbled into the publishing world a little over two years ago thanks to the trust and tutelage of Mr. Al Regnery, now publisher for The *American Spectator*. It has been my honor and pleasure from that day on to work with Jeff Carneal, Marji Ross, Harry Crocker, Paula Decker, and Patricia Jackson. They are absolutely the best. I thank Al Regnery for having the trust and patience to give me a shot. I thank Jeff and Marji for their continued faith, confidence, and honest consideration. I thank Harry and Paula for their editorial expertise, wise counsel, and the occasionally needed vector change. Harry's thrown me some curve balls and I, in turn, have thrown them at Paula. Hopefully, we hit the curve as well as we hit the fastball. I thank Patricia for taking care of me, the media, and speaking engagements with professional devotion and a personal touch.

I wrote my first book, *Dereliction of Duty*, motivated to understand my experiences and observations while serving in the Clinton White House. I also felt an obligation to deliver a message I thought all Americans should hear clearly, despite the cacophony of elite media spin and bias, that of failed leadership at the highest level of our government. I write *Reckless Disregard* with much more concern for my country, for the challenges we face in this post–September 11 world, and, most importantly, for the men and women of the United States armed forces, the greatest military on earth.

231

As a military officer, I was trained not to voice my political opinions and was legally constrained from doing so. As a retired officer, I've realized that it's essential for our military to have a voice. Now, more than ever, it's important for Americans to more fully understand the lives and sacrifices of our soldiers, sailors, airmen, and Marines within the political context. For it is our military "whom we shall send" in this war for the preservation of our way of life.

I salute every man and woman of the 2.3 million currently serving on active duty, in the National Guard or the Reserves, and all of their families. While I can't speak with depth to the life and experience of the soldier, sailor, and Marine, I pray I captured their spirit, their strength, and their will. For the airmen, I'm proud to have been counted in your numbers. Huuah! Fair winds and following seas! Fly Safe! Semper Fi!

I'm deeply indebted to my parents, Bob and Sandy Patterson. My father, Major General Bob Patterson, taught me how to lead and how to take care of my troops, and showed me the way. My mother is the other half of the military family service commitment. She raised my brother, sister, and me while my dad was leading men and fighting wars. My brother, Mike, and sister, Kris, and their families have been undyingly supportive. I love you all.

I'm also thankful to my wife's family, Phil and Christie LaGrow, Russ, Becca, and Jackie. When I asked Phil and Chris for their daughter's hand, they opened their hearts and their home. They've been loving, supportive, and a constant source of counsel.

Most especially, I want to thank my beautiful wife, Nichole, and our children, Kylie and Tanner. Nichole is my angel who supports me in every endeavor and raises our children when their father is sequestered in a library or yelling at his computer. She is the other half of this writing experience and I love her deeply. Kylie and Tanner are my daily reminders that our God is a great and loving God.

Chapter 1
A Soldier Knows

1. Testimony of John F. Kerry, Legislative Proposals Relating to the War in Southeast Asia, United States Senate, Committee on Foreign Relations, Washington, D.C., April 22, 1971.
2. Nick Anderson, "Buoyant Kerry Embraces Role of Frontrunner," *Los Angeles Times*, February 4, 2004.
3. *This Week*, ABC, February 1, 2004.

Chapter 2
The Politics of Treason I

1. J. Michael Waller, "Kerry Exploits Vets for Hanoi," *Insight* magazine, March 16, 2004.
2. Michael Kranish, "Kerry Faces Questions Over Purple Heart," *Boston Globe*, April 14, 2004.
3. Ibid.
4. Byron York, "Kerry Purple Heart Doc Speaks Out," *National Review*, May 4, 2004.
5. Kranish, "Kerry Faces Questions Over Purple Heart."
6. Charles Hurt, "Records on Medals Spark Questions," *Washington Times*, April 22, 2004.
7. Stephen Crump, "Purple Hearts: Three and Out," *The Nation*, May 10, 2004.

8. Kranish, "With Antiwar Role, High Visibility," *Boston Globe*, June 17, 2003.
9. Ibid.
10. Brian Ross and Chris Vlasto, "Discarded Decorations: Videotape Contradicts John Kerry's Own Statements Over Vietnam Medals," ABCNEWS.com, April 26, 2004.
11. Marc Morano, "Kerry in 1971: 'Our Democracy is a Farce'," Newsmax.com, April 22, 2004.
12. Scott Camil, University of Florida Oral History Archive, October 20, 1992.
13. David Freddoso, "Navy Vets: Kerry Unfit to Serve," *Human Events*, May 7, 2004.

Chapter 3
The Politics of Treason II: Hillary Clinton at the Front

1. J. Michael Waller, "When Does Politics Become Treason?" *Insight* magazine, December 23, 2003.
2. Dick Morris, "Hillary's Badwill Tour," *New York Post*, December 2, 2003.
3. Kenneth R. Timmerman, "Hillary Rodham Clinton's Disloyal Opposition," *Insight* magazine, December 23, 2003.
4. Geoff Metcalf, "Were Hillary's Words Treasonous?" NewsMax.com, December 1, 2003.
5. Timmerman, "Hillary Rodham Clinton's Disloyal Opposition."
6. "Hillary: 'Right Wing Apparatus' to Blame for Troop Comment Firestorm," Newsmax.com, December 7, 2003.
7. Dan Balz, "Kerry Angers GOP in Calling For 'Regime Change'," *Washington Post*, April 4, 2003.
8. Mort Kondracke, "Gore, Dean Form 'Anti-Clinton' Party, Well Left of Center," RealClearPolitics.com, December 12, 2003.
9. Vicki Allen, "Kennedy Says Bush Broke Faith in Iraq," Reuters, January 14, 2004.

10. Lolita Baldor, "Kennedy Says Iraq War a Political Product," Associated Press, January 14, 2004.

11. Ross Mackenzie, "Observations On The War in Iraq That Was," Townhall.com, April 29, 2003.

12. Ibid.

13. "Clarke Questions Bush's Patriotism," Newsmax.com, January 13, 2004.

14. "Clarke Calls for Bush Impeachment Probe," Newsmax.com, January 18, 2004.

15. "Clarke: Bush 'Never Intended' to Get Bin Laden," Newsmax.com, January 13, 2004.

16. Waller, "Soros Resolves to Bring Bush Down," *Insight* magazine, December 9, 2003.

17. Waller, "Victories in the War Against Terrorism," *Insight* magazine, November 11, 2003.

18. Diana West, "Fighting Terror," *Washington Times*, April 2, 2004.

Chapter 4
The Politics of Treason III: The Only Spending Liberals Hate

1. Richard W. Stevenson and Adam Nagourney, "Bush's Campaign Emphasizes Role of Leader in War," *New York Times*, March 17, 2004.

2. Transcript of President Bush's remarks, CBS News, September 7, 2003.

3. Susan Milligan, "Among the White House Hopefuls, It's 3 Opposed, 2 in Favor," *Boston Globe*, October 18, 2003.

4. "Kerry Voted Against Body Armor for U.S. Troops," Newsmax.com, March 8, 2004.

5. Chad Allen, "The Only Spending Democrats Hate," *Washington Dispatch*, September 12, 2003.

6. Ibid.

7. Dave Eberhart, "Kerry on the Record: Bashing Reagan," Newsmax.com, March 15, 2004.

8. Ibid.

9. Joshua Muravchik, "Kerry's Inner Dove," *Washington Post*, February 23, 2004.

10. S.3189, Congressional Quarterly Vote #273, October 15, 1990.

11. Charles R. Smith, "Kerry's Real Defense Record," Newsmax.com, March 4, 2004.

12. Senate Congressional Resolution 106.

13. John Solomon, "Kerry's 1994 Effort to Cut Defense Eyed," Associated Press, March 19, 2004.

14. Ibid.

15. Ibid.

16. Eberhart, "Kerry on the Record: Bashing Reagan."

17. Smith, "Kerry's Real Defense Record."

18. Charles Hurt, "Kerry Opposed Key Weapons," *Washington Times*, February 24, 2004.

19. "The 1994 Kerry Amendment," *Washington Times*, April 1, 2004.

20. Barbara Comstock, "Leading to Disaster," *National Review*, March 10, 2004.

21. Ibid.

22. Matthew Continetti, "The Many Faces of Kerry," *Weekly Standard*, February 9, 2004.

Chapter 5
Where Have All the Flowers Gone?

1. Mary Hynes, "Ace in the Hole: A Special Welcome for Pilot Ace Steve Ritchie," *Las Vegas Review Journal*, April 25, 1997.

2. Brad Wright and Jennifer Yuille, "Kennedy: Iraq is George Bush's Vietnam," CNN.com, April 6, 2004.

3. Max Cleland, "Mistakes of Vietnam Repeated with Iraq," *Atlanta Journal-Constitution*, September 18, 2003.

4. Robert L. Bartley, "Iraq: Another Vietnam?" *Wall Street Journal*, November 3, 2003.

5. Mona Charen, *Useful Idiots: How Liberals Got It Wrong in the Cold War and Still Blame America First* (Washington, D.C.: Regnery, 2003), 42.

6. Daniel Henninger, "Primary Democrats Find Perfect Vessel in John Kerry," *Wall Street Journal*, February 13, 2004.

7. Stephen Young, "How North Vietnam Won the War," *Wall Street Journal*, August 3, 1995.

8. Ibid.

9. Ibid.

10. David Horowitz, "How the Left Undermined America's Security Before 9/11," FrontPageMagazine.com, March 24, 2004.

11. Ibid.

12. For more on the point, see Brandon Crocker, "What Really Matters": http://www.spectator.org/dsp_article.asp?art_id=6545

13. John Podhoretz, "Beyond the Pale—Trashing the Troops for Political Points," *New York Post*, May 11, 2004.

14. Les Blumenthal, "Senators Decry Abuse of Prisoners in Iraq," *News Tribune*, May 5, 2004.

15. David Gelernter, "It's America's War," *Weekly Standard*, May 24, 2004.

16. Jeff Jacoby, "The Images We See—and Those We Don't," *Boston Globe*, May 13, 2004.

17. John Kerry for President, fund-raising e-mail, May 7, 2004.

Chapter 6
War Torn: The Liberals' War with the U.S. Military

1. Sophocles, *Oedipus at Colonus*.

2. Interview with USAF lieutenant, February 28, 2004.

3. Thomas E. Ricks, "Challenging of Overseas Ballots Widens Divide Between Military, Democrats," *Washington Post*, November 21, 2000.

4.   Tom Donnelly, "Why Soldiers Dislike Democrats: In the Mythology of Military Life, the Democratic Party is the Enemy," *Weekly Standard*, December 4, 2000.

5.   Matthew Continetti, "One Soldier, One Vote," *National Review Online*, September 3, 2002.

6.   Harold Kennedy, "Study Probes Civilian-Military Disconnect," *National Defense*, August 2000.

7.   Byron York, "Don't the Democrats Care Even a Little About Terrorism?" *The Hill*, October 23, 2003.

8.   William J. Bennett, "The Democratic Party and the Politics of War," The Claremont Institute, March 15, 2004.

9.   Joseph Curl, "Clinton Calls Terror a U.S. Debt to Pay," *Washington Times*, November 8, 2001.

10.   "Clinton's National Security Policy: A Critique," Empower America Issue Briefing.

Chapter 7
Desert Tortoise or GI Joe?

1.   Somerset Maugham, *Then As Now* (New York: Doubleday, 1948).

2.   Linda de France, "Navy Leader Blasts Environmentalists for Activism, Training Restrictions," *Aerospace Daily*, April 18, 2001.

3.   Ibid.

4.   "Rev. Jackson to Conduct 'Free Vieques Rally' at St. Cecilia Church in NY," *Oakland Post*, September 19, 1999.

5.   Brad Knickerbocker, "Military Gets Break From Environmental Rules," *Christian Science Monitor*, November 24, 2003.

6.   Harold Kennedy, "Military Training Gets Break From Environmental Rules," *National Defense*, August 2003.

7.   Testimony of Deputy Assistant Secretary (Installations and Facilities) Wayne Arny, U.S. Navy, before the U.S. House of Representatives Subcommittee on Readiness, Armed Services Committee, Washington, D.C., March 13, 2003.

8. Knickerbocker, "Military Gets Break From Environmental Rules."

Chapter 8
The Clinton Catastrophe I: The Anti-Military Presidency

1. "International Perspectives," *Newsweek*, December 11, 2000.

2. Rich Lowry, *Legacy: Paying the Price for the Clinton Years* (Washington, D.C.: Regnery, 2003), 251.

3. Phil Brennan, "David Horowitz: How Democrats Undermined America's Security," Newsmax.com, July 18, 2002.

4. Robert J. Samuelson, "The Peace Dividend," *Newsweek*, January 26, 1998.

5. Center for Military Readiness, "'Legacy Project' Launches Spin Campaign to Obscure Clinton Record on Military Readiness," January 24, 2002.

6. Anthony H. Cordesman, *The Crisis in U.S Defense Spending: A Reality Check* (Washington, D.C.: Center for Strategic and International Studies, 1999).

7. Carl von Clausewitz, *On War*, Michael Howard and Peter Paret, translators, (Princeton, N.J.: Princeton University Press, 1976).

8. David H. Hackworth, "Clinton Can Undo the Damage to the Military," *Newsweek*, June 28, 1993.

9. Major Robert L. Stephenson, "Hollow Force of the 1990s?" research report submitted to Air Command and Staff College, Maxwell AFB, Alabama, April 1999.

10. Richard Grenier, "Bill Clinton's Armchair Warriors," *Washington Times*, November 18, 1997.

11. Ibid.

12. Kingsley Browne, "Women at War: An Evolutionary Perspective," *Buffalo Law Review*, Winter 2001.

13. Walter Russell Mead, "See Bush's Strong Hand—and Raise the Ante," *Los Angeles Times*, February 1, 2004.

14. Robert L. Maginnis, "Restoring Military Morale," *The World & I*, February 1995.

15. "Hillary: Bush Should Thank Bill For Military: Insists Clinton Administration Deserves Credit for U.S. Successes," WorldNet Daily.com, February 28, 2004.

Chapter 9
The Clinton Catastrophe II: Corruption, Cowardice, and the Fraud of Richard Clarke

1. Niccolò Machiavelli, *The Prince*, 1513.
2. President Ronald Reagan, *Speaking My Mind* (New York: Simon & Schuster, 1989), 352.
3. John T. Correll, "Visionaries and Their Visions," *Air Force Magazine*, May 1990.
4. Ronald Reagan, speech delivered from the White House, March 23, 1983.
5. Austin Bay, "Prepared for War and Peace," *Houston Chronicle*, December 25, 2003.
6. Public Broadcasting System, "The American Experience: War Letters," www.pbs.org/wgbh/amex/warletters.
7. John A. Gentry, "Complex Civil-Military Operations," *Naval War College Review*, September 22, 2000.
8. William J. Taylor, "Pax Clintonia," *The World and I*, July 2001.
9. Center for Security Policy, No. 93-D 14.
10. Phil Brennan, "David Horowitz: How Democrats Undermined America's Security," Newsmax.com, July 18, 2002.
11. Norman Kempster, "Truck Bomb Kills 23 Americans at an Air Base in Saudi Arabia," *Los Angeles Times*, June 26, 1996.
12. Steve Hayward, *The Age of Reagan, 1964–1980: The Fall of the Old Liberal Order* (New York: Prima, 2001).
13. Chuck Morse, "Jimmy Carter Sold Out Iran," HenchPac, February 16, 2003, www.hench.net.
14. For an excellent and overdue account of the Carter presidency, see Steven F. Hayward's *The Real Jimmy Carter: How Our Worst Ex-President Undermines American Foreign Policy, Coddles Dicta-*

tors, and Created the Party of Clinton and Kerry (Washington, D.C.: Regnery, 2004).

15. Jeff Jacoby, "The War Didn't Begin on 9/11," *Boston Globe*, September 11, 2003.

16. Byron York, "Master of His Game," *National Review*, October 15, 2001.

17. Susan Page, "Why Clinton Failed to Stop bin Laden," *USA Today*, November 12, 2001.

18. Rich Lowry, *Legacy: Paying the Price for the Clinton Years* (Washington, D.C.: Regnery, 2003), 301.

19. "Clinton Administration Freed Bin Laden's Banker," Newsmax.com, January 4, 2004.

20. http://prorev.com/wwstats.htm. For details on these scandals see: Edward Timperlake and William C. Triplett II, *The Year of the Rat: How Bill Clinton and Al Gore Compromised U.S. Security for Chinese Cash* (Washington, D.C.: Regnery, 1998); Timperlake and Triplett II, *Red Dragon Rising: Communist China's Military Threat to America* (Washington, D.C.: Regnery, 1999); and David Limbaugh, *Absolute Power: The Legacy of Corruption in the Clinton-Reno Justice Department* (Washington, D.C.: Regnery, 2001).

21. Byron York, "Clinton Has No Clothes," *National Review*, December 17, 2001.

22. Ibid.

23. Richard Miniter, *Losing bin Laden* (Washington, D.C.: Regnery, 2003). Miniter has a remarkably accurate and complete look at the many ways the Clinton administration mishandled terrorism and bin Laden during the 1990s.

24. York, "Clinton Has No Clothes."

25. Barry Schweid, "Suspicion Centers on Bin Laden," Associated Press, October 13, 2000.

26. "Blast Kills U.S. Sailors in Likely Terrorist Attack," *Bradenton Herald*, October 13, 2000.

27. "New Attack From the Write on Bubba," *New York Daily News*, March 18, 2003.

28. John Michael Loh, General, USAF (Ret.) and Gerald Kauvar, "FAA: A Failure on Aviation Security," *Aviation Week & Space Technology*, October 8, 2001.

29. Joseph Farah, "How Gore Aborted Air Safety," WorldNet Daily.com, September 24, 2001.

30. Daniel C. Twining, "Richard Clarke is Far Tougher on the Clinton Failures Than Advertised," *Weekly Standard*, April 12, 2004.

Chapter 10
Winning: George W. Bush and the Art of Command

1. George Neumayr, "Midland Ministers to the World," The American Spectator Online: http://www.spectator.org/dsp_article.asp?art_id=5870. I am indebted to Neumayr's piece, which captures the essence of Midland values.

2. Ibid.

3. Oliver North, "Democrats for Bush," Townhall.com, January 30, 2004.

4. "Koch Explains Why He's Bolting for Bush, Newsmax.com, January 10, 2004.

5. General Douglas MacArthur, "Duty, Honor, Country," Speech to the Corps of Cadets, U.S. Military Academy, West Point, New York, May 12, 1962.

Chapter 11
Who Would Osama Vote For?

1. General Douglas MacArthur, Speech to the Corps of Cadets, U.S. Military Academy, West Point, New York, May 12, 1962.

2. Jimmy Carter, "Just War—Or Just A War?" *New York Times*, March 9, 2003.

3. Paul Jacob, "The Democratic Candidates are Too Dumb to Be President," Townhall.com, November 23, 2003.

4. Notra Trulock, "Kerry and the Unaccounted For," Newsmax.com, March 17, 2004.

5. "Al Jazeera Praises Kerry," Newsmax.com, March 16, 2004.

6. Amir Taheri, "John Kerry: The Arab Hope?" *New York Post*, March 28, 2004.

7. Kenneth R. Timmerman, "Kerry Will Abandon War on Terrorism," Insight on the News, March 16, 2004.

8. Taheri, "John Kerry: The Arab Hope?"

9. For Carter's role see Steven F. Hayward's *The Real Jimmy Carter: How Our Worst Ex-President Undermines American Foreign Policy, Coddles Dictators, and Created the Party of Clinton and Kerry* (Washington, D.C.: Regnery, 2004).

10. Michael Manville, "French Going Wild for Senator Kerry in Election Fever," *New York Sun*, March 15, 2004.

11. Ben Shapiro, "The Distinguished List of Kerry Supporters," Townhall.com, March 17, 2004.

12. Timmerman, "Kerry Will Abandon War on Terrorism."

13. Joseph L. Galloway, "We Must Act More Like a Nation at War," *Miami Herald*, April 8, 2004.

Collins, Tom, 30
Columbia University, 90
Communism: Democratic Party
  and, 32; fear of, 123; Kerry
  and, 6, 9; VVAW and, 46
Congo, 119
Congressional Black Caucus,
  119
Congressional Research Service,
  124
conservatives: military and, 15;
  national security and, 151. *See
  also* Republican Party, Repub-
  licans
Constitution, U.S., 25, 97
Conyers, John, 15–16
Council on Foreign Relations,
  154
Council on Human Rights, 62
Couric, Katie, 23
Cox, Chris, 17
Cranmer, Hal, 98–99
Cronkite, Walter, 87–88
Cuba, 45
Czechoslovakia, 89

D
D'Agostino, Joseph, 18
Daschle, Tom, 49, 70, 71
Dean, Howard, 29, 31, 68, 69,
  71, 86, 124
DeBellevue, Chuck, 85
DeConcini, Dennis, 80–81

Defend America Act of 1996,
  79
defense: Carter and, 12; Democratic Party and, 26; funding
  for, 75–81, 114–17, 122–23;
  liberals and, 26; missile,
  12–14; nuclear freeze policy
  and, 12–13
Defense Authorization Bill
  (2004), 109
Defense Department, 45, 79,
  115, 122
Defense Science Board, 117
Dellums, Ron, 29
Democracy Corps, 101
Democratic Party, Democrats,
  1–2; American Left and, 5;
  antiwar protesting and,
  29–32; Communism and, 32;
  defense and, 26; intelligence
  and, 24; national security and,
  22–23, 26–27; nuclear freeze
  policy and, 13; patriotism of,
  9–12; terrorism and, 32, 36;
  Vietnam War and, 39, 86–90,
  90–91; War on Terror and,
  15–17. *See also* American
  Left; liberals
Denton, Jeremiah, 7, 54–55
Dereliction of Duty (Patterson),
  133
Dhahran, Saudi Arabia, 24
Dick Cavett Show, 56